The Royal Commission on Historical Manuscripts

Guides to Sources for British History
based on the National Register of Archives

4

Private Papers of
BRITISH DIPLOMATS
1782 – 1900

London   Her Majesty's Stationery Office

ISBN 0 11 440188 8

HER MAJESTY'S STATIONERY OFFICE

Government Bookshops

49 High Holborn, London WC1V 6HB
13a Castle Street, Edinburgh EH2 3AR
Brazennose Street, Manchester M60 8AS
Southey House, Wine Street, Bristol BS1 2BQ
258 Broad Street, Birmingham B1 2HE
80 Chichester Street, Belfast BT1 4JY

Government Publications are also available
through booksellers

Preface

This fourth volume in the Commission's series of Guides based on information in the National Register of Archives presents the results of a survey of the surviving private papers of British diplomats, consuls and Foreign Office officials in post between the establishment of the Foreign Office in 1782 and the beginning of the present century.

The survey began by identifying every head or acting head of a British diplomatic mission during the period, from ambassadors, plenipotentiaries and special emissaries to chargés d'affaires and those left in charge without formal accreditation. To these were added the senior officials of the Foreign Office with whom they corresponded, and every secretary of state for foreign affairs, under secretary and assistant under secretary.[1] Of the 700 men identified, 278 were found to have left material relevant to foreign affairs within the period. They included three-quarters or more of the diplomats fully accredited to the key European courts. By contrast, papers survive of less than half the diplomats who were posted to more remote parts in the Far East or South America where less paperwork was generated, climatic conditions were less favourable to its preservation, and greater difficulties hindered its safe transport home. Where it was readily available, information has also been included about the papers of 104 other men who served as slave trade and boundary commissioners, junior diplomats, clerks in the Foreign Office, and as consuls and agents, especially those who exercised diplomatic functions in places where their posts were barred from the status of missions, as in Spanish America or the outposts of the Ottoman Empire. Emissaries of the government of India were not considered for inclusion, with the exception of those sent to Persia, coverage of which would otherwise have been intermittent.

For most of the 382 individuals noticed the intention has been to describe all those private papers that remained in their possession at their death, whatever the subject matter. The diverse papers of a number of diplomats better known in other capacities, as colonial governors, explorers or men of letters, have therefore been included. Only in the case of those whose papers have already been fully dealt with in the first volume in this series, *Papers of British Cabinet Ministers 1782-1900* (HMSO, 1982), has the description been limited to material relating to foreign affairs.[2]

Among the diplomatic papers to be found in these collections are drafts or copies of despatches or diplomatic notes retained by the diplomat for his own reference, as well as his personal journals, memoranda and other papers. Of most importance, however, are the private letters exchanged between diplomats and their superiors in London and colleagues abroad. Although this confidential correspondence was often used as a means of supplementing the information contained in despatches, the letters remained the property of their recipients and no record of them was normally kept in the Foreign Office. The archives of the Foreign Office itself are excluded from the Guide, but papers originally in private possession which later passed to it for safekeeping and were subsequently transferred to the Public Record Office have been noticed.[3] The great majority of the 728 groups of papers described in the Guide are now to be found in libraries and record offices throughout the world. Only 91 are known to remain in private hands. The present location of 34 groups, most of which surfaced recently in the saleroom, has not yet emerged.

The Commission gratefully acknowledges the help it has received from the many owners and custodians who have made their collections available to its staff or responded generously to its requests for information. Preliminary research for the Guide was undertaken by Dr RJ Palmer, and the main work of compilation has been carried out by Dr JG Parker and Dr SG Roberts under the direction of Miss Sonia P Anderson.

BS SMITH
Secretary
21 September 1984

Quality House, Quality Court
Chancery Lane, London WC2A 1HP

---

[1] DB Horn, *British Diplomatic Representatives 1689-1789* (Royal Historical Society, Camden 3rd series, xlvi, 1932); ST Bindoff *et al, British Diplomatic Representatives 1789-1852* (ibid, l, 1934); JM Collinge, *Foreign Office Officials 1782-1870* (University of London Institute of Historical Research, 1979); *Foreign Office List; Royal Kalendar; Imperial Kalendar; Almanach de Gotha.* In general the biographical details at the head of each entry in the Guide note only the senior diplomatic posts held, with the outside and therefore sometimes overlapping dates of appointment or of taking up or leaving office.

[2] Cross-references are given in the form 'See also *Cabinet Ministers*'.

[3] *The Records of the Foreign Office 1782-1939* (HMSO, Public Record Office Handbooks No 13, 1969), pp 86-8, 149-50, 163-74. Examples of Foreign Office concern about papers in private hands are cited in *Foreign Office confidential papers and information: control over unauthorised publication*, 1923 (PRO, FO 370/379, file 602).

Contents

Access to privately owned papers

Privately owned collections of papers that have been deposited on loan by their owners in libraries, record offices and other public institutions are normally available for research without restriction. Special conditions, however, may sometimes apply to their use, particularly if they are to be cited in published works. All enquiries on this point should be addressed to the institutions concerned.

Permission to see other privately owned collections should, in the first instance, be sought from their owners in writing. Applicants are reminded that such papers can normally be made available for use only at considerable personal inconvenience and expense to their owners, and that access for purposes of research is a privilege, not a right. The conditions of access to individual collections were those prevailing in December 1983. Enquiries about papers described simply as in private or family possession should be addressed to the Commission.

Unpublished lists of which copies may be consulted in the National Register of Archives are cited by their number there, eg NRA 23627.

Private papers of British diplomats 1782-1900

[1] **ABBOTT, Charles Stuart Aubrey** (1834-1882), 3rd Baron Tenterden 1870
Assistant under secretary for foreign affairs 1871-3, permanent under secretary 1873-82.

Letters to him as under secretary, with draft letters from him 1873-82 (5 vols).
Public Record Office (FO 363). Transferred from the Foreign Office Library 1921. NRA 23627.

[2] **ABERCROMBY, Ralph** (1803-1868), 2nd Baron Dunfermline 1858
Secretary of legation in Prussia 1831-6 (intermittently in charge); minister resident in Tuscany 1836-9; minister to the Germanic Confederation 1839, to Sardinia 1840-52, to the Netherlands 1852-8.

Letters from his father 1828-53 (1 vol); family corresp 1828-68 (1 vol); letter books 1847-52 (2 vols); misc family papers 1854-71 (1 vol).
National Library of Scotland (MSS 13172-5, 13180). Purchased 1958 from his widow's great-great-nephew the 5th Earl of Minto. NRA 10476.

Letters to him, Sardinia 1850-2, mainly from the Marchese Massimo d'Azeglio, with summaries of letters from London, Vienna and Berlin and a few drafts or extracts of letters from him (1 vol).
Cambridge University Library (Add 6627). Presented by the Revd TA Walker 1929.

ABERDEEN, Earl of, see Hamilton-Gordon.

[3] **A'COURT, Sir William** (1779-1860), 2nd Bt 1817, 1st Baron Heytesbury 1828
Secretary of legation in the Two Sicilies 1801-7 (intermittently in charge); joint commissioner to enquire into the affairs of Malta 1812; on a special mission to the Barbary states 1813; minister to the Two Sicilies 1814-22, to Spain 1822-4; ambassador to Portugal 1824-8, to Russia 1828-32.

Draft report and other corresp and papers, Malta 1812 (1 vol); instructions and papers, Barbary states 1813 (2 vols); despatches to him from Lord Castlereagh and draft despatches from him 1814-22 (8 vols); corresp with ministers of the Two Sicilies 1814-22 (5 vols), with consular officials at Palermo and Naples 1815-22 (3 vols), with Sir Thomas Maitland, Lord Stewart, Sir Charles Stuart and others 1814-22 (9 vols), with successive foreign secretaries 1822-32 (23 vols); misc papers 1814, 1820-1 (2 vols).
British Library (Add MSS 41511-63). Sold among the contents of Heytesbury House by Hampton & Sons 27 Apr 1926, lot 1674, and purchased by the British Museum 1927.

Misc letters and papers as lord lieutenant of Ireland 1844-6 (12 items).
Wiltshire RO (WRO 635). Deposited by the 6th Baron Heytesbury 1975. NRA 0671.

[4] **ADAIR, Sir Robert** (1763-1855)
Minister *ad interim* to Austria 1806-8; plenipotentiary to Turkey 1808-9, ambassador 1809-10; on a special mission to Belgium 1831-5, to Prussia 1835-6.

Copies of despatches from him 1806-8 and of a few private letters, with despatches and papers rel to British pensioners on the Continent (1 vol); 'Déclaration de la Cour de Vienne à la Cour de France' 1809 (1 vol); copies of despatches to and from him 1831-5 (4 vols).
Trustees of the Bedford Estates. Enquiries to the Archivist, Bedford Office, 29A Montague Street, London WC1B 5BL. The papers passed from Adair into the possession of the 7th Duke of Bedford. NRA 26179.

Accounts and vouchers, Belgium 1831-5 and Prussia 1835-6 (2 boxes).
Public Record Office (FO 95/503-4).

Letters from Lord Grey 1806-42 (25 items).
Durham University Department of Palaeography and Diplomatic (Grey of Howick Collection). Deposited by the 5th Earl Grey 1955. NRA 6228.

[5] **ADAM, Charles Fox Frederick** (1852-1913)
Secretary of legation in Brazil 1888-92 (in charge
1890-1), in Belgium 1892-7 (intermittently in
charge); secretary of embassy in the United States
1897-8 (in charge 1897), in Spain 1898-1904
(intermittently in charge).

Personal corresp 1869-1913, mainly letters from
his mother, wife and children, but incl a few
letters from diplomats and others (c3,000 items);
appointments, circulars, press cuttings, etc mainly
rel to his diplomatic career 1853-1912 (c240
items).
RK Adam Esq. Enquiries to NRA (Scotland).
NRA 9954.

[6] **ADAMS, Sir Francis Ottiwell** (1826-1889)
Secretary of legation in Japan 1868-72 (in charge
1871-2); secretary of embassy in Germany 1872-4
(in charge 1873, 1874); secretary of embassy in
France 1874-81 (intermittently minister *ad interim*
1875-81); minister to Switzerland 1881-8.

Draft despatches to Lord Granville, Japan 1871-2
(3 vols); draft despatches to Lords Derby,
Granville and Salisbury, with drafts and copies of
private corresp with Granville, Sir Charles Dilke
and others, France 1878-81 (1 vol); scrap book,
mainly press cuttings 1874-85.
Untraced. Sold at Phillips's 7 June 1984, lot 655.

[7] **ADDINGTON, Henry Unwin** (1790-1870)
Secretary of legation in Switzerland 1814-18 (in
charge 1814-15, 1816), in Denmark 1821-2 (in
charge), in the United States 1822-6 (in charge
1823-5); minister to the Germanic Confederation
1828-9, to Spain 1829-33; permanent under
secretary for foreign affairs 1842-54.

Drafts of despatches sent, copies of those received,
and printed papers, Germany and Switzerland
1813-17, Denmark 1821-2, United States 1823-9,
1840-2, Germanic Confederation 1828-9, Spain
and Gibraltar 1830-4 and China 1839-41
(6 boxes); diaries and travel journals 1809-14,
1821-8, 1839-40 (10 vols).
Devon RO (152M/33-8,67). Deposited by the 6th
Viscount Sidmouth 1955. NRA 8747.

Letters from his brother-in-law Major-General JB
Bucknall Estcourt 1842-55, mainly rel to the
boundary between the United States and British
N America 1843-6 (180 items).
Gloucestershire RO (D1571/F471-7,486).
Deposited by TDG Sotheron-Estcourt 1958-73.
NRA 2630.

[8] **AINSLIE, Sir Robert** (c1730-1812),
1st Bt 1804
Ambassador to Turkey 1776-94.

Copies of official letters to British diplomats,
consuls and others 1776-94, and to foreign
secretaries 1783-7 (7 vols).

Public Record Office (FO 261/1-7). Presented to
the Foreign Office 1917, 1930.

Copies of letters to the Levant Co 1776-93 (1
vol).
Public Record Office (PRO 30/26/72). Presented
by the Revd FJ Bywaters 1929.

[9] **ALCOCK, Sir Rutherford** (1809-1897)
Member of the mixed British and Portuguese
claims commission 1840-4; consul at Fuchow
1844-6, at Shanghai 1846-54, at Canton 1854-8;
consul-general at Tokyo 1858-9; minister to Japan
1859-65, to China 1865-71.

Corresp, testimonials, general orders, etc 1824-46,
mainly rel to his service as an army surgeon in
Portugal and Spain 1832-7 and as a member of
the Anglo-Portuguese commission 1840-4 (1 vol).
Bristol University Library (DM 142). Purchased
from J Stevens Cox, bookseller, 1949. NRA
25818.

[10] **ALSTON, Edward Gardiner** (1872-1897)
Vice-consul in S. Nyasa 1896-7.

Diaries as an officer with the British Central
Africa forces, rel to the training of troops, the
building of forts, and expeditions against hostile
chiefs and Arab slave-traders 1894-6 (4 vols).
National Archives of Zimbabwe, Harare (AL4).
*Guide to the historical manuscripts in the National
Archives of Rhodesia*, p4.

[11] **AMHERST, William Pitt** (1773-1857), 2nd
Baron Amherst 1797, 1st Earl Amherst 1826
Minister to the Two Sicilies 1809-11; ambassador
to China 1816-17.

Corresp and papers c1789-1835, mainly as
governor-general of Bengal 1822-8, but incl copies
of corresp rel to the Two Sicilies, and a few
papers rel to China (9 boxes); letters from his
wife 1814-22 (1 bundle); travel notes and
drawings, Italy, Switzerland and Germany 1791,
1795-6 (3 vols).
India Office Library and Records (MSS Eur F
140). Deposited by the 5th Earl Amherst 1968,
1973.

Journal of his embassy to China 1816-17 (5 vols).
Untraced. Sold by the 5th Earl Amherst at
Sotheby's 13 Feb 1968, lot 523.

AMPTHILL, Baron, see Russell OWL.

[12] **ARBUTHNOT, Charles** (1767-1850)
Secretary of legation in Sweden 1795-9 (in charge
1795-7); on an extraordinary mission to
Württemberg 1798; consul and chargé d'affaires
in Portugal 1800-1; envoy to Sweden 1802-4;
ambassador to Turkey 1804-7.

Letters, mainly drafts and copies, to statesmen, diplomats and others 1804–49 (29 items); corresp with his second wife 1813–34, his son Charles 1816–50 and his mother-in-law Mrs Lisle 1802–6 (989 items); misc family and general corresp mainly 1805–49 (117 items); misc papers 1804–49, incl political memoranda 1830–1 and an autobiographical sketch (7 items).
Aberdeen University Library (MSS 3029). Deposited by Sir John Arbuthnot Bt 1980. NRA 25353.

Letters to him and his second wife from the Duke of Wellington 1819–34 (632 items).
The Duke of Wellington. Returned to the 1st Duke by Colonel CGJ Arbuthnot after his father's death. See *Wellington and his friends,* ed Duke of Wellington 1965.

Letters to him and CGJ Arbuthnot from the Duke of Wellington 1822–51 (82 items); letters to him from CGJ Arbuthnot and others 1841–50 (16 items).
Untraced. Sold by Miss Marcia Arbuthnot at Sotheby's 17 Dec 1951, lots 208–9.

Letters to him mainly from Lord and Lady Clanwilliam 1848–50 (16 items).
Public Record Office of Northern Ireland (D3044/G/1/72–87). Returned to Lady Clanwilliam by CGJ Arbuthnot 1851, and deposited by the 6th Earl of Clanwilliam 1973. NRA 21971.

[13] **ARCHIBALD, Sir Edward Mortimer** (1810–1884)
Consul at New York 1857–71, consul-general 1871–83, judge in the mixed court of New York for suppression of the slave trade 1862–70.

Corresp 1839–82, mainly rel to the American civil war, Fenian raids into Canada and the *Alabama* dispute (1 vol); commissions and addresses received 1832–83 (2 vols); press cuttings and other biographical material (1 vol); misc family papers 19th–20th cent (1 vol).
Public Archives of Canada, Ottawa (MG27 IH1). *General inventory: manuscripts,* v, p126.

[14] **ARDAGH, Major-General Sir John Charles** (1840–1907)
Commissioner for the delimitation of the Bulgarian boundary 1878 and of the Turco-Greek boundary 1881; military delegate to the Hague peace conference 1899 and the conference for the revision of the Geneva convention 1906.

Diary 1862, private corresp and misc papers 1862–1906 (3 boxes); private and official corresp, memoranda, reports, journals, etc rel to the defences of Constantinople and the Bulgarian boundary 1876–81 (1 box); to the Turco-Greek boundary 1879–83 (1 box); to his military service in Egypt and the Sudan 1882–7 (1 box); as private secretary to the viceroy of India 1888–96 (3 boxes); as director of military intelligence

1888–1903 (2 vols, 1 box); rel to the Hague peace conference 1899 (1 box); to the S African war and subsequent claims commission 1899–1902 (2 boxes); to various law and boundary commissions, treaties, etc 1894–1908 (4 boxes); to the British Women's Emigration Association 1901–2 (1 box); other journals, diaries, notebooks and memoranda 1867–1906 (2 boxes); biographical material collected by his widow (1 box).
Public Record Office (PRO 30/40). Bequeathed by his widow the Dowager Countess of Malmesbury 1936. NRA 8649.

ARRAN, Earl of, see Gore.

ASHBURTON, Baron, see Baring A.

[15] **ASTON, Sir Arthur Ingram** (1798–1859)
Secretary of legation in Brazil 1826–33 (in charge 1826–7, 1828); secretary of embassy in France 1833–9 (intermittently minister *ad interim* 1833–5); minister to Spain 1840–3.

Private corresp with Woodbine Parish and William Parry 1829–30, Lords Granville, Howard de Walden and Palmerston, GWF Villiers and others 1833–43, and officials at Gibraltar, the Admiralty and the Spanish foreign ministry 1840–3 (2 boxes); drafts and copies of despatches from him, with misc memoranda and corresp with Brazilian ministers, the French foreign ministry, etc 1827–39 (2 boxes); drafts of despatches and of letters to Spanish ministers and others 1840–3 (3 boxes).
Public Record Office (FO 355). Presented to the Foreign Office by his executor 1860.

AUCKLAND, Baron, see Eden W.

[16] **BACKHOUSE, John** (1784–1845)
Acting under secretary for foreign affairs 1822–3, permanent under secretary 1827–42.

Corresp rel to his career as a merchant, as private secretary to George Canning 1816–21, as a commissioner of excise 1823–7, as permanent under secretary 1827–42, and as an art collector, with corresp and papers of his sons and other members of his family, and a large quantity of printed material, 1740–1956 (7 vols, 4,473 items).
William R Perkins Library, Duke University, Durham, N Carolina. Presented 1968. NRA 24155.

Corresp and papers rel to his mission to Don Carlos of Spain at Portsmouth 1834 (1 vol).
Public Record Office (FO 323/6). Presented to the Foreign Office by his great-grandson the Revd FL Sheppard 1939.

[17] **BADGER, Revd George Percy**
(1815-1888)
Attached to the commission of investigation into
the dispute between Muscat and Zanzibar 1860-1;
secretary to Sir HBE Frere's mission to Zanzibar
1872-3.

Corresp and papers rel to Abyssinia, Aden, Persia
and Zanzibar 1856-67, to the Muscat-Zanzibar
commission 1859-69, to Frere's mission to
Zanzibar 1872-3, etc.
Cambridge University Library (Add 2887-2915).
N Matthews and MD Wainwright, *Guide to
manuscripts and documents in the British Isles
relating to Africa*, 1971, p165.

Letters mainly from Sir James Outram c1854-63
(1 vol).
British Library (Add MS 38775). Purchased 1913.

Journal of his service with the British
expeditionary force to Persia 1856-7 and of his
travels in Egypt 1857-62.
India Office Library and Records (MSS Eur B
377). Presented by the Ministry of Defence
Library 1982.

[18] **BAGOT, Sir Charles** (1781-1843)
Under secretary for foreign affairs 1807-9;
minister to France 1814-15, to the United States
1815-19; ambassador to Russia 1820-4, to the
Netherlands 1824-32; on a special mission to
Austria 1835.

Official and private corresp, United States incl
material rel to British N America 1816-19 (7
vols), Russia 1820-4 (6 vols), Netherlands 1824-
32 (9 vols); corresp and papers as governor-in-
chief of British N America c1840-3 (1 box);
letters from George Canning, Edward Nicholas,
Henry Wellesley, William Wellesley-Pole and
others 1808-36, with misc papers rel to his career
1805-43 (1 box); papers rel to the Mint 1812-19,
and the treaty of Ghent 1814 (2 vols); journals
1821-4 (2 vols).
OR Bagot Esq. Enquiries to Cumbria Record
Office, Kendal. NRA 6234.

Letters, petitions and addresses received, mainly
as governor-in-chief of British N America, 1838-
42 (5 vols).
Public Archives of Canada, Ottawa (MG24 A13).
Presented by JF Bagot 1910. *General inventory:
manuscripts*, iv, pp138-9.

[19] **BAKER, Colonel George** (1794-1859)
Commissioner for the delimitation of the Greek
boundary 1830-6.

Despatches and official letters to him 1830-8 (1
vol); copies of despatches and official letters from
him 1830-6 (3 vols); letters from the French and
Russian commissioners 1831-6, and from his
assistants 1834-6 (1 vol); report from his assistant
Captain FB Dunne 1834 (1 vol); corresp rel to
his military career, notes and reports on Greece,
and other papers, 1809-49 (1 vol); letters from

him to his wife 1830-6, and other family corresp
1828-36 (4 vols); protocols and other papers
1830-6 (1 vol); abstracts of the commission's
expenses 1830-6 (1 vol); journals 1830-5 (8 vols);
journals of his wife 1832-6 (5 vols); itineraries in
Greece (1 vol); printed material rel to Greece
1827-36, 1853 (9 vols and items).
Bodleian Library, Oxford (MSS Dep. b.136,
c.263-72, d.215-18, e.52-64, f.26-7). Presented by
JEA Baker 1966.

[20] **BANDINEL, James** (1783-1849)
Foreign Office clerk 1799-1845, superintendent of
the slave trade department 1824-45.

Personal and family papers 1763-1906, incl letters
from him to his wife, papers rel to Foreign Office
business incl African exploration and suppression
of the slave trade, and a volume of his poems and
translations from the Spanish (6 vols, 403 items).
*William R Perkins Library, Duke University,
Durham, N Carolina.* Presented 1970. NRA 25903.

[21] **BARCLAY, Anthony** (d 1877)
Commissioner for the delimitation of the
boundary between British N America and the
United States 1816-28; consul at New York
1842-56.

See Barclay T.

[22] **BARCLAY, Thomas** (1753-1830)
Consul-general at New York 1799-1816;
commissioner for the delimitation of the boundary
between British N America and the United States
1816-28.

Papers of Thomas and Anthony Barclay as
boundary commissioners, incl corresp with
diplomats, surveyors and others, c1764-1827 (7
boxes).
Maine Historical Society, Portland.

Corresp, accounts and lists of prisoners as
commissioner for British prisoners-of-war at New
York 1812-14 (6 vols, 11 boxes).
New York Historical Society.

[23] **BARING, Alexander** (1774-1848), 1st
Baron Ashburton 1835
On a special mission to the United States 1842.

Corresp and papers rel to the Ashburton treaty
1842, incl despatches and private letters from
Lord Aberdeen, corresp with Sir Charles Bagot,
John Tyler, Daniel Webster and others, two letter
books, drafts and copies of the treaty, memoranda
and press cuttings (2 vols, 14 bundles).
The Marquess of Northampton. Enquiries to the
Historical Manuscripts Commission. NRA 24219.

See also *Cabinet Ministers.*

[24] **BARING, Evelyn** (1841-1917), 1st Baron Cromer 1892, 1st Viscount Cromer 1899, 1st Earl of Cromer 1901
Commissioner for the Egyptian public debt 1877-9, comptroller-general 1879-80; agent and consul-general in Egypt 1883-1907.

Corresp as chief secretary to the viceroy of India 1872-3 (1 vol); papers rel to Egypt 1840, 1866, 1877-1910, incl corresp and telegrams, memoranda, reports, etc, and rel to his *Modern Egypt* 1908 (29 vols); political, literary and personal corresp 1907-15 (8 vols); memoranda rel to the Russian military threat 1876-7 (1 vol); speeches, pamphlets, articles and press cuttings 1872-1917 (34 vols and boxes); command papers, Egypt 1876-1914 (40 vols).
Public Record Office (FO 633). Presented by the 3rd Earl of Cromer 1958 (NRA 5961) and 1980. Mainly Cromer's printed or typescript copies.

Typescript drafts of *Modern Egypt*, incl unpublished material, 1895-1915 (9 vols).
British Library (Add MSS 44903-11). Presented by the 2nd Earl of Cromer 1936.

Autograph collection, mainly letters to him, 1788-1916 (4 vols).
The Earl of Cromer. Enquiries to the Archivist, Baring Bros & Co Ltd, 88 Leadenhall Street, London EC3A 3DT. NRA 11212.

[25] **BATHURST, Henry** (1762-1834), styled Lord Apsley 1775-94, 3rd Earl Bathurst 1794
Foreign secretary 1809.

Corresp as foreign secretary 1809, with other corresp rel to foreign affairs during his terms as a cabinet minister, incl many letters from George Canning 1807-27.
British Library (MS Loan 57, vols 3-23). Deposited by the 8th Earl Bathurst 1965. NRA 20952.

See also *Cabinet Ministers*.

BEACONSFIELD, Earl of, see Disraeli.

BEAUVALE, Baron, see Lamb.

[26] **BEKE, Charles Tilstone** (1800-1874)
Acting consul at Leipzig 1837-8; on an unofficial mission to Abyssinia to secure release of European prisoners 1865-6.

Corresp of Beke and his wife with statesmen, scholars, scientists and others 1838-1909, mainly rel to his schemes for the exploration and commercial development of Abyssinia 1839-67, and to attempts to gain public recognition of his services 1867-85 (over 100 items); journals 1833-8, 1843-53, 1861-74 (7 vols); literary MSS, incl his unpublished autobiography 1871, notes and printed material mainly rel to Abyssinia 1846-69.

Wellcome Historical Medical Library, London (Acc 69764). NRA 25910.

Travel journals, Abyssinia 1840-3 (7 vols); corresp and papers, Abyssinia, mainly 1840-5, incl collections rel to history and topography, sketches and maps (4 vols, 2 rolls).
British Library (Add MSS 30247-58). Purchased 1877.

Letters from CH Purday, secretary of the Abyssinian Captives Liberation Fund, 1865-9 (20 items); account of his mission to Abyssinia and extracts from his corresp with Purday 1865-6 (1 bundle); extracts from official corresp rel to Abyssinia 1836-74 (1 vol), and other material rel to his public services collected by his wife.
John Rylands University Library of Manchester (Eng MSS 888-90). Presented by Mrs E Hartland 1936. *Supplementary hand-list of western manuscripts*, p26.

[27] **BENTINCK, Lieutenant-General Lord William Henry Cavendish** (1774-1839)
Commander-in-chief in Sicily and minister to the Two Sicilies 1811-14.

Corresp, letter books, journals and papers mainly rel to his military service in Flanders and Italy 1793-1802, and in the Peninsula 1808-11 (36 vols, 838 items); corresp with the Sicilian royal family, generals, politicians and informers, and with British statesmen, diplomats and military and naval officers 1810-15 (c5,620 items); official and private letter books and registers 1811-15 (14 vols); memoranda, intelligence reports, etc, Sicily 1810-21 (c850 items); journals, notebooks and accounts 1811-14 (14 vols); corresp, letter books, journals, memoranda, etc rel to his career in India mainly 1803-7, 1827-35 (175 vols, 312 bundles, c3,200 items); corresp and papers rel to his career in Britain 1814-27, 1833-9, partly as MP for King's Lynn and Glasgow (18 vols, 1 bundle, 1,527 items).
Nottingham University Library (PwJ). Deposited by the 7th Duke of Portland 1949-68. NRA 7628.

[28] **BERTIE, Francis Leveson** (1844-1919), 1st Baron Bertie of Thame 1915, 1st Viscount Bertie of Thame 1918
Entered the Foreign Office 1863; assistant under secretary for foreign affairs 1894-1903; ambassador to Italy 1903-5, to France 1905-18.

He bequeathed his personal and political papers to Lady Algernon Gordon Lennox. His diaries 1914-18 edited by her in 1924 have not been traced.

Semi-official corresp and papers 1894-1918, mainly 1903-18, incl confidential memoranda, and corresp with HH Asquith, AJ Balfour, Sir MWE de Bunsen, Sir Edward Grey, Sir Douglas Haig,

Lords Hardinge of Penshurst and Lansdowne, Sir L du P Mallet, Sir Arthur Nicolson and other statesmen, diplomats, Foreign Office officials and military commanders (43 vols).
British Library (Add MSS 63011-53). Purchased 1980 from the Pierpont Morgan Library, to which they had been sold by Lady Algernon Gordon Lennox.

Letter books arranged by country 1896-1918 (22 vols); corresp 1903-18 (9 vols); indexes to letter books and corresp (2 vols).
Public Record Office (FO 800/159-91). NRA 23627.

BERWICK, Baron, see Noel-Hill.

BEXLEY, Baron, see Vansittart.

[29] BLACKWELL, Joseph Andrew (1798-1886)
Diplomatic agent in Hungary 1843-4, 1847-8, 1849; vice-consul at Lübeck 1854-7; consul at Stettin 1857-80.

Copies of and extracts from letters and despatches from him rel to Hungary (399ff); copies of his memoranda for Lord Palmerston 1850 (69ff) and for Count Emanuel Zichy-Ferraris nd (42ff); poems and translations by him (372ff).
Hungarian Academy, Budapest (MSS 10.003, 10.005, 10.008-9). Bequeathed by Blackwell.

[30] BLIGH, Sir John Duncan (1798-1872)
Secretary of legation in Tuscany 1829-31 (in charge 1830), in the Netherlands 1831-2 (minister *ad interim* 1832); minister *ad interim* to Russia 1832-5; minister to Sweden 1835-8, to Hanover 1838-56.

Diplomatic corresp mainly with Lord Palmerston 1832-57 (2 vols); draft despatches to foreign secretaries, with a few letters to him, 1830-56 (16 vols); letters from his family 1817-54 (1 vol); journal of a tour from Hanover to Prague and Dresden 1840 (1 vol).
British Library (Add MSS 41268-87). Presented by his son-in-law the 4th Earl of Chichester 1888.

[31] BLOOMFIELD, Lieutenant-General Benjamin (1768-1846), 1st Baron Bloomfield 1825
Minister to Sweden 1823-33.

Copies of despatches from him 1823-33 (4 vols).
Public Record Office (FO 356/34-7). Acquired with the papers of the 2nd Baron Bloomfield. NRA 23631.

[32] BLOOMFIELD, John Arthur Douglas (1802-1879), 2nd Baron Bloomfield 1846
Secretary of legation in Württemberg 1825-6, in Sweden 1826-39 (intermittently in charge 1827-38); secretary of embassy in Russia 1839-44 (intermittently minister *ad interim* 1840-2); minister to Russia 1844-51, to Prussia 1851-60; ambassador to Austria 1860-7, to Austria-Hungary 1867-71.

Private corresp with the Foreign Office 1833-59 (2 boxes); private letters to him 1844-71 (3 boxes); private letter books 1861-71 (4 vols); drafts mainly of despatches sent 1840-71, and registers of despatches sent 1852-71 (29 boxes, vols and bundles).
Public Record Office (FO 356/1-33, 38-42). NRA 23631.

[33] BOND, Phineas (1749-1815)
Consul and commissioner at Philadelphia 1786-92, consul-general 1792-1812; chargé d'affaires in the United States 1795-6.

Corresp and papers rel to the American revolution and to his career as a lawyer and a representative of British commercial interests in the United States *c*1770-*c*1815 (40 boxes).
Historical Society of Pennsylvania, Philadelphia (Cadwalader Collection). Presented by the Cadwalader family mainly in 1947. *Guide to the manuscript collections*, 1949.

[34] BOOTHBY, Sir Brooke (1856-1913), 11th Bt 1865
Third secretary in Greece 1884 (in charge 1884), in Belgium 1884-6 (in charge 1884); second secretary in Bavaria 1895-6 (in charge 1895, 1896), in France 1896-8 (in charge 1898); secretary of legation in Brazil 1898-1901 (in charge 1900-1), in Japan 1901-2, in Belgium 1902-5 (intermittently in charge); counsellor of embassy in Austria 1905-7 (in charge 1905, 1906); minister to Chile 1907-13.

Corresp and papers rel to his career, and to family and business matters.
Glamorgan Archive Service.

[35] BOSANQUET, George Jacob (1791-1866)
Secretary of legation in Spain 1824-30 (in charge 1824-5, 1827-30).

Diplomatic and personal corresp and papers 1824-31 (18 items); personal, local and estate corresp and memoranda *c*1820-66 (*c*90 items); diary *c*1825-7.
Hertfordshire RO (D/EBb). Deposited 1960 by Baylis Pearce & Co, solicitors. NRA 15819.

[36] **BOWRING, Sir John** (1792-1872)
Consul at Canton 1849-54; acting plenipotentiary
and superintendent of trade in China 1852-3,
plenipotentiary and superintendent 1853-7; on a
special mission to Siam 1855.

Some of his papers descended through his eldest
son to his great-grandson CGA Bowring, and
were sold at Sotheby's 3 Apr 1950, lots 193-7, and
4 Apr 1977, lot 249. Others descended through
his third son to his great-granddaughter Mrs
NHA Taylor, and were sold at Christie's 25 July
1958, lots 240-1, and 8 Dec 1958, lot 286. Further
papers were sold anonymously at Sotheby's 29 Oct
1962, lot 211, and 15 May 1967, lots 221-226A.

Papers rel to his missions to China c1839-1857,
incl corresp with Sir George Balfour, Lord
Clarendon, Richard Cobden, Lord Dalhousie,
William Miller, Sir GT Staunton, Sir James
Stirling, Sir HG Ward and HH Wilson, literary
MSS and related printed material (623 items).
University of California Library, Los Angeles. See
National union catalog, MS 71-842.

Letters to him and papers 1822-64, mainly as
governor of Hong Kong 1854-9 (223 items);
letters from his son Frederick 1837-64 (65 items).
John Rylands University Library of Manchester
(Eng MSS 1229-30). Purchased at Christie's
8 Dec 1958, lot 286. *Hand-list of additions to the
collection of English manuscripts 1952-1970,* p26.

Corresp with RC Wyllie and others, instructions,
texts of treaties, etc rel to his diplomatic service
on behalf of the kingdom of Hawaii 1859-71 (8
vols).
Bancroft Library, University of California, Berkeley.
Purchased at Christie's 25 July 1958, lot 240.
National union catalog, MS 65-1777.

Letters from statesmen, politicians and others, incl
Lord Auckland, George Canning and Lords
Clarendon, Dalhousie and Palmerston 1816-65
(119 items); letters from correspondents in
Europe rel to his literary work, with copies of
poems, etc 1821-53 (39 items); papers rel to
Serbian popular poetry (1 vol).
*Houghton Library, Harvard University, Cambridge,
Massachusetts* (b MS Eng 1247). Acquired
1966-71. NRA 20033.

Letters from political, religious and literary
figures, incl letters from Roman Catholic bishops
to members of his family after his death,
1795-1908 (176 items).
Huntington Library, San Marino, California.
Purchased 1967 from Francis Edwards Ltd, by
whom they had been acquired at Sotheby's
15 May 1967, lot 222. *National union catalog,*
MS
71-1046.

Autograph collection c1691-c1910, mainly letters
to him c1814-69 (c250 items).
University College London (MS Ogden 62).
Purchased from CK Ogden 1953.

Misc corresp and papers mainly as executor of
Jeremy Bentham, incl letters from Bentham and
Edwin Chadwick, MSS on utilitarianism and on
international law, notes and extracts rel to
European languages and literature, and reports of
the Greek committee 1825.
University College London (Bentham Papers).
Presented by him among the Bentham papers.
Catalogue of the manuscripts of Jeremy Bentham.

Corresp and misc papers, incl some rel to China,
1810-71 (c45 items).
Wellcome Historical Medical Library, London.
Purchased from Glendining & Co Ltd 29 Apr
1935, lot 334 and 27 May 1935, lot 419.

Misc corresp, verses and papers 1831-72 (c50pp).
King Library, University of Kentucky, Lexington.
Purchased at Sotheby's 4 Apr 1977, lot 249.

[37] **BOYLE, Harry** (1863-1937)
Vice-consul at Massawa 1890-9; oriental secretary
at Cairo 1899-1909; consul-general at Berlin
1909-14.

Letters from him to Sir JR Rodd 1902, 1907,
confidential despatch to Sir Edward Grey 1908,
memorandum on the background to the British
occupation of Egypt (1 file); personal corresp and
papers incl letters from him while in Germany
1909-10, letters from Sir Horace Rumbold
1928-31, and press cuttings 1888-1932 (1 file);
memorandum on his visit to Egypt with Lord
Milner's mission 1921, and letters from him in
Egypt to his wife 1921 (2 files); letters from him
mainly to his mother 1866-1910 (9 files).
Middle East Centre, St Antony's College, Oxford.
Bequeathed by his widow 1966.

Corresp mainly with his wife 1910-15 (2 boxes).
St Antony's College Library, Oxford. Bequeathed
by his widow 1966.

[38] **BRAME, Joseph** (fl 1786-99)
Consul at Genoa 1786-99 (in charge 1793-4,
1794-5, 1795-7).

See Noel-Hill.

[39] **BRANT, James** (d 1861)
Vice-consul at Trebizond 1830-6, consul at
Erzerum 1836-55, at Damascus 1855-61.

Corresp 1830-61, incl letters from Colonel FR
Chesney 1832-9, Sir John McNeill 1834-42, Sir
CA Murray 1855, Lord Stratford de Redcliffe
1846-55 and Sir WF Williams 1850-6 (3 vols).
British Library (Add MSS 42512, 42565-6).
Presented by Commander James Brant 1931.

Travel journal, Armenia and Asia Minor 1836.
Royal Geographical Society.

BRISTOL, Marquesses of, see Hervey FW and
HAR.

[40] **BRODRICK, William St John Fremantle**
(1856-1942), 9th Viscount Midleton 1907, 1st
Earl of Midleton 1920
Under secretary for foreign affairs 1898-1900.

Corresp and minutes mainly rel to the War Office
1885-98 (3 vols); corresp with Lords Cromer,
Lansdowne and Salisbury and others 1898-1900,
incl many letters rel to the S African war and the
Boxer rebellion (2 vols); with Edward VII,
political colleagues, senior army officers and
others as secretary of state for war 1900-3 (13
vols); with Lords Curzon and Kitchener and
others as secretary of state for India 1903-5, and
related press cuttings (4 vols); misc political
corresp, memoranda, etc 1906-33 (4 vols); corresp
and papers rel to Irish politics 1893-1941, mainly
1916-22 (31 vols).
Public Record Office (PRO 30/67). Deposited by
his daughter Lady Moyra Loyd 1967. NRA
23461.

Corresp with Lord Curzon 1903-6 (6 vols).
British Library (Add MSS 50072-7). Acquired
1959.

Letters to him and his wife from Joseph
Chamberlain, Lords Cromer and Rosebery and
other public figures 1890-1933 (1 vol).
*William R Perkins Library, Duke University,
Durham, N Carolina.* Purchased 1969. *Guide to the
cataloged collections*, pp62-3.

Letters from Joseph Chamberlain, Lord Milner
and others, mainly rel to the S African war,
1897-1902 (48 items).
Untraced. Sold at Sotheby's 1 July 1968, lots
377-81.

[41] **BROOKE, Sir James** (1803-1868)
Rajah of Sarawak 1841-68; governor of Labuan
and consul-general in Borneo 1847-56; on a
special mission to Siam 1850.

Letters mainly from his nephew JB Brooke
1849-66 (146 items); copies of corresp 1851-3 and
press cuttings 1849-52 rel to Siam (1 vol); notes
and copies of letters and memoranda rel to
negotiations with Great Britain, France and the
Netherlands about the future of Sarawak 1859-63
(24 items); papers mainly rel to charges against
him 1847-64, copies of letters from him 1852-62,
and verses c1830-48 (c50 items).
Rhodes House Library, Oxford (MSS Pac. s. 90).
Presented by Vice-Admiral BCB Brooke 1975.
NRA 21238.

[42] **BRUCE, Sir Frederick William Adolphus**
(1814-1867)
Chargé d'affaires and consul-general in Bolivia
1848-52, in Uruguay 1851-3; agent and consul-
general in Egypt 1853-8; secretary to Lord Elgin's
mission to China 1857-8; minister to China
1858-65, to the United States 1865-7.

Copies of despatches from him to Lord Clarendon
1852-4 and Lord Russell 1864 (1 bundle); corresp
mainly with the Foreign Office 1857-8 (1
bundle); draft despatches to Russell 1859-61 (2
vols); drafts of misc official letters from him 1859-
60 (1 vol); copies of his despatches to Russell and
Lord Elgin 1860-1 (2 bundles); copies of
despatches received 1860-1 (1 bundle); corresp
and papers rel to China, incl the Chinese
Maritime Customs and the activities of CG
Gordon 1863-4 (1 bundle); official corresp with
Pierpont Edwards and others 1865-7 (1 vol); misc
letters to him 1866-7, and papers rel to his death
1867 (1 bundle); family corresp 1834-60 (2
bundles); diaries 1858-60 (3 vols); accounts for
purchases of items to be taken to China 1857.
The Earl of Elgin. Access restricted.

Copies of letters from him to Lords Clarendon,
Russell and Stanley 1865-7 (1 vol).
Untraced. Sold at Sotheby's 29 Oct 1973, lot 405,
and exported. A photocopy is in the British
Library (RP 950).

[43] **BRUCE, James** (1811-1863), styled Lord
Bruce 1840-1, 8th Earl of Elgin 1841
On a special mission to the United States 1854;
plenipotentiary to China 1857-9, 1860-1.

Official and family corresp and papers as governor
of Jamaica 1842-6 (c2 boxes); corresp and papers
rel to British N America 1823-58, mainly as
governor-in-chief 1846-54, incl draft despatches
1846-55 (c6 bundles); drafts and copies of his
private letters to Lord Grey 1847-51 (1 vol, 5
bundles); despatches from Lords Clarendon and
Malmesbury, HS Parkes and others 1857-9 (10
bundles); draft despatches and copies of
enclosures 1857-9 (5 bundles); corresp with the
Chinese authorities 1857-9 (1 bundle); private
letters from Lord Malmesbury 1858-9 (1 bundle);
drafts and copies of despatches to and from him
1860-1 (3 bundles); copies of his despatches from
China, and extracts from the French Yellow Book
(c12 vols); private official corresp 1857-61 (2
boxes, 4 bundles); letters from Sir FWA Bruce
1857-63 (1 box); copies of journal-letters to his
wife 1857-9, 1860-1 (1 bundle); memoranda rel to
Chinese affairs 1857-9, and drafts of letters from
Baron Gros to the Chinese authorities (1
bundle); commission and credentials 1860 (1
bundle); notebooks kept while at Oxford 1830-2
(8 vols); press cuttings rel to India 1862-4 (1
vol); letters rel to him 1811-63 collected by his
widow (1 bundle).
The Earl of Elgin. Access restricted. A microfilm
of the Canadian papers is in the Public Archives
of Canada (MG24 A16).

See also *Cabinet Ministers.*

[44] **BRUCE, General Thomas** (1766-1841), 7th Earl of Elgin 1771
On a special mission to Austria 1790-1; envoy to the Southern Netherlands 1792-3, 1793-4; minister to Prussia 1795-9; ambassador to Turkey 1799-1803.

Official corresp with JB Burges, Lord Grenville and the Duke of Leeds, corresp with Sir George Don, MF Eden, Joseph Ewart, Lord Malmesbury, Sir James Murray, John Trevor, Lord Whitworth, William Wickham and other British and foreign diplomats and army officers, intelligence reports, memoranda, accounts and other diplomatic papers 1789-99 (*c*780 vols, bundles etc); corresp with Lord Grenville, Lord Hawkesbury, JS Smith, Sir WS Smith, Alexander Straton, Francis Werry and Turkish ministers and officials, intelligence reports, accounts and other papers 1798-1803 (*c*240 bundles and items); corresp and papers rel to the Egyptian campaign 1798-1802 (125 bundles and items), to Afghanistan, India, Persia, and trade in the Near East 1799-1803 (54 bundles and items), to his imprisonment in France 1803-6 (36 bundles and items), to the Elgin marbles and other works of art 1793-1837 (8 vols, 2 boxes, 33 bundles and items), to the Elgin Fencibles 1794-7 (29 bundles and items); general and personal corresp and papers, incl family corresp, papers rel to elections of Scottish representative peers, notebooks and accounts 1770-1837 (*c*200 vols, bundles and items).
The Earl of Elgin. Access restricted. NRA 26223 (partial list).

Copies of his instructions as minister to Prussia, of despatches and private letters from Lord Grenville and George Hammond, and of misc papers 1795-9 (1 vol).
Beinecke Library, Yale University, New Haven, Connecticut (Osborn Collection MS c 206). Purchased at Sotheby's 28 June 1965, lot 90 (Phillipps MS 12342). NRA 18661.

Corresp and papers mainly rel to Turkey 1799-1803 (1 vol).
Untraced. Sold at Sotheby's 26 June 1974, lot 2913 (Phillipps MS 23772), and exported. A microfilm is in the British Library (RP 1016).

Corresp and accounts rel to Turkey 1801-6.
Untraced. Photocopies are in the British Library (RP 1542).

[45] **BRYCE, James** (1838-1922), Viscount Bryce 1914
Parliamentary under secretary for foreign affairs 1886; ambassador to the United States 1907-13.

Corresp with American scholars, politicians and diplomats 1871-1922 (23 vols); corresp and papers as ambassador to the United States 1906-13 (7 vols); corresp, press cuttings and other papers rel to *The American Commonwealth* 1881-1921 (3 vols); corresp and papers rel to Armenia 1876-1922 (7 bundles).

Bodleian Library, Oxford (MSS Bryce). Presented by Miss MV Bryce 1944-61. NRA 6716.

Corresp rel to foreign affairs 1904-21 (4 vols); maps of Hungary (1 bundle).
Public Record Office (FO 800/331-5).

See also *Cabinet Ministers.*

BRYDGES, see Jones.

[46] **BUCHANAN, Sir Andrew** (1807-1882), 1st Bt 1878
Secretary of legation in Tuscany 1841-4 (in charge 1842-3, 1844), in Russia 1844-52 (intermittently in charge 1844-51); minister to Switzerland 1852-3, to Denmark 1853-8, to Spain 1858-60, to the Netherlands 1860-2; ambassador to Prussia 1862-4, to Russia 1864-71, to Austria-Hungary 1871-7.

Diplomatic corresp 1827-35, incl copies of his letters from Corfu to Stratford Canning 1828 (2 vols); corresp, Russia 1844-56 (3 vols); copies of letters to Lord Malmesbury, Switzerland 1852 (1 vol); corresp, Denmark 1853-8 (7 vols, 1 item); letters to him, Spain 1859-60 (6 vols); letters to him and copies of his despatches to Lord Russell, mainly Netherlands, 1861-2 (3 vols); corresp, mainly Prussia, 1863-4 (4 vols), and Russia 1864-71 (8 vols); letters to him, Austria-Hungary 1872-7 (4 vols).
Major Sir CJ Buchanan Bt. NRA 8677.

[47] **BUCKLEY-MATHEW** (formerly **MATHEW**), **Sir George Benvenuto** (1807-1879)
Consul at Charleston 1850-3, at Philadelphia 1853-6; consul-general and chargé d'affaires in Guatemala 1861, minister 1861-6; minister to the Argentine Republic 1866, to Paraguay 1866-7, to Brazil 1867-79.

Despatch book as governor of the Bahamas 1844-50 (1 vol); letter books 1863-4 (2 vols); diary of a tour in South and Central America 1866 (1 vol); letters of appointment; papers rel to his W Indian estate.
Glamorgan Archive Service (D/D/Mw). Deposited 1968. *Annual report 1982,* p20.

Letters from WE Gladstone, GPR James, the 2nd Marquess of Salisbury, the 7th Earl of Shaftesbury and other statesmen, diplomats and authors 1831-79 (68 items).
Liverpool RO (Acc 2463). Presented by his son-in-law Arthur Earle 1906. NRA 25880.

[48] **BUCKNALL ESTCOURT** (formerly **ESTCOURT**), **Major-General James Bucknall** (1802-1855)
Commissioner for the delimitation of the boundary between the United States and British N America 1843-6.

Letters from him to his family 1811-55, with press cuttings and misc papers 1817-55, mainly rel to his service on the Euphrates expedition 1834-7, on the N American boundary commission 1843-6, and in the Crimea 1854-5 (540 items, 1 bundle); letters and copies of letters to his brother-in-law HU Addington 1842-55, mainly rel to the N American boundary commission (180 items); journals 1835, 1837, 1843-4, 1851, 1853-5 (5 vols, 3 bundles); biographical material collected by his widow, incl memoranda and account book kept by him in the Crimea (6 vols, 113 items).
Gloucestershire RO (D1571). Deposited by TDG Sotheron-Estcourt 1958-73. NRA 2630.

[49] **BULWER, William Henry Lytton Earle** (1801-1872), Baron Dalling and Bulwer 1871
On a special mission to Belgium 1830, secretary of legation 1832-3, 1835-7 (in charge 1835-6, 1836-7); secretary of embassy in Turkey 1837-9, in France 1839-43 (intermittently minister *ad interim*); minister to Spain 1843-8, to the United States 1849-52, to Tuscany and Modena 1852-5; commissioner in the Danubian principalities 1856-8; ambassador to Turkey 1858-65.

Private corresp, draft despatches, memoranda, etc, Prussia, Austria and the Netherlands 1828-30 (2 bundles), Belgium 1835-7 (2 bundles), Turkey 1837-8 (2 bundles), France 1839-43 (2 bundles), Spain 1843-8 (58 bundles), the United States 1849-52 (19 bundles), Tuscany 1852-5 (11 bundles), the Danubian principalities 1856-8 (43 bundles), Turkey 1858-65 (206 bundles); corresp and papers rel to his parliamentary career 1830-7, 1868-9 (9 bundles), to business matters in S America and elsewhere *c*1850-60 (23 bundles); general corresp 1865-*c*1872 (12 bundles); literary MSS and papers (24 bundles); personal and misc papers (10 bundles).
Norfolk RO. Deposited by Brigadier Hetherington Long and Mrs Long, his great-great-niece 1968, 1982. NRA 6790.

Corresp and papers, United States, mainly rel to the Clayton-Bulwer treaty, incl letters from British consuls 1850-3, drafts of letters to JM Clayton 1849-50 and Daniel Webster 1850-1, memoranda and drafts of the treaty 1848-51 (1 vol).
Public Record Office (FO 800/232). Acquired by the Foreign Office from Lieutenant-Colonel EAE Bulwer 1931.

Letters from various correspondents rel to politics, slavery, etc in the United States 1850-3 (23 items).
William R Perkins Library, Duke University, Durham, N Carolina. Acquired 1932. *Guide to the cataloged collections,* p72.

Family corresp *c*1839-72, incl some letters to him from his nephew ERL Bulwer-Lytton as consul at Belgrade 1860 (2 bundles, etc); misc corresp, incl letters to him from diplomats 1844 (*c*30 items) and letters from him to the editors of *The Examiner c*1830-71 (2 bundles); misc printed papers (1 box).

Hon David Lytton Cobbold. Not open for research. NRA 25520.

Letters mainly from ERL Bulwer-Lytton 1864-72 (*c*55 items); misc literary and other papers 1832-71 and nd, incl MS novels, a memoir (in French) and a biography of him begun by HEG Bulwer (11 vols, 3 bundles, 23 items).
Hertfordshire RO (D/EK). Deposited by his great-great-niece Lady Cobbold at various dates since 1953. NRA 4598.

[50] **BULWER-LYTTON, Edward Robert Lytton** (1831-1891), 2nd Baron Lytton 1873, 1st Earl of Lytton 1880
Consul at Belgrade 1860-3; chargé d'affaires in Denmark 1863-4; secretary of legation in Greece 1864-5; chargé d'affaires in Portugal 1865-8; secretary of legation in Spain 1868; secretary of embassy in Austria 1868-72 (in charge 1869, 1871), in France 1872-4 (minister *ad interim* 1873, 1874); minister to Portugal 1874-6; ambassador to France 1887-91.

Corresp with diplomats, politicians, literary figures, his family and others 1864-87 and nd (6 vols, 7 boxes, 2 bundles, etc); letter books 1871-88 (3 vols); corresp and papers, India 1873-99 (5 bundles); misc corresp and papers 1858-91 (1 vol, 1 bundle, 2 items); financial papers 1873-87 (4 vols, 1 bundle, 2 items).
Hertfordshire RO (D/EK). Deposited with other family papers by his granddaughter Lady Cobbold 1953, 1962. NRA 4598.

Corresp mainly as viceroy of India 1850-85 (62 vols, *c*56 bundles); corresp and papers rel to Afghanistan 1863-90 (9 vols), to famine in India 1877-9 (9 vols) and to other subjects rel to India 1858-88 (16 vols); speeches 1876-82 (6 vols); press cuttings 1876-9 (5 vols); corresp and papers 1876-9 collected by his daughter Elizabeth (4 vols); misc papers 1859-87 (7 vols).
India Office Library and Records (MSS Eur E 218). Deposited by Lady Cobbold 1955.

Family and misc corresp *c*1840-91, mainly letters from his father *c*1840-72 and his uncle Lord Dalling (4 vols, *c*150 items, etc); literary papers, incl MSS of his published works, notes for speeches, etc (8 vols, 7 boxes, 2 bundles, etc).
Hon David Lytton Cobbold. Not open for research. NRA 25520.

Letters from him to his wife *c*1868-1891, with misc family corresp, verses by him, etc (3 vols); draft of *Marah,* a collection of poems (1892).
British Library (Add MSS 44873, 59611-13). Partly presented by the 2nd Earl of Lytton 1936 and partly purchased at Sotheby's 29 Oct 1975, lot 189.

[51] **BURGES** (afterwards **LAMB**), **Sir James Bland** (1752-1824), 1st Bt 1795
Under secretary for foreign affairs 1789-95.

Letters to him mainly from British diplomats and agents 1789-95 (17 vols); copies of letters from him 1790-3 (3 vols); general corresp 1773-1824, incl list of letters received 1788-94 (12 vols); family corresp 1772-1824 (16 vols); misc official and other papers rel to Foreign Office and diplomatic business 1749-1804, incl notebooks of RC Etches, Russian commissary-general of marine 1789 (8 vols); copies of official Foreign Office corresp, memoranda and other papers 1762-95 (15 vols); account of political events of December 1783, and memoirs (3 vols); literary papers 18th-19th cent (4 vols).
Bodleian Library, Oxford (MS Dep. Bland Burges). Deposited 1958 by Mrs M Morris Davies, a descendant of his sister Frances Head. NRA 19920.

Letters from Sir William Hamilton 1774-98 (14 items).
Fitzwilliam Museum, Cambridge. Bequeathed by SG Perceval 1922.

BURGHERSH, Baron, see Fane J.

[52] **BURTON, Sir Richard Francis**
(1821-1890)
Consul at Fernando Po 1861-5, at Santos 1865-9, at Damascus 1869-71, at Trieste 1872-90.

His oriental MSS and other collections were destroyed by fire in 1861. His diaries were destroyed by his widow after she had written the *Life* (1893).

His books mainly rel to travel and exploration, many containing his annotations, and with letters to him, literary MSS, maps and press cuttings inserted (*c*2,000 vols).
Royal Anthropological Institute. Transferred in 1955 from Kensington Central Library, to which they had been given in 1898 by Lady Burton's executors.

Notebook kept during his journey from the E African coast to Ujiji 1858, and log kept at Santos 1868 and Damascus 1870-1 (2 vols).
Royal Geographical Society.

Misc literary corresp and papers 1865-90 (62 items).
Syracuse University Library, New York. Presented by FP Hier 1955, and purchased 1956-66.
National union catalog, MS 66-1956.

BUTE, Marquess of, see Stuart J.

[53] **BYNG, George** (1740-1812), 4th Viscount Torrington 1750
Chargé d'affaires in the Southern Netherlands 1782-3, minister 1783-92.

Corresp 1782-92, incl letters from foreign secretaries, diplomats and others (8 vols); copies of letters from various European correspondents

1787-9 (5 vols); memoranda and copies of corresp rel to diplomatic affairs at Brussels from 1782 (1 vol); précis of official letters 1782-8 (1 vol); notes on events in the Southern Netherlands copied from corresp with his daughters and Lord John Russell 1787 (2 vols); registers of correspondents.
The Earl of Bradford (a descendant of his eldest daughter). Access through Staffordshire RO. *HMC Second Report, Appendix,* 1871, p30.

Unbound corresp, reports, accounts, etc 1785-94; misc family corresp 1788-1812.
Staffordshire RO (D 1287). Deposited 1978 by the 6th Earl of Bradford. NRA 0430.

[54] **CAMPBELL, Sir John Nicoll Robert**
(1799-1870), 2nd Bt 1858
Assistant to the E India Co envoy to Persia 1826-30, acting envoy 1830-1, envoy 1831-3, consul-general and plenipotentiary 1833-5.

Corresp and papers, *c*1826-41, incl translations of letters from the Persian court (1 vol, 11 bundles).
India Office Library and Records (MSS Eur D 556). Presented by Mrs E Barrington Haynes 1958.

Corresp with his father, diplomatic colleagues and Indian administrators, memoranda and other papers 1814-41, mainly rel to Persia, incl efforts to stabilise the Persian government, relations with India, Russia and Turkey, and charges against his conduct of affairs (260 items).
William R Perkins Library, Duke University, Durham, North Carolina. Acquired 1962. *Guide to the cataloged collections,* p82.

[55] **CANNING, Charles John** (1812-1862), 2nd Viscount Canning 1837, Earl Canning 1859
Parliamentary under secretary for foreign affairs 1841-6.

Corresp with diplomats and statesmen incl Lord Aberdeen, WHLE Bulwer and WE Gladstone, memoranda and other papers rel to foreign affairs mainly 1841-6 (*c*90 bundles and items).
West Yorkshire Archive Service, Leeds (Earl of Harewood's Archives 177 C-X). Deposited in 1963 by his great-great-great-nephew the 7th Earl of Harewood. NRA 7618.

See also *Cabinet Ministers.*

[56] **CANNING, George** (1770-1827)
Under secretary for foreign affairs 1796-9; foreign secretary 1807-9, 1822-7; ambassador to Portugal 1814-15.

Corresp as foreign secretary 1807-9 with British diplomats and foreign diplomats and statesmen (17 bundles); corresp, Portugal 1814-15 (3 bundles); corresp as foreign secretary 1822-7 with Sir William A'Court, Sir Charles Bagot, Stratford Canning, Lord Granville and other diplomats, Foreign Office officials and foreign diplomats and statesmen (24 bundles); royal, political and

personal corresp 1787-1827, incl letters from
diplomats and Foreign Office officials (76
bundles); letter book 1807-9 (1 vol); memoranda
and other papers rel to foreign affairs c1794-1813,
incl corresp of the Comte d'Antraigues 1802-9 (5
bundles); cabinet notes and minutes 1807-9 (1
bundle); diaries 1792-1815, 1818-21, 1823.
West Yorkshire Archive Service, Leeds (Earl of
Harewood's Archives: Canning Papers).
Deposited in 1963 by his descendant the 7th Earl
of Harewood. NRA 9205.

Copies and précis of despatches to and from him
as foreign secretary 1807-9 (57 vols); as
ambassador to Portugal 1814-15 (7 vols); as
foreign secretary 1822-7 (101 vols).
The Earl of Harewood. Access through West
Yorkshire Archive Service, Leeds. NRA 9205.

Misc corresp and papers of Canning and his
private secretary AG Stapleton rel to French,
Greek, Portuguese and Spanish affairs 1823-7 (73
items); copies of corresp of Canning and
Stapleton with Lords Granville and Liverpool
1824-7 (123 items).
West Yorkshire Archive Service, Leeds (Stapleton
MSS). Purchased by Leeds City Council 1972.
NRA 23599.

Notebook rel to Spain 1824-5, and memoranda rel
to Greece 1824-7 (3 vols).
Public Record Office (FO 800/229-31).

See also *Cabinet Ministers.*

[57] **CANNING, Stratford** (1786-1880),
Viscount Stratford de Redcliffe 1852
Secretary of embassy in Turkey 1809-12 (minister
ad interim 1810-12); minister to Switzerland
1814-19, to the United States 1820-5; on a special
mission to Russia 1824-5; ambassador to Turkey
1825-7; plenipotentiary to Greece 1828;
ambassador on a special mission to Turkey
1831-2; on an extraordinary mission to Spain
1832-3; ambassador to Turkey 1841-58; on special
missions to Belgium, Hanover, Prussia, Saxony,
Austria, Bavaria, Greece 1848, to Turkey 1858.

Private corresp, drafts, copies and précis of
despatches, memoranda, notes, etc rel to Turkey
1809-12 (4 boxes), Switzerland 1813-19 (4
boxes), the United States 1820-5 and Russia
1824-5 (7 boxes), Turkey 1825-8 (18 boxes),
Greece 1828-9 (5 boxes), Turkey, Spain, etc
1829-42 (6 boxes), Turkey 1841-64 (53 boxes),
and misc diplomatic matters c1807-63 (6 boxes).
Public Record Office (FO 352). Presented to the
Foreign Office by his daughter 1897 and by his
biographer Stanley Lane-Poole 1930. NRA 23623.

Letters from politicians, diplomats and others
mainly rel to Greek and Turkish affairs 1812-58
(1 vol).
Untraced. C & IK Fletcher Ltd, catalogue 182,
1958, item 19.

Letters from AH Layard 1845-6 mainly rel to his
excavations at Nimrud (1 vol).

British Library (Add MS 40637). Presented by C
Paget 1921.

[58] **CARADOC** (formerly **CRADOCK**),
General John Hobart (1799-1873), 2nd Baron
Howden 1839
Envoy to Egypt 1827; military commissioner with
the French army 1832, with the Spanish army
1834-5; minister to Brazil 1847-50, to Spain
1850-8.

Corresp, papers and accounts while attached to
the Queen of Spain's army in the Basque
provinces 1834-5 (1 vol).
Public Record Office (FO 323/3). Presented to the
Foreign Office 1932 by Miss CI Meade, daughter
of his cousin ER Meade.

Copies of despatches from him 1850-8 (8 vols);
copies of private letters to Lord Palmerston and
others 1850-8 (2 vols); copies of letters to Spanish
officials, etc 1850-8 (6 vols).
Captain JW Alston-Roberts-West. NRA 4349.

CARLISLE, Earl of, see Howard G.

CARMARTHEN, Marquess of, see Osborne.

CARNOCK, Baron, see Nicolson.

[59] **CARTWRIGHT, Sir Fairfax Leighton**
(1857-1928)
Second secretary in Persia 1887-9, in Spain
1889-93, in Austria 1893-4, in Italy 1894-9;
secretary of legation in Mexico 1899-1902 (in
charge 1900-1), in Portugal 1902-5
(intermittently in charge 1903-4); chargé
d'affaires in Spain 1905-6; minister resident in
Bavaria 1906-8; ambassador to Austria-Hungary
1908-13.

Personal and diplomatic corresp from 1880 (10
boxes); despatches 1900-11 (1 box); personal,
family, diplomatic and literary papers (7 boxes);
accounts and receipts (2 boxes); misc corresp and
papers 1883-c1928 (3 boxes).
Northamptonshire RO. Deposited by Miss
Elizabeth Cartwright (afterwards Mrs Cartwright
Hignett) at various dates since 1960. NRA 21333.

[60] **CARTWRIGHT, Sir Thomas** (1795-1850)
Secretary of legation in Bavaria 1821-9
(intermittently in charge 1821-7); secretary of
embassy in the Netherlands 1828-30 (minister *ad
interim* 1829); on special service in Belgium and
joint commissioner from the Conference of
London 1830; minister to the Germanic
Confederation 1830-8, to Hesse-Cassel 1831-8, to
Sweden 1838-50.

Copies of despatches from him, Belgium 1830 (1
vol); corresp with Lord Palmerston and the

Foreign Office 1830-6 (2 vols), copies of despatches and letters from him 1830-8 (9 vols) and translation in French of a resolution of the diet at Frankfurt 1834 (1 vol); letters from Palmerston and the Foreign Office 1838-9 (1 vol), copies of despatches from him 1838-45, 1849 (4 vols); misc family and diplomatic corresp, draft despatches, press cuttings, etc c1828-49 (2 boxes, etc).
Northamptonshire RO. Deposited by Miss Elizabeth Cartwright 1960. NRA 21333.

CARYSFORT, Earl of, see Proby.

[61] **CASEMENT, Sir Roger David** (1864-1916)
Consul at Lourenço Marques 1895-8, at Luanda 1898-1902, at Boma 1902-6, at Santos 1906-8, at Para 1908-9; consul-general at Rio de Janeiro 1909-13.

Corresp and papers, partly of his cousin Gertrude Bannister, 1889-1935, incl letters to him from family, friends and political and literary figures c1900-15, corresp with the Foreign Office 1911-13, letters from him to Gertrude Bannister 1889-1915, papers rel to his investigations in the Congo 1903-4 and in Putumayo c1909-13, his Irish nationalist activities and journeys to the United States and Germany 1914-15, and his trial 1916, and literary MSS 1882-1916 (c4,000 items); journal 1899 (1 vol); memorandum book 1901 (1 vol); diaries 1914-16 (2 vols).
National Library of Ireland (MSS 1689-90, 12114-18, 13073-92). *Manuscript sources for the history of Irish civilisation,* ed RJ Hayes, i, Boston 1965, pp509-10 and *Supplement,* i, 1979, pp107-12.

Diaries 1901-11 (5 vols).
Public Record Office (HO 161). Access restricted.

[62] **CATHCART, General William Schaw** (1755-1843), 10th Lord Cathcart 1776, 1st Viscount Cathcart 1807, 1st Earl Cathcart 1814
Ambassador to Russia 1812-20; plenipotentiary to the congresses of Châtillon, Paris and Vienna 1814-15.

Corresp, letter books, order books and other papers rel to his military commands 1791-1812 (14 vols, 28 bundles); corresp and papers 1812-20, incl despatches and letters to and from Lord Castlereagh, British agents and naval and military officers (3 vols, 30 bundles, etc); corresp with Colonel EP Lygon, the Duke of Wellington and others 1820-37 (3 bundles); personal and family corresp 1776-1843 (41 bundles); diaries 1839-43 (5 vols).
Major-General the Earl Cathcart. NRA 3946.

[63] **CECIL, Robert Arthur Talbot Gascoyne-** (1830-1903), styled Viscount Cranborne 1865-8, 3rd Marquess of Salisbury 1868

Special ambassador to the conference of Constantinople 1876-7; foreign secretary 1878-80, 1885-6, 1887-92, 1895-1900; joint plenipotentiary to the congress of Berlin 1878.

Royal corresp c1874-1902 (c20 boxes); political corresp c1852-1903 (15 vols, c220 boxes); corresp and memoranda as foreign secretary 1878-80 (34 vols), 1885-6 (10 vols), 1887-92 (38 vols), 1895-1900 (58 vols); letters from foreign correspondents (3 boxes); Cabinet and departmental papers, mostly printed (36 boxes, 22 files); guest lists, Foreign Office and Hatfield House (1 box).
The Marquess of Salisbury. Enquiries to the Librarian/Archivist, Hatfield House, Hatfield, Hertfordshire. NRA 9226 (Foreign Office corresp only).

See also *Cabinet Ministers.*

[64] **CHAD, George William** (1784-1849)
Chargé d'affaires in the Netherlands 1816-17, secretary of embassy 1817-24 (intermittently minister *ad interim*); minister to Saxony 1824-8, to the Germanic Confederation 1829-30, to Prussia 1830-2.

Diaries 1807-49 (32 vols).
British Library (Add MSS 59705-36). Purchased from Henry Bristow Ltd 1976.

Letters from James Bandinel and other Foreign Office officials and diplomats 1815-17 (1 vol).
British Library (Add MS 61836). Presented 1980 by Vizards, solicitors.

Notes of conversations with the Duke of Wellington 1820-48 (1 vol).
The Duke of Wellington. See *Conversations of the first Duke of Wellington with George William Chad,* ed Duke of Wellington, Cambridge 1956.

[65] **CHAMBERLAIN, Sir Henry** (1773-1829), 1st Bt 1828
Consul-general at Rio de Janeiro 1814-29 (chargé d'affaires in Brazil 1815-19, chargé d'affaires and plenipotentiary 1826).

Letters from Vice-Admiral Sir TM Hardy rel to the Brazilian war of independence 1820-31, mainly 1822-3 (19 items).
Untraced. John Wilson, catalogue 49, 1982, item 147.

[66] **CHAMBERLAIN, Joseph** (1836-1914)
Plenipotentiary to the United States for the N American fisheries conference 1887-8.

Papers rel to the fisheries conference 1887-8, incl private corresp, copies of official corresp, diary, printed papers and press cuttings, and misc American corresp 1881-97 (2 vols, 349 items).
Birmingham University Library (JC 3). Presented by the Chamberlain family 1960. NRA 12604.

See also *Cabinet Ministers.*

[67] **CHICHELE-PLOWDEN, Sir Trevor John Chichele** (1846-1905)
Resident and political agent in Turkish Arabia and consul-general at Baghdad 1880-5.

Corresp, memoranda, reports, etc, Baghdad 1879-85 (31 items); notebook *c*1880; official and private corresp and papers, Kashmir 1885-91 (1 vol, 4 bundles, etc), Hyderabad *c*1893-1910, incl material rel to the Nizam's Guaranteed State Railways Co 1900-10 (44 items); misc personal and Indian corresp and papers *c*1836-1901 (56 items).
Hertfordshire RO (D/EK/O41-73). Deposited by his granddaughter Lady Cobbold 1962. NRA 4598.

[68] **CHRISTIE, William Dougal** (1816-1874)
Agent and consul-general on the Mosquito Coast 1848-51; secretary of legation in Switzerland 1851-4 (intermittently in charge); chargé d'affaires and consul-general in the Argentine Republic 1854-6, minister 1856-9; on a special mission to Paraguay 1858; minister to Brazil 1859-63.

Corresp and papers of Christie and his family *c*1835-*c*1900, incl letters to him from politicians, diplomats, scholars, university friends and others, with related papers (several hundred items).
Untraced. Sold at Sotheby's 8 Dec 1983, lots 140, 372, 377.

Letters from Sir Arthur Helps 1835-72 (20 items).
John Rylands University Library of Manchester. Presented by Professor JR De Bruyn 1983 following purchase at Sotheby's 3 Nov 1969, lot 278.

Letters from Lord Houghton 1863-4 and nd (20 items).
Untraced. Sold at Sotheby's 3 Nov 1969, lot 279.

Letters from JS Mill 1864-71 (23 items).
Cornell University Libraries, Ithaca, New York. Purchased at Sotheby's 3 Nov 1969, lot 277.

CLANDEBOYE, Baron, see Hamilton-Temple-Blackwood.

CLANRICARDE, Marquess of, see De Burgh.

CLANWILLIAM, Earl of, see Meade RCFC.

CLARENDON, Earl of, see Villiers GWF.

CLEVELAND, Duke of, see Vane HG.

[69] **COLLET, John** (d 1786)
Consul at Genoa 1776-86.

See Noel-Hill.

[70] **COLNAGHI, Sir Dominic Ellis** (1834-1908)
Acting consul at Mytilene 1854-7; vice-consul at Missolonghi 1859-62; consul at Bastia 1862-4, at Larnaca 1864-5, at Turin 1865-72; consul at Florence 1872-81, consul-general 1881-96; consul-general at Boston 1896-9.

Letters to his parents 1852-81 interspersed with notes by him on his career, sketches and copies of other letters from him (3 vols); letters, press cuttings, photographs, etc rel to the Mont Cenis tunnel 1868-71 (1 vol).
British Library (Add MSS 59502-5). Purchased 1975.

[71] **COLQUHOUN, Sir Robert Gilmour** (1803-1870)
Consul at Bucharest 1834-7, consul-general 1837-51; agent and consul-general in Romania 1851-8, in Egypt 1858-65.

Diary as consul-general at Bucharest, covering the revolution in Wallachia 1848, etc.
Central State Library, Bucharest (St George's MSS CCVI/4). B Marinescu, *Romanian-British political relations 1848-1877,* Bucharest 1983, p21.

[72] **COOPER, Colonel Harry** (1847-1928)
Vice-consul in Bosnia 1877-8, in Anatolia 1879-80.

Letters to him 1877-80 (1 bundle); copies of reports and letters sent, Bosnia 1877-8 (4 bundles); corresp, reports and other papers rel to the Nile expedition 1898 (12 vols, bundles and items); corresp, letter books, telegram books, etc as commandant of the Namaqualand Frontier Force 1902 (9 vols, 3 bundles and 5 items); misc military corresp and papers 1864-1922, rel to the Ashanti war 1873-4, the Territorial Army, etc (*c*32 vols, bundles and items).
National Army Museum (6111/156, 6112/190, 475, 595-6, 7003/21, 7303/6). Presented by his daughter Mrs B Cunliffe 1961, 1970 and by Mrs D Cooper 1973. NRA 25756.

[73] **COPE, Walter** (d 1871)
Consul at Guayaquil 1827-54; plenipotentiary to Ecuador 1838-51, chargé d'affaires and consul-general 1854-61.

Misc letters, despatches, etc mainly from the Foreign Office and other consuls in S America 1829-37 (1 vol).
Untraced. Deighton, Bell & Co, catalogue 229, autumn 1984, item 82.

[74] **CORBETT, Sir Vincent Edwin Henry**
(1861-1936)
Second secretary in Turkey 1891-4, in Denmark
1894-5 (in charge 1895), in Greece 1895-1900 (in
charge 1895, 1899); secretary of legation in
Greece 1900-3; financial adviser to the
Government of Egypt 1904-7; minister to
Venezuela 1907-10, to Bavaria and Württemberg
1910-14.

Letter book 1892-3, mainly comprising copies of
his fortnightly reports to the Foreign Office.
Public Record Office (PRO 30/26/124). Presented
by the British Records Association 1956. NRA
23347.

Letters mainly from Foreign Office staff
1898-1936 (20 items); letters to him on his
resignation from Egypt 1907-8 (15 items); papers
rel to honours and appointments 1898-1921 (10
items); miscellanea and photographs (1 bundle).
Hampshire RO (17M78). Deposited 1978 by
Lieutenant-Commander MR de Halpert and Mrs
BS Dufort, grandchildren of his sister Beatrix.
NRA 20230.

[75] **CORNWALLIS, General Charles**
(1738-1805), styled Viscount Brome 1753-62, 2nd
Earl Cornwallis 1762, 1st Marquess Cornwallis
1792
Plenipotentiary to the congress of Amiens 1801-2.

Corresp with Joseph Bonaparte, Lord
Hawkesbury and CM de Talleyrand, drafts of
protocols and articles, and other papers rel to the
congress of Amiens 1800-2 (384 items).
Kent AO (U269/O199). Deposited among the
papers of Earl Whitworth by the 4th Baron
Sackville in 1950. NRA 8575.

Drafts and copies of his despatches and letters to
Lord Hawkesbury 1801-2 (2 vols, 1 bundle);
letters from Henry Addington, Hawkesbury and
Lord St Vincent 1801-2 (1 bundle).
Public Record Office (PRO 30/11/264-7).
Presented by his great-great-great-grandson the
9th Baron Braybrooke in 1947. NRA 8658.

See also *Cabinet Ministers.*

[76] **COSSINS, Richard Brown** (1823-1898)
Acting vice-consul at Marsala 1860.

Corresp with Garibaldi, Stefan Türr and others
rel to Garibaldi's campaign in Sicily 1860, with
related papers 1860-6 (30 items).
Untraced. Sold at Sotheby's 17 Nov 1983, lot 258.
NRA 16964.

[77] **COURTENAY, Vice-Admiral George
William Conway** (1795-1863)
Consul at Port-au-Prince 1832-42; plenipotentiary
to negotiate slave trade treaty with Haiti 1838-9.

Journal as commander of HMS *Bann* on anti-
slave trade patrol, W Africa 1823-5 (1 vol).

University of Illinois Library, Chicago (Sierra
Leone Collection). NRA 22949.

COWLEY, Baron and Earl of, see Wellesley H
and HRC.

[78] **COWPER, George Augustus Frederick**
(1806-1856), styled Viscount Fordwich 1806-37,
6th Earl Cowper 1837
Parliamentary under secretary for foreign affairs
1834.

Letters to him mainly from his family and friends,
incl his mother, his brother Spencer, RC Bingham
and AD Craven, 1828-55 (64 items); accounts of
his election expenses, Canterbury 1830 (1 vol);
misc legal and financial corresp and papers
1836-48 (1 vol, 1 bundle).
Hertfordshire RO (D/EP, boxes 34, 40-1).
Deposited by his great-great-granddaughter Lady
Salmond and JJW Salmond 1952. NRA 26283.

Travel journals 1825, 1828-9 (2 vols).
Bedfordshire RO (L31/418-19). Deposited by his
great-granddaughter Baroness Lucas 1961. NRA
6283.

[79] **COX, Major-General Sir Percy Zachariah**
(1864-1937)
Vice-consul and assistant political resident at Zeila
1893-4, at Berbera 1894-5; consul and political
agent at Muscat 1899-1904; consul-general at
Bushire 1904-14; political resident in the Persian
Gulf 1909-14; minister *ad interim* to Persia
1918-20; high commissioner in Iraq 1920-3.

Journals, Somaliland 1894, 1898-9, and Persian
Gulf 1902-7 (4 vols).
Royal Geographical Society.

[80] **CRAMPTON, Sir John Fiennes Twisleton**
(1805-1886), 2nd Bt 1858
Attaché in Belgium 1834-9 (in charge 1836,
1837), in Austria 1839-44 (in charge 1842);
secretary of legation in Switzerland 1844-5;
secretary of legation in the United States 1845-52
(in charge 1847-9, 1851-2), minister 1852-6;
minister to Hanover 1857-8, to Russia 1858-60, to
Spain 1860-9.

Corresp mainly with his father Sir Philip
Crampton 1819-59 (*c*400 items); other family and
estate papers.
Trinity College, Dublin (MSS 4176-4217).
Presented 1967 by Miss Doreen Boyle, heiress of
his great-niece Selina Boyle. NRA 20226.

Letters to him rel to the Codex Sinaiticus 1860
(20 items).
British Library (Add MS 61835). Presented by JA
Green 1979.

CROMER, Earl of, see Baring E.

[81] **CROWE, Sir Joseph Archer** (1825-1896)
Consul-general at Leipzig 1860-72, Düsseldorf
1872-80; commercial attaché in Germany and
Austria 1880-2, for Europe (based in France)
1882-96.

MSS of his published works on the history of art,
related notes, sketches, etc c1852-86 (20 vols, 10
boxes, etc).
Victoria and Albert Museum Library. See *Catalogue
of English non-illuminated manuscripts*, pp37-8.

MS of his *Reminiscences of thirty-five years of my
life* (1865), and three chapters of an unpublished
sequel 1860-1 (3 vols).
British Library (Add MSS 41309, 44059-60).
Presented by EB Crowe 1926, 1935.

[82] **CURRIE, Philip Henry Wodehouse**
(1834-1906), Baron Currie 1899
Assistant under secretary for foreign affairs
1882-9, permanent under secretary 1889-93;
ambassador to Turkey 1893-8, to Italy 1898-1903.

Intelligence reports, mainly summaries in French
of telegrams and corresp between the Turkish
foreign ministry and its diplomats 1893-6 (1 vol).
Public Record Office (FO 800/114).

[83] **CURZON, George Nathaniel** (1859-1925),
Baron Curzon 1898, Earl Curzon 1911, Marquess
Curzon 1921
Parliamentary under secretary for foreign affairs
1895-8; foreign secretary 1919 (*ad interim*),
1919-24.

General corresp 1880-1905; letters from the
British and Belgian royal families 1899-1924; misc
corresp and papers as under secretary for foreign
affairs, incl material rel to Anglo-Turkish
relations and the Triple Alliance 1895-8; corresp
and papers rel to India c1870-1924, mainly during
his viceroyalty 1898-1905; corresp and papers rel
to Oxford University, women's suffrage, Irish
home rule, the National Gallery, etc 1906-25; as
lord privy seal and leader of the House of Lords
1914-24; as a member of the War Cabinet, incl
papers rel to Irish and foreign affairs 1915-19; as
foreign secretary, incl papers rel to Europe, the
Middle and Far East, the first Lausanne Peace
Conference 1919-24 and the Imperial Conferences
1921-3; printed papers 1880-1923, mainly rel to
his viceroyalty and membership of the War
Cabinet; corresp, papers and journals rel to his
travels in Afghanistan, Persia, the Far East, etc
c1881-1910; literary papers and speeches c1880-
1925; scrap books, albums and press cuttings
1879-1925; personal, family, household and estate
corresp and papers c1866-1925.
India Office Library and Records (MSS Eur F 111-
12). Deposited by the Kedleston Trustees 1962,
1966, 1977. NRA 20536.

Corresp as under secretary for foreign affairs
1895-8 (2 vols); corresp of Curzon, Sir James
Fergusson and JW Lowther as under secretaries
1886-97 (1 vol); general corresp as foreign
secretary 1919-24 (7 vols); corresp rel to
particular countries and miscellanea 1919-23 (3
vols).
Public Record Office (FO 800/28, 147-58). Mainly
deposited in the Foreign Office Library through
Sir IZ Malcolm 1926. NRA 23627.

Corresp and papers rel to the purchase and
restoration of Tattershall Castle 1911-25 (2 vols,
10 bundles, 980 items).
Lincolnshire AO (NT/1-5). Deposited by the
National Trust 1958. NRA 19642.

Letters from Lord Carmichael, Sir William
Foster, BA Gupte, the 4th Earl of Minto and
others, with misc notes and memoranda, rel to the
Victoria Memorial Hall, Calcutta, 1912-26 (50
items).
University of Alberta Library, Edmonton (MS Coll
Box 96-88). Presented by JP Custis 1973. NRA
26023.

Corresp with Sir HEA Cotton and others 1895,
1911-25, mainly rel to paintings and sculptures
for the Victoria Memorial Hall, Calcutta (36
items).
*William R Perkins Library, Duke University,
Durham, N Carolina.* Acquired 1968-71. NRA
25900.

Corresp, draft speeches, press cuttings, etc rel to
the National Service League 1908-15.
Untraced. J Browning, catalogue 1, 1983, item 27.

[84] **CURZON, Robert** (1810-1873), 14th Baron
Zouche 1870
Joint commissioner for the delimitation of the
Turco-Persian boundary 1843-4.

Corresp with Sir Stratford Canning 1836-46 (1
vol); diary 1830.
In family possession. NRA 0637.

DALLING AND BULWER, Baron, see Bulwer.

[85] **DALRYMPLE, John** (1749-1821), styled
Viscount Dalrymple 1768-89, 6th Earl of Stair
1789
Envoy to Saxony 1782 (did not proceed);
minister to Poland 1782-4, to Prussia 1785-7.

Copies of despatches sent 1782-7 (2 vols); of
letters to Lord Carmarthen 1786 (1 vol); of
corresp 1778-86 (2 vols); family corresp and
papers 1707-1821 (2 vols).
Scottish Record Office (GD 135). Deposited by the
13th Earl of Stair 1965. NRA 10017.

[86] **DAWKINS, Edward James** (1792-1865)
Secretary of legation in Tuscany 1816-23
(intermittently in charge); resident and consular
agent in Greece 1828-33, minister 1833-5.

Corresp, Greece 1828-35 (8 vols).
Norfolk RO. Deposited with papers of his wife's
family the Petres of Westwick by JFB Petre 1979.

[87] **DE BUNSEN, Sir Maurice William Ernest**
(1852-1932), Bt 1919
Chargé d'affaires in Japan 1892-4, in Siam 1894-6;
secretary of embassy in Turkey 1897-1902 (in
charge 1898, 1900-1, 1902), in France 1902-5
(minister *ad interim* 1903); minister to Portugal
1905-6; ambassador to Spain 1906-13, to Austria-
Hungary 1913-14; on a special mission to S
America 1918.

Letters from diplomatic colleagues and friends,
incl Sir Arthur Nicolson and Frederick Penfield,
*c*1888-1920 (12 bundles); letters from his family
*c*1870-1902 (4 bundles); misc diplomatic papers
1877-1918, incl corresp with the Foreign Office
rel to promotions 1877-96, and papers on the
outbreak of war 1914 and his mission to S
America 1918 (5 bundles); misc papers mainly rel
to foreign affairs 1919-31 (10 bundles); personal
papers 1852-1934, incl diaries 1862-3, 1885, 1918
and 1926, and a Madrid embassy visitors' book
1907-13 (11 bundles); press cuttings and other
printed material 1881-1930 (3 bundles).
Lady Salisbury-Jones (his daughter). NRA 20352.

[88] **DE BURGH, Ulick John** (1802-1876), 14th
Earl of Clanricarde 1808, 1st Marquess of
Clanricarde 1825
Under secretary for foreign affairs 1826-7;
ambassador to Russia 1838-41.

General corresp 1824-*c*1830, incl letters from
George Canning and others 1826-7 (*c*7 bundles);
draft despatches from him 1838-41, with misc
related papers (8 bundles); register of despatches
received and sent 1838-41 (1 vol); misc corresp
rel to foreign affairs, mainly Italy, 1846-7, 1857-60
(1 vol, 4 bundles).
West Yorkshire Archive Service, Leeds (Earl of
Harewood's Archives: Clanricarde Papers).
Deposited in 1963 by his great-great-great-nephew
the 7th Earl of Harewood. NRA 16182.

See also *Cabinet Ministers.*

DE GREY, Earl, see Robinson GFS.

[89] **DENYS** (afterwards **DENYS-BURTON**),
Sir Francis Charles Edward (1849-1922),
3rd Bt 1881
Third secretary in Belgium 1873-5 (in charge
1875); secretary of legation in Mexico 1887-90 (in
charge 1889-90), in Denmark 1890-5 (in charge
1891, 1892-3).

Corresp, reports, press cuttings, etc mainly rel to
the introduction of railways to Mexico 1886-92 (1
vol).
Untraced. B Marshall, catalogue 10, 1982, item 36.

DERBY, Earl of, see Stanley EH.

[90] **DERING, Sir Henry Nevill** (1839-1906),
9th Bt 1896
Secretary to Lord Odo Russell during the
congress of Berlin and acting chargé d'affaires in
Germany 1878; secretary of legation in the
Argentine Republic 1882-3 (in charge 1883);
chargé d'affaires in Saxe-Coburg-Gotha 1883-6;
secretary of embassy in Russia 1886-8 (in charge
1886-7, 1888), in Italy 1888-92 (in charge 1889,
1891-2); agent and consul-general in Bulgaria
1892-4; minister to Mexico 1894-1900, to Brazil
1900-6.

A few papers incl 'A day to day diary of the
Berlin Congress, 1878'.
Lady Dering.

[91] **DES GRAZ, Sir Charles Louis**
(1860-1940)
Chargé d'affaires in Greece 1888; second secretary
in the Netherlands 1891-4 (intermittently in
charge), in Russia 1894-1901; secretary of legation
in Persia 1901-03 (in charge 1902), in Greece
1903-05 (in charge 1903-04); counsellor of
embassy in Italy 1905-08 (in charge in Italy 1905,
1906, 1907, and in Montenegro 1906); minister to
Ecuador and Peru 1908-13, to Serbia 1914-21.

Misc corresp and papers 1893-1940, incl diary
1914-16.
Cambridge University Library (Add 7450).
Presented by the executors of CGM Des Graz
1954. NRA 10589.

[92] **DICKSON, John** (d 1906)
Vice-consul at Mosul 1872-6 (acting vice-consul
at Damascus 1875-6), at Beirut 1876-82 (acting
consul-general 1880-1); vice-consul at Damascus
1882-4, consul 1884-90; consul at Jerusalem
1890-1906.

Papers rel to his appointments to Mosul and
Beirut 1872-6 (1 bundle); corresp, Beirut and
Damascus, incl letters from British diplomats,
consuls, travellers and others 1876-90 (1 bundle);
corresp, Jerusalem, incl letters from the Palestine
Exploration Fund, Gertrude Bell, Ann and WS
Blunt, British diplomats and consuls, and others
1891-1906 (5 bundles); family papers from 1854
(2 bundles); diaries, Damascus 1882-8 (2 vols).
Middle East Centre, St Antony's College, Oxford.
Partly presented by Mrs Violet Dickson 1970.

[93] **DILKE, Sir Charles Wentworth**
(1843-1911), 2nd Bt 1869
Parliamentary under secretary for foreign affairs
1880-2.

Corresp with Lords Dufferin, Granville and
Lyons, Sir RBD Morier, Sir Julian Pauncefote,
Lord Tenterden and French diplomats and
statesmen 1880-2 (7 vols); political diary 1880-4
(2 vols); drafts, notes and other papers mainly rel
to foreign affairs 1882-1908 (1 vol).
British Library (Add MSS 43878-84, 43924-5,
43944). Presented by his niece Miss GM
Tuckwell 1935.

See also *Cabinet Ministers.*

[94] **DISRAELI, Benjamin** (1804-1881), Earl of
Beaconsfield 1876
Joint plenipotentiary to the congress of Berlin
1878.

Corresp and papers rel to the congress of Berlin
1878, incl letters of congratulation, memoranda,
protocols and other official papers (273 items);
corresp and papers rel to the Eastern Question,
incl letters from British diplomats and statesmen
and members of the Austrian, Russian and
Turkish governments 1875-81, and cabinet notes,
telegrams, Foreign Office memoranda and
pamphlets 1867-80 (899 items); misc papers rel to
foreign affairs 1848-81, incl the expansion of
Russia, and Egyptian and Turkish finances (220
items); corresp with Queen Victoria 1874-81
(1,737 items).
Bodleian Library, Oxford (MS Disraeli dep.).
Deposited by the National Trust 1978. NRA
0842.

Corresp with Queen Victoria 1877-81 (13 vols).
The Royal Archives, Windsor Castle. Returned to
Queen Victoria after his death. Access restricted.

See also *Cabinet Ministers.*

[95] **DODSON, John William** (1869-1933), 2nd
Baron Monk Bretton 1897
Attaché in France 1894-5, in Turkey 1895-7;
assistant private secretary to the foreign secretary
1899-1900.

Corresp, misc papers, journals and diaries, France
and Turkey 1894-9 (1 box); corresp rel to foreign
and colonial affairs 1895-1904 (1 box); corresp
and papers mainly rel to the Colonial Office 1895-
1908 (21 boxes); papers rel to local government
in London and E Sussex 1899-1932 (6 boxes);
private and misc corresp 1887-1930 (2 boxes);
diaries 1904-30 (7 vols); press cuttings 1893-1926
(1 vol); misc papers c1867-1925 (2 boxes);
further papers of his and his father's, mainly
printed, 1860-1930 (11 boxes).
Bodleian Library, Oxford (MS Dep. Monk
Bretton). Deposited by the 3rd Baron Monk
Bretton 1960, 1967. NRA 9224 (partial list).

Corresp and papers, mainly estate and local
government 1887-1933 (11 vols, 31 bundles, c120
items).
East Sussex RO (D 350, D 871). Deposited by
the 3rd Baron Monk Bretton 1959, 1968. NRA
21871.

[96] **DONALD, William Macalister** (d 1880)
Vice-consul at Ferrara 1834-62.

Corresp of the Donald and Macalister families
1780-1848, incl letters to him as vice-consul rel to
personal and business matters, Italian politics, etc,
with misc family and estate papers 17th-19th cent
(8 bundles).
Mrs RE Salvesen (née Donald). Enquiries to NRA
(Scotland). NRA 19459.

DONOUGHMORE, Earl of, see Hely-
Hutchinson.

DORSET, Duke of, see Sackville.

[97] **DOUGLAS, Andrew Snape** (d 1869)
Secretary of legation in the Two Sicilies 1809-11,
1813-24 (intermittently in charge 1811-22);
secretary of embassy in the Netherlands 1824-9
(minister *ad interim* 1824; 1825).

Draft despatches from him, and corresp with
Sicilian ministers, and with British diplomats,
army commanders and colonial governors 1811,
1813-14, 1816-18, 1822 (2 vols).
Public Record Office (PRO 30/7). Bequeathed to
his private secretary John Fowle, sold after
Fowle's death in 1906, and presented by Captain
CJP Cave in 1920. NRA 23633.

[98] **DRAKE, Francis** (1764-1821)
Secretary of legation in Denmark 1790-3 (in
charge 1790-2); minister to Genoa 1793-7, to
Parma 1794-7; envoy to Bavaria 1800-2, minister
1802-4; minister to the diet of Ratisbon 1800-4.

Corresp as chargé d'affaires in Denmark 1790-2,
and with the Foreign Office 1791-1814 (1 vol);
corresp with John Trevor, envoy to Sardinia,
1793-1800 (2 vols); corresp 1793-1815, mainly
letters and intelligence reports, Genoa (8 vols);
letters to him 1800-13, mainly Bavaria (1 vol);
general and family corresp 1696-1861 (4 vols);
misc papers 1793-1807 (2 vols).
British Library (Add MSS 46822-46838B).
Presented by the Revd HM Drake 1948.

Corresp 1790-1820, mainly Denmark, Italy and
Bavaria (c750 items); misc family corresp and
papers c1773-1850 (c200 items).
Devon RO (1700 M). Deposited 1968 by Lady
Nicholson, daughter of the Revd HM Drake.
NRA 13842.

Corresp mainly rel to his diplomatic missions and to local and national politics, with some related papers 1785-1820 (*c*19 bundles, 37 items); family and estate corresp and papers 1694-1854 (*c*7 bundles, 23 items).
Somerset RO (DD/NE). Deposited 1967 by Squadron Leader BH Newton. NRA 22739.

Letters from Lord Nelson 1793-1800 mainly rel to the blockade of the Genoese coast, with a letter from Pasquale di Paoli 1793 (28 items).
Untraced. Sold at Sotheby's 28 Apr 1969, lots 306-9.

[99] DRUMMOND-HAY, Edward William Auriol (1785-1845)
Agent and consul-general in Morocco 1829-45.

Family corresp and papers, early 19th cent (1 box); corresp and papers, Morocco 1830-46, incl letters to EWA and JH Drummond-Hay from John Davidson 1835-6 and others 1831-44, and from JH Drummond-Hay to Sir FWE Nicolson 1845-6, translations of Moorish letters, memoranda on Moroccan geography, Berber grammar, etc (2 bundles); journals of EWA Drummond-Hay 1829, 1830, 1832, 1844 (9 vols), and of JH Drummond-Hay 1838, 1840, 1846 (3 vols); notebook rel to African geography (1 vol); extracts from JH Drummond-Hay's journals and letters to his mother 1846-64 (1 vol); translation into French of journal kept by Faki Mohammed ben Mahlouf during JH Drummond-Hay's mission to Fez 1880 (1 vol).
Bodleian Library, Oxford (Drummond-Hay Papers). Presented by Robert Drummond-Hay 1980. NRA 26116.

[100] DRUMMOND-HAY, Sir John Hay (1816-1893)
Agent *ad interim* in Morocco 1845-6, agent and consul-general 1846-7, chargé d'affaires and consul-general 1847-60, minister resident 1860-72, minister 1872-86.

See Drummond-Hay EWA.

[101] DRUMMOND-HAY (afterwards HAY-DRUMMOND-HAY), Sir Robert (1846-1926)
Attaché in Morocco 1869-75; consul at Mogador 1876-9, at Stockholm 1879-89; consul at Tunis 1889-91, consul-general 1891-4; consul-general at Beirut 1894-1908.

Letters to him 1895-9, mainly from his elder son Arnold in Nyasaland (*c*50 items); letters from him, mainly to his parents *c*1858-65, 1893-6 (1 bundle); memoranda and travel notes (1 bundle); journals and notebooks, Syria and Palestine 1895-7 (3 vols).
Bodleian Library, Oxford (Drummond-Hay Papers). Presented by Robert Drummond-Hay 1980. NRA 26116.

[102] DUFF, Sir James (d 1815), 1st Bt 1813
Consul at Cadiz 1790-1815.

Foreign account rolls 1808-13 (5 items).
National Library of Wales, Aberystwyth (Harpton Court MSS 2898-2902). Deposited by Sir DF Duff Gordon Bt 1953. NRA 22798.

DUFFERIN AND AVA, Marquess of, see Hamilton-Temple-Blackwood.

DUNFERMLINE, Baron, see Abercromby.

[103] DURAND, Sir Henry Mortimer (1850-1924)
Foreign secretary to the government of India 1884-94; minister to Persia 1894-1900; ambassador to Spain 1900-3, to the United States 1903-6.

Corresp and papers, India, Afghanistan and Morocco 1840-1906, incl letters from Lords Curzon and Lansdowne, Sir CM MacGregor, Lord Roberts and others (2 boxes); corresp, speeches, press cuttings, etc, United States (2 boxes, etc); letter books 1902-9 (4 vols); despatches, corresp, telegrams to and from the Foreign Office 1901-6 (1 box); corresp rel to his parliamentary candidacy for Plymouth 1910 (1 box); personal, literary, biographical and family corresp and papers 1812-96 and nd (6 vols, 5 boxes, etc); diaries 1870-1907 (15 vols); printed material *c*1852-1917 (3 vols, 1 box).
School of Oriental and African Studies, London (Acc No 257247). Purchased from his family 1969. NRA 14595.

Letter books 1876-1903 (7 vols); letter books as foreign secretary to the government of India 1885-94 (5 vols); letters to him, India 1885-8 (3 vols); corresp and papers mainly rel to Afghanistan and the Afghan boundary commission 1884-1908 (3 bundles).
India Office Library and Records (MSS Eur D 729). NRA 27462.

DURHAM, Earl of, see Lambton.

[104] EASTWICK, Edward Backhouse (1814-1883)
Secretary of legation in Persia 1860-3 (in charge 1862-3); commissioner for arranging loans to Venezuela 1864, 1867.

Letters to him 1839-79 (1 vol); notes on Gujerat *c*1840-6 (1 vol); registers of European monumental inscriptions in India and Burma *c*1880 (4 vols).
India Office Library and Records (MSS Eur A 28, E 144-7, F 18/1). *Catalogue of European manuscripts,* ii, pt 2, pp1457-64.

[105] **EDEN, Morton Frederick** (1752-1830),
1st Baron Henley 1799
Minister to Bavaria 1776-9; envoy to Denmark
1779-83; envoy to Saxony 1783-9, minister
1789-91; minister to Prussia 1791-3; envoy and
plenipotentiary to Austria 1793-4, 1794-9.

Nine volumes of his copies of official diplomatic
correspondence 1777-99, with other papers, were
disposed of by the 2nd Baron Henley as waste
paper. They were subsequently offered for auction
by Evans of Pall Mall (19 June 1833, lots 928,
930-1). The Foreign Office obtained an
injunction preventing the sale, took possession of
the papers and may have incorporated them in
the official records.

Corresp with his brother Lord Auckland, incl
some original letters to him from Auckland,
1772-1814 (c410 items).
British Library (Add MSS 34412-60). Purchased
1893.

Despatches from Lord Grenville 1794-5, 1797-8,
with a few private letters from George Canning,
Grenville and George Hammond and misc related
papers (3 bundles).
Trustees of the Bedford Estates. Enquiries to the
Archivist, Bedford Office, 29A Montague Street,
London WC1B 5BL. Acquired from Sir Robert
Adair. NRA 26179.

Travel journal and accounts 1788-91 (1 vol).
Revd Canon JH Adams.

Diplomatic instructions 1776-83 and misc letters
mainly from Lord Grenville 1792-1821 (12
items).
Northamptonshire RO (Northington Papers).
Deposited by the 6th Baron Henley 1954. NRA
14944.

[106] **EDEN, William** (1744-1814), 1st Baron
Auckland 1789
Under secretary for the northern department
1772-8; envoy to France 1786-8; ambassador to
Spain 1788-9, to the Netherlands 1790-4.

Diplomatic, political and general corresp 1660-
1861, mainly 1761-1814, and many transcripts of
despatches of other diplomats 1790-3 (50 vols);
papers rel to the commercial treaty with France
1786, and Paris newsletters 1786-8 (2 vols);
journal in the form of letters to his mother 1788-9
(1 vol); corresp and papers rel to the E India Co
1776-1802 (4 vols); copies of corresp between
Robert Liston and Lord Carmarthen 1786-7, and
extracts from the letters of Swedish conspirators
1792-4 (1 vol).
British Library (Add MSS 34412-69). Purchased
1893.

Letters to Lord Sheffield 1781-c1814 (2 vols);
corresp as under secretary 1775-9, incl intercepted
corresp of American diplomats, corresp with
William Pitt 1785-c1801, and other personal and
family corresp and papers 1688-1899 (4 vols).

British Library (Add MSS 45728-30, 46490-1,
46519). Presented by OE and Miss VM
Dickinson, grandchildren of the 3rd Baron
Auckland, 1941, 1948.

Letters from peers, statesmen and others to him
and his son George 1768-1827 (1 vol).
British Library (Add MS 29475). Purchased 1873.

Misc papers of Auckland and his family (1 vol).
British Library (Add MS 54328). Purchased 1968.

Letters from Lord Clare 1784-1801 (40 items);
letters rel to Irish affairs from British and Irish
politicians 1784-7, 1795-1802 (72 items).
Keele University Library (S21). Purchased from
the collector Raymond Richards 1957. NRA 1248.

ELGIN, Earls of, see Bruce J and T.

[107] **ELIAS, Ney** (1844-1897)
Member of the Anglo-Siamese boundary
commission 1889-90; consul-general at Mashhad
1891-6.

Draft letters, reports, etc to the Indian
government 1873-90; literary corresp and papers
c1895-7; journals, Dresden 1857-60; travel
journals, field notebooks and observations, mainly
China and Mongolia 1867-87, and as a member of
the Anglo-Siamese boundary commission 1889-90.
Royal Geographical Society.

[108] **ELIOT, Edward Granville** (1798-1877),
styled Lord Eliot 1823-45, 3rd Earl of St Germans
1845
Envoy extraordinary to Spain 1834-5.

Drafts of the Eliot convention on the treatment of
prisoners of war, copies of despatches and letters
from him, despatches from the Duke of
Wellington and letters from GWF Villiers and
Spanish generals 1835 (1 vol); other papers incl
commonplace book c1823-45.
Lord Eliot.

[109] **ELIOT, William** (1767-1845), 2nd Earl of
St Germans 1823
Secretary of legation in Prussia 1791-3 (in charge
1793); secretary of embassy in the Netherlands
1793-5 (minister *ad interim* 1793-4);
plenipotentiary on a special mission to Brunswick
1794; minister to the diet of Ratisbon 1796-8;
under secretary for foreign affairs 1804-5.

Copies of despatches to and from him, Prussia
and the Netherlands 1793-4 (1 vol, 3 bundles);
letters from Lord Malmesbury 1793-4 (14 items);
personal accounts and vouchers 1812-23 (1 vol, 2
bundles).
Lord Eliot.

[110] **ELLIOT, Admiral Sir Charles**
(1801-1875)
Chief superintendent of trade in China 1837-41,
plenipotentiary to China 1840-1; consul-general
and chargé d'affaires in Texas 1842-6.

Family corresp 1763-1892, copies of despatches
sent 1841, reports to Lord Aberdeen 1842 and
Lord Palmerston 1846 (2 boxes); notes on
Demerara 1831, papers rel to W Indian slavery
1832-3, memoranda and other papers, Canton
1840-2, and miscellanea (1 box); corresp as
governor of Trinidad and St Helena 1856-70,
general corresp 1856-74, returns, addresses, etc,
with corresp of the Ouseley family, 1851-91 (*c*300
items).
National Library of Scotland (Acc 5534, 7287).
Purchased 1972, and at Sotheby's 16 Oct 1978, lot
209. NRA 18510, and *Annual Report 1978-9*, p72.

[111] **ELLIOT, Hon George Francis Stewart**
(1822-1901)
Attached to Lord John Russell's mission to
Austria 1855; private secretary to Russell as
foreign secretary 1859-65 and prime minister
1865-6.

Letters from Admiral Sir CGJB Elliot 1859-81,
Sir HG Elliot 1859-60 and other members of his
family 1845-98 (3 vols); corresp and papers
mainly rel to his antiquarian and genealogical
interests *c*1857-*c*1901 (12 vols).
National Library of Scotland (MSS 13089-13103).
Purchased from the 5th Earl of Minto 1958, 1960.
NRA 10476.

Corresp 1879-96 as Russell's executor, and rel to
accusations that in 1860 Russell had planned to
advance Sir HG Elliot at the expense of Sir James
Hudson (1 box).
Public Record Office (PRO 30/22/118A).
Bequeathed by Gertrude Russell 1942. NRA
8659.

[112] **ELLIOT, Sir Henry George** (1817-1907)
Secretary of legation in the Netherlands 1848-53
(intermittently in charge 1850-3), in Austria
1853-8 (in charge 1855); minister to Denmark
1858-9, to the Two Sicilies 1859-61; on special
missions to Greece 1862-3; minister to Italy
1863-7; ambassador to Turkey 1867-77, to
Austria-Hungary 1877-84.

Private corresp with successive foreign secretaries,
Foreign Office officials, diplomats and others
1870-7 (9 vols) and 1878-84 (6 vols); draft
despatches from him 1870-6 (8 vols); registers of
corresp 1875-6 (2 vols); misc corresp and papers
1822-1904 (1 vol); printed parliamentary papers
rel to Italy 1860 and the Ottoman Porte 1876-7,
and printed official corresp rel to Austria-
Hungary 1878-80 (3 vols).
National Library of Scotland (MSS 13060-88).
Purchased from the 5th Earl of Minto 1958, 1960.
NRA 10476.

Letters from CG Gordon 1872-3 (15 items).
Untraced. Sold at Sotheby's 15 Dec 1980, lot 164.

[113] **ELLIOT, Hugh** (1752-1830)
Minister to Bavaria and the Imperial diet 1774-7;
envoy to Prussia 1777-82, to Denmark 1783-91;
minister to Saxony 1791-1803, to the Two Sicilies
1803-6.

Despatches to and from him and misc diplomatic
papers 1772-1802 (6 vols); corresp and papers,
Two Sicilies 1802-7, incl despatches, intelligence
reports and corresp with British and foreign
diplomats, British army and naval officers, and
Neapolitan ministers (31 vols); private diplomatic
and general corresp 1772-1814 (42 vols); corresp
and papers as governor of the Leeward Islands
1809-13, (5 vols); papers as governor of Madras
1814-17 (1 vol); family corresp 1771-1823 (12
vols); financial and business corresp and papers
1774-1820 (11 vols).
National Library of Scotland (MSS 12952-13059).
Purchased from the 5th Earl of Minto 1958, 1960,
except MS 13040 presented by HM Colvin 1965.
NRA 10476.

Corresp and papers, Two Sicilies 1803-6, incl
letters from Admiral Collingwood, Lord Nelson
and others, drafts and copies of replies, and
intelligence reports (2 vols, *c*175 items).
National Maritime Museum (ELL/300-10).
Presented by Sir James Caird, who had purchased
them from the 5th Earl of Minto in 1941. *Guide
to the manuscripts*, i, pp53–4.

[114] **ELLIOT-MURRAY-KYNYNMOUND**
(formerly **ELLIOT**), **Sir Gilbert** (1751-1814),
4th Bt 1777, 1st Baron Minto 1797, 1st Earl of
Minto 1813
Civil commissioner at Toulon 1793; viceroy of
Corsica 1794-6; minister to Austria 1799-1801.

Corresp and papers, Toulon, Corsica and Italy
1793-1803, incl letters from Sir JC Hippisley and
Count Pozzo di Borgo, and intercepted French
corresp (14 vols); corresp with and rel to French
emigrés 1794-1806 (3 vols); letters and despatches
from successive foreign secretaries and under
secretaries, Austria 1799-1801 (5 vols); copies of
letters and despatches to and from foreign
secretaries 1799-1801 (6 vols); papers formerly
enclosed in despatches 1799-1801 (2 vols);
corresp with British diplomats, consuls and army
and naval officers, accounts and misc diplomatic
and military papers 1799-1801 (33 vols); political
corresp and papers 1776-1806 (16 vols); corresp
and papers as president of the Board of Control
1806 and governor-general of India 1806-14 (468
vols); family and general corresp of Minto and his
wife 1773-1820 (115 vols); financial and legal
corresp and papers 1767-1816 (29 vols); travel
journals 1781-1807 and political journal 1793 (7
vols); verses and masques 1783-1810 (7 vols);
corresp and papers, mainly his and his son
Gilbert's rel to Roxburghshire elections 1777-1877
and local defence 1776-1819 (45 vols, etc).
National Library of Scotland (MSS 11042-11739,
12824-30, 13330-52, 13356-77). Purchased from
the 5th Earl of Minto 1958, 1960. NRA 10476.

Official corresp, Toulon and Corsica 1793-6,
corresp with Lord Nelson and Lady Hamilton,
account of the seizure and defence of Toulon
1793, journal 1794 and misc papers (62 vols).
National Maritime Museum (ELL/100-66).
Presented by Sir James Caird, who had purchased
them from the 5th Earl of Minto in 1941. *Guide
to the manuscripts,* i, pp52-3.

Corresp with JWJanssens and TS Raffles, treaties
and other papers rel to Java 1808-14 (48 vols).
India Office Library and Records
(MSS Eur F148). Presented 1969 by the
Malaysia-Singapore Commercial Association after
purchase from A Dickson-Wright, to whom they
had been sold by the 5th Earl of Minto.

[115] **ELLIOT-MURRAY-KYNYNMOUND,
Gilbert** (1782-1859), styled Viscount Melgund
1813-14, 2nd Earl of Minto 1814
Minister to Prussia 1832-4; on an extraordinary
mission to Switzerland, Sardinia, Tuscany, the
Vatican and the Two Sicilies 1847-8.

Letters to him, Prussia 1832-4, mainly from Lord
Palmerston and other diplomats (11 vols); copies
of despatches to him 1832-4 (11 vols); drafts and
copies of his letters and despatches to Palmerston,
and of letters to Foreign Office officials and other
diplomats 1832-4 (9 vols); corresp and papers rel
to his mission to Italy and to his support for
Italian unification 1847-59 (50 vols); corresp and
papers as first lord of the Admiralty 1835-41, and
rel to naval affairs 1822-56 (40 vols); political
corresp c1806-59 (22 vols); family and general
corresp 1789-1859 (103 vols); financial and legal
corresp and papers 1808-59 (58 vols); scientific
corresp and papers (13 vols); political and travel
journals 1812, 1816-23, 1829-30, 1842-3, 1848-59
(30 vols); cabinet papers c1835-52 (78 vols);
notes and speeches (6 vols).
National Library of Scotland (MSS 11740-77,
11789-11844, 11909-12005, 12017-12237).
Purchased from the 5th Earl of Minto 1958, 1960,
except MSS 12064A-B purchased 1975. NRA
10476.

See also *Cabinet Ministers* and the preceding
entry.

[116] **ELLIS, Charles Augustus** (1799-1868),
6th Baron Howard de Walden 1803
Under secretary for foreign affairs 1824-8;
minister to Sweden 1832-3, to Portugal 1833-46,
to Belgium 1846-68.

Corresp, memoranda, etc rel to foreign affairs,
incl letters from British diplomats and from
Count Gustav Wetterstedt, 1817-34 (2 vols);
copies, translations and deciphers of intercepted
foreign despatches and private letters 1824-8 (3
vols).
Public Record Office (FO 360). Transferred from
the Foreign Office Library 1921. NRA 23467.

Letters from Lord Palmerston 1834-40, Lord
Aberdeen 1842, Lord Clarendon 1842-5, and Lord
Stanley 1867 (2 vols).
Bodleian Library, Oxford (MSS Eng. lett. d.42,
e.3). Purchased 1932.

Letters from Lord Palmerston 1835-64, Lord
Canning 1842-6, and Lord Stanley 1867 (1 vol).
British Library (Add MS 45176). Presented 1938
by the surviving executor of his son CA Ellis.

[117] **ERRINGTON, Sir George** (1839-1920),
Bt 1885
On a special mission to the Vatican 1881-5.

Corresp 1881-5 (5 vols).
Public Record Office (FO 800/235-9). Transferred
from the Foreign Office Library.

ESTCOURT, see Bucknall Estcourt.

[118] **EVERETT, Colonel Sir William**
(1844-1908)
Vice-consul at Erzerum 1879-82, consul 1882-8;
employed on several boundary commissions in
Turkey 1879-83, and in W Africa 1895-1900.

Reports on Erzerum and surrounding districts,
itineraries in Turkey and Persia, notes and
printed papers 1876-83, and letters from the War
Office, the British embassy at Constantinople, etc
1880-6 (2 files); corresp rel to famine relief in
Armenia 1881, and to boundary commissions
1879-83 (1 file); letters from consulates 1886-8,
misc consular and private accounts, etc (1 file);
letters to his wife 1884, and corresp rel to his
career 1884-8 (1 file); corresp and papers rel to
the assault on him 1885, his resignation and his
claim for compensation 1888-92 (1 file); corresp
and papers mainly rel to his promotion in the
army 1887-92 (1 file); diaries 1879-82 (1 file);
maps of the Balkans, Turkey and Central Asia
1876-91 (1 file).
Middle East Centre, St Antony's College, Oxford.
Deposited by his granddaughter Mrs FM Bailey
1970-1.

[119] **EWART, Joseph** (1759-1792)
Secretary to Sir John Stepney in Prussia 1782-4;
chargé d'affaires in Prussia 1784-5, secretary of
legation 1785-8, envoy 1788-9, minister 1789-91.

Letters mainly from diplomats incl Lord
Auckland, Hugh Elliot, FJ Jackson, Sir RM
Keith, Robert Liston and Charles Whitworth,
with copies of his replies, 1782-92 (21 bundles);
commissions and misc papers 1774-92 (4
bundles).
Sir HSP Monro (his great-great-great-grandson).
Enquiries to NRA (Scotland). NRA 11854
(bundles 129-33, 137-8, 144-61).

[120] **FAGAN, Robert** (*c*1745-1816)
Consul-general at Palermo 1809-16.

Letters to him from Queen Caroline of Naples
1812-13, copies of letters from Lord William
Cavendish Bentinck to King Ferdinand and
Queen Caroline of Naples, political memoranda
and notes, etc 1812-14 (1 vol).
British Library (Add MS 36730). Purchased 1902.

[121] **FANE, General John** (1784-1859), styled
Lord Burghersh 1784-1841, 11th Earl of
Westmorland 1841
Military commissioner to the allied armies
1813-14; minister to Tuscany 1814-31; on special
missions to the Vatican 1823, 1829 and to the
Two Sicilies 1825; minister to Prussia 1841-51;
ambassador to Austria 1851-5; on a special mission
to Belgium 1856.

Some papers were burnt by his widow in 1860.
Extensive diplomatic correspondence and papers
were sold by the Westmorland Trustees at
Sotheby's 31 July 1950, lots 548-9. His personal
papers, with those of his wife, descended to his
granddaughter Miss Rachel Weigall, who sold
some at Sotheby's 1 Mar 1965, lots 452-67. The
remainder were inherited by her nephew the
Revd AF Weigall who deposited them in Kent
Archives Office in 1968.

Corresp with diplomats, statesmen and others
1808-58, incl the 4th Earl of Clarendon, Lords
Lyons, Palmerston, Raglan and Stuart de
Rothesay and Sir HG Ward (27 vols); drafts and
copies of despatches sent 1813-30, 1843-56 (37
vols); papers formerly enclosed in corresp 1815-28
(2 vols); papers rel to his missions to Rome and
Naples 1823-9 (1 vol); to his mission to Belgium
1856 (1 vol); to India, parliamentary reform, etc
1806-55 (1 vol); guest lists, printed material and
other papers rel to Italy 1740-1836 (5 vols);
memoranda of conversations 1850-1 (1 vol);
school notebook (1 vol); literary MSS with some
letters from the Duke of Wellington 1808-11 (4
vols, *c*4 bundles).
Untraced. Exported to Cuba 1957 following sale at
Sotheby's 31 July 1950, lots 548-9. A microfilm is
in the British Library (M/509-29).

Corresp and papers, Denmark and Schleswig-
Holstein 1845-51, incl corresp with Lord
Bloomfield, Sir Thomas Cartwright, Lord Cowley,
WTH Fox Strangways, GL Hodges, Sir HWW
Wynn and Danish and Prussian statesmen, copies
and précis of despatches from Bloomfield, Cowley,
Hodges, Westmorland and Wynn to Lord
Palmerston, and misc memoranda (6 vols).
Danish National Archives, Copenhagen (Private
Archives No 6870). Purchased 1952. NRA 26043.

Copies of his despatches and enclosures 1814-15
(2 vols); copies of memoranda on the congress of
Vienna 1814-15 (1 vol); letters from AC Magenis,
Lord Ponsonby and George Samuel 1848-9 (1
vol); misc corresp and papers rel to his diplomatic
career, his memoirs and his music 1815-*c*1859 (*c*60

items); corresp and papers rel to military business
1805-7, 1831-2 (1 vol, 22 items); family and
personal corresp 1827-54 (44 items).
Kent AO (U 1371). Deposited by the Revd AF
Weigall 1968. NRA 15266.

Corresp with Lords Aberdeen and Palmerston
and Sir George Shee 1830-2, and account of
expenses of his return from Tuscany (1 bundle);
misc commissions and warrants 1830-57 (7
items); bank books from 1837 and cheque books
*c*1851-5 (2 bundles).
Northamptonshire RO (Westmorland (Apethorpe)
MSS, boxes 1, 7). Deposited by the 15th Earl of
Westmorland 1950.

Corresp of Leopold I, King of the Belgians, with
him and his wife 1830-65 (27 items); memoranda
by him of two conversations with King Leopold
1838.
Archives Générales du Royaume, Brussels.
Purchased at Sotheby's 1 Mar 1965, lot 460.

Letters to him and his wife from Lords Clarendon
and Palmerston and other diplomats and
statesmen 1837-76 (22 items).
*William R Perkins Library, Duke University,
Durham, N Carolina.* Purchased at Sotheby's
1 Mar 1965, lot 455. NRA 25906.

Letters to him and his wife from the 1st and 2nd
Dukes of Cambridge and their families 1842-73
(*c*130 items); corresp with Prince Albert 1842-57
(27 items).
The Royal Archives, Windsor Castle. Purchased at
Sotheby's 1 Mar 1965, lots 452, 458. Access
restricted.

Scores of his vocal and instrumental compositions
(19 vols).
British Library (Add MSS 33297-33315).
Purchased from CS Palmer 1887.

[122] **FANE, Hon Julian Henry Charles**
(1827-1870)
Secretary of legation in Russia 1856-8; secretary of
legation in Austria 1858-60 (intermittently in
charge), secretary of embassy 1860-5 (in charge
1860-1, 1862); secretary of embassy in France
1865-8 (in charge 1867, intermittently minister *ad
interim*).

Letters from his mother and sister 1846-68 (98
items); appointment as secretary of legation in
Austria 1858 (2 items).
Kent AO (U 1371/C49-50, O18). Deposited by
the Revd AF Weigall 1968. NRA 15266.

[123] **FEATHERSTONHAUGH, George
William** (1780-1866)
Commissioner for the delimitation of the
boundary between the United States and British
N America 1839; consul at Le Havre 1844-66.

Corresp, journals and other papers of him and his
family 1771-1952, incl his journals as boundary
commissioner.

Albany Institute of History and Art, Albany, New York. Presented by JD Featherstonhaugh. *National union catalog,* MS 82-1044.

Corresp 1827-65, mainly letters on geological matters from William Buckland, Sir Charles Lyell, Sir RI Murchison, Sir Richard Owen and Adam Sedgwick (c170 items).
Cambridge University Library (Add 7652). Deposited by the Sedgwick Museum of Geology to which the correspondence had been presented by Featherstonhaugh's family after his death.

[124] **FERGUSSON, Sir James** (1832-1907), 6th Bt 1849
Parliamentary under secretary for foreign affairs 1886-91.

Corresp as under secretary 1886-91, with misc corresp of JW Lowther and GN Curzon 1891-7 (4 vols).
Public Record Office (FO 800/25-8).

Memorandum book as governor of S Australia 1869-72 (1 vol); copies of minutes 1869-70 (1 vol).
State Library of South Australia Archives Department, Adelaide. Deposited among the Governor's Office records 1968. *South Australiana,* viii, no 1, Mar 1969, p28.

Official and private corresp as governor of Bombay 1880-5 (2 vols, 19 files); private letter books 1880-5 (3 vols).
India Office Library and Records (MSS Eur E 214). The correspondence was presented by Sir James Fergusson Bt 1954 and the letter books transferred from the official records 1967.

Some papers, mainly late 19th cent.
Sir Charles Fergusson Bt. Many papers are reported to have been destroyed after Sir James's death. C Cook, *Sources in British political history 1900-1951,* iii, 1977, p156.

[125] **FITZGERALD, Lord Robert Stephen** (1765-1833)
Secretary of embassy in France 1789-91 (minister *ad interim* 1789-90); minister to Switzerland 1792-5; envoy to Denmark 1796-1802; minister to Portugal 1802-8.

Corresp and misc family papers 1786-1832, mainly letters from him to the Duke of Richmond 1786-1802 (31 items).
Public Record Office of Northern Ireland (D3151). Deposited by Mrs P Anderton 1976. NRA 25890.

FITZGERALD AND VESEY, Baron, see Vesey-Fitzgerald.

[126] **FITZHERBERT, Alleyne** (1753-1839), Baron St Helens 1791
Minister resident in Flanders 1777-82, minister 1782; minister to France 1782-3, to Russia 1783-7, to the Netherlands 1789-90; ambassador to Spain 1790-4, to the Netherlands 1794-5, to Russia 1801-2; plenipotentiary to Denmark and Sweden 1801-2.

Despatches 1777-1802, diplomatic corresp 1781-1804, reports on draft treaties, notes, credentials, etc 1777-1817 (458 items); family and other corresp 1785-1839, papers rel to parliamentary elections 1805-32, accounts and other personal papers (2,840 items); papers as a privy councillor 1801-19 and as a lord of the bedchamber 1802-30 (169 items).
Derbyshire RO (D239M). Deposited by Sir JRF Fitzherbert Bt 1963.

FITZMAURICE, Baron, see Petty-Fitzmaurice.

FORDWICH, Viscount, see Cowper.

[127] **FORESTI, Spiridion** (d 1822)
Consul at Corfu 1793-1803; minister resident in the Septinsular Republic 1803-13.

Official letter books mainly containing copies of his letters to the Foreign Office, British diplomatic and consular representatives, naval and military officers, and local authorities in the Seven Islands 1793-1813 (7 vols).
Public Record Office (FO 348). Presented to the Foreign Office by Sir ETF Crowe 1937.

[128] **FOSTER, Sir Augustus John** (1780-1848), 1st Bt 1831
Secretary of legation in Sweden 1808-10 (in charge 1808, 1809-10); minister to the United States 1811-12, to Denmark 1814-24, to Sardinia 1824-40.

Corresp mainly with his mother 1794-1826 (8 vols); diaries and journals 1798-1844, mainly Sardinia (64 vols).
Library of Congress, Washington. Purchased at Sotheby's 25 Mar 1929, lot 875, and from Sir AV Foster Bt 1933.

Corresp 1794-1848, mainly with his mother 1798-1824 (478 items); diaries, journals and sketch book c1805-1848 (20 vols).
Public Record Office of Northern Ireland (D3618). Deposited by Mrs AC May 1983. NRA 27263.

[129] **FOX, Charles James** (1749-1806)
Foreign secretary 1782, 1783, 1806.

Corresp with George III and with diplomats 1782-3, 1806, and misc papers rel to foreign affairs 1770-1804 (8 vols); Foreign Office secret service accounts mainly 1806-7 (4 vols).

British Library (Add MSS 47559, 47562-3, 51457-65). Partly presented by Professor GM Trevelyan 1951, and partly purchased from the trustees of the 5th Earl of Ilchester 1960.

See also *Cabinet Ministers.*

[130] **FOX, General the Hon Henry Edward** (1755-1811)
Commander-in-chief in Sicily and minister to the Two Sicilies 1806-7.

Letters from his wife and children 1786-1805 (44ff).
Bodleian Library, Oxford (MS Eng. lett. c.234). Presented 1962-3 by WF Bruce and JN Russell, descendants of his younger daughter. NRA 13979.

Letter book as governor of Minorca 1802 (1 vol).
Wigan RO (D/DZ EHC13). Presented by Edward Hall 1949.

Letters to him and misc papers mainly rel to affairs in the Mediterranean 1802-7 (1 vol, etc).
British Library (Add MSS 37050, 37053). Purchased with papers of his son-in-law Sir HE Bunbury Bt 1905.

Misc letters and papers as commander-in-chief in Ireland 1803 (1 vol).
National Library of Ireland (MS 57). *Manuscript sources for the history of Irish civilisation,* ed RJ Hayes, ii, Boston 1965, p193.

Defence of his actions during the Dublin rising 1803 (22pp); letter book, Sicily 1806-7 (1 vol).
Suffolk RO, Bury St Edmunds (E18). Deposited by Sir CHN Bunbury Bt 1949. NRA 2582.

[131] **FOX, Henry Edward** (1802-1859), 4th Baron Holland 1840
Secretary of legation in Sardinia 1832-5 (in charge 1834-5); secretary of embassy in Austria 1835-7 (minister *ad interim* 1835-6); minister to the Germanic Confederation 1838-9, to Tuscany 1838-46.

Special corresp with foreign secretaries, Foreign Office officials, diplomats, politicians and others 1811-59 (27 vols); 'correspondance politique', reports by a French agent in Paris 1854-5 (5 vols); general corresp *c*1810-1859 (6 vols); family corresp 1809-57 (62 vols); letter books 1831-2, 1834-5, 1850-1 (3 vols); journals 1814-56 (23 vols); engagement books 1813-45, dinner books 1835-59, and commonplace books (17 vols).
British Library (Add MSS 51748-78, 52001-52112). Purchased in 1960 from the trustees of the 5th Earl of Ilchester, to whom they had passed on the death of Lady Holland in 1889.

Letters from Lady Northampton 1825-6, 1829 (41 items).
John Rylands University Library of Manchester (Eng MS 1287). Acquired 1963. *Hand-list of additions to the collection of English Manuscripts 1952-1970,* p43.

[132] **FOX, Henry Stephen** (1791-1846)
Secretary of legation in Sardinia 1824-6 (in charge 1824-5), in Sicily 1826-8 (in charge 1827-8); minister to the Argentine Republic 1830-2, to Brazil 1832-6, to the United States 1835-44.

Letters from diplomats, politicians and others 1823-42 (*c*205ff), and from relatives 1815-40 (*c*70ff); draft letters from him and legal papers rel to the United States 1835-41 (19ff).
Bodleian Library, Oxford (MSS Eng. lett. c.234-5; MS Eng. misc. b.96). Presented 1962-3 by his great-nephews WF Bruce and JN Russell, and by W Nell, husband of his great-great-niece Rachel Russell. NRA 13979.

Official and private corresp with the United States government, British governors in Canada and New Brunswick and others 1836-44 (3 vols); corresp and papers rel to the Canadian rebellion and the Maine-New Brunswick boundary dispute 1837-42, incl letters to him from Lord Palmerston, British governors and others, and copies of intelligence reports about the rebellion received by the United States government (1 vol).
Public Record Office (FO 97/16-19).

[133] **FOX-STRANGWAYS, William Thomas Horner** (1795-1865), 4th Earl of Ilchester 1858
Secretary of legation in Tuscany 1825-8 (in charge 1825, 1825-6), in Naples 1828-32; secretary of embassy in Austria 1833-5 (in charge 1833, minister *ad interim* 1834-5); parliamentary under secretary for foreign affairs 1835-40; minister to the Germanic Confederation 1840-8.

Letters and misc papers rel to Poland 1857-63, mainly from WL Birkbeck and Charles Szulczewski of the Literary Association of the Friends of Poland (1 vol); general and family corresp, mainly 1830-63 (1 vol); MS 'Lay of Meliadoc' (1 vol).
British Library (Add MSS 51366-8). Purchased from the trustees of the 5th Earl of Ilchester 1960.

Misc testamentary and other papers 1857-65 (1 bundle).
Dorset RO. Deposited by the 7th Earl of Ilchester 1961.

[134] **FRASER, Colonel Alexander John** (d 1866)
On a special mission to Syria 1860; member of the international commission of enquiry into the massacres in Syria 1861-2.

Corresp and papers 1853-66, incl corresp in Syria with Sir WHLE Bulwer, Lord Dufferin, Lord John Russell and others 1860-2 (3 vols); diary 1856 (1 vol).
British Library (Add MSS 44912-44913C). Presented by Mrs Peter Duguid and Mrs Clotilda Marson 1936.

[135] **FREEMAN, Edward Bothamley**
(1838-1921)
Chancellor to the consulate at Diyarbakir
1858-60, at Sarajevo 1860-76; vice-consul at
Mostar 1876-9; intermittently acting consul at
Sarajevo 1863-79, consul 1879-91, consul-general
1891-1905.

Journals 1858-1921, incl copy of his journal rel to
the Austrian occupation of Sarajevo 1878 (25
vols); list of visitors 1894-c1904 (1 vol).
British Library (Add MSS 57470, 59746-70).
Presented 1971 and bequeathed 1976 by his
daughter Mrs EHAM Cahen.

[136] **FRERE, Sir Henry Bartle Edward**
(1815-1884), 1st Bt 1876
On a mission to Zanzibar to negotiate a slave
trade treaty 1872-3.

Returns and memoranda rel to the revenues of
Sind as chief commissioner 1848-57 (1 bundle);
misc corresp, reports and memoranda 1793-1877
incl material rel to public works (2 bundles, etc).
India Office Library and Records (MSS Eur D
710). Transferred from the official records 1967.

Misc corresp and papers, partly his wife's, mainly
rel to personal and Indian affairs 1816-84 (1 vol,
245 items).
India Office Library and Records (MSS Eur F 81).
Presented by P Frere 1944-5. NRA 27516.

Copies of letters from him to Lord Salisbury rel
to the North West Frontier 1876, with related
papers 1859 (1 vol).
India Office Library and Records (MSS Eur E
218/175). Deposited among the papers of the 1st
Earl of Lytton by Lady Hermione Cobbold 1955.

Notes on African affairs and constitutions.
London University Library (MSS 947-9).

[137] **FRERE, John Hookham** (1769-1846)
Under secretary for foreign affairs 1799-1800;
minister to Portugal 1800-2, to Spain 1802-4,
1808-9.

Corresp, intelligence reports and misc papers rel
to Spain and France 1804-14 (82 items).
National Army Museum (6807/400). Transferred
from the Royal United Service Institution 1968.
NRA 20817.

Letters and verses from George Canning 1800-26
(1 vol).
British Library (Add MS 38833). Purchased 1914.

Translations of literary works by Aristophanes
and Gonzalo de Berceo (2 vols).
British Library (Add MSS 39668, 40057).
Bequeathed by Baroness Zouche 1917, and
purchased 1921.

[138] **GABRIEL, Edmund** (1821-1862)
Arbitrator in the court of mixed commission at
Luanda 1845-56, acting commissioner 1856-9,
commissioner 1859-62; acting consul at Luanda
1859-60.

Letters from David Livingstone 1854-5 (1 vol).
British Library (Add MS 37410). Purchased 1906.

[139] **GOLDSMID, Major-General Sir Frederic
John** (1818-1908)
Commissioner for the delimitation of the Perso-
Baluch frontier and special commissioner to
arbitrate in the Perso-Afghan boundary dispute
1870-3; on a mission to Turkey 1882.

Corresp, despatches and telegrams rel to the
Perso-Baluch and Perso-Afghan boundary
commissions 1870-2 (5 vols, 2 boxes); account
book (1 vol); diaries and misc printed papers (1
box); literary papers (1 box); misc notes and
papers (1 box).
India Office Library and Records (MSS Eur F
134). Presented by Mrs JM White 1942. NRA
25897.

Literary notes c1839 (1 vol); diary 1854 (1 vol).
India Office Library and Records (MSS Eur C
168a-b). Acquired 1963.

Corresp rel to his military career 1842-80 (45
items).
India Office Library and Records (MSS Eur D
642). Acquired 1965.

[140] **GOODWIN, John** (d 1869)
Consul at Palermo 1834-69.

MS of Palmieri's *Saggio Storico e Politico sulla
Costituzione del Regno di Sicilia* ... (1847), with
Goodwin's translation and 'Review' of Sicilian
history based on it (4 vols); MS works by him on
the political, economic and social condition of
Sicily (6 vols).
British Library (Add MSS 42143-52). Found
among the official records at the Palermo
consulate and presented by the foreign secretary
1930.

[141] **GORDON, Sir Robert** (1791-1847)
Secretary of embassy in the Netherlands 1813-15
(minister *ad interim* 1814-15), in Austria 1815-26
(intermittently minister *ad interim*); minister to
Brazil 1826-8; ambassador to Turkey 1829-33, to
Austria 1841-6.

Corresp with Lord Aberdeen, mainly private,
1811-25, 1827-31, 1841-7 (3 vols); with the 3rd
Marquess of Londonderry 1815-46 (1 vol); letters
from Terrick Hamilton, WR Hamilton and Lord
Strangford 1821-3 (1 vol); corresp with Lord
Ponsonby, the Foreign Office and naval officers
on the S American station 1826-8 (2 vols); with
Sir Stratford Canning and Sir Edmund Lyons
1839-46 (1 vol); general corresp 1809-46, incl
brief travel journals 1809, 1812-13 (2 vols); copies
of his despatches 1817-19, 1841-6 (4 vols).

British Library (Add MSS 43209-22). Presented by the 1st Marquess of Aberdeen 1932, except Add MSS 43220-2 presented by the 2nd Baron Stanmore.

Journal as attaché to the British mission to Persia 1810-11 (1 vol).
British Library (Add MS 49273). Presented by his great-nephew the 2nd Baron Stanmore 1953. NRA 20961.

[142] **GORE, Philip Yorke** (1801-1884), 4th Earl of Arran 1837
Attaché in Sweden 1820-5, in France 1825-6, in Portugal 1826-7; secretary of legation in the Argentine Republic 1827-37 (in charge 1832-4).

Corresp with his parents and misc papers rel to his diplomatic career 1822-36, 1845, 1849 (44 items); political and personal corresp and papers 1837-c1859, incl papers rel to Irish representative peerage elections 1837-41 (73 items); corresp and papers rel to his Irish estates 1837-56 (375 items).
Trinity College, Dublin (MSS 7602-15). Purchased from the 8th Earl of Arran 1977. NRA 20404.

[143] **GOSCHEN, George Joachim** (1831-1907), 1st Viscount Goschen 1900
Ambassador to Turkey 1880-1.

Copies of his telegrams to Lord Granville 1880-1 (1 vol).
Bodleian Library, Oxford (MS Dep. c.182). Deposited 1957 by his granddaughter Mrs Francis Balfour.

See also *Cabinet Ministers.*

[144] **GOSCHEN, Sir William Edward** (1847-1924), 1st Bt 1916
Secretary of legation in China 1885-8, in Denmark 1888-90, in Portugal 1890-3; secretary of embassy in the United States 1893-4, in Russia 1894-8 (minister *ad interim* 1897); minister to Serbia 1898-1900, to Denmark 1900-5; ambassador to Austria-Hungary 1905-8, to Germany 1908-14.

Diaries 1891-1914 (24 vols); misc corresp and papers, incl letters from his brother Lord Goschen c1896-8.
Sir EC Goschen Bt.

[145] **GOULBURN, Henry** (1784-1856)
Joint plenipotentiary to treat with the United States 1814.

Corresp and papers 1813-14 rel to the negotiation of the treaty of Ghent, incl letters to him from Lords Bathurst, Castlereagh and Liverpool, copies of letters from him, notes exchanged with the United States commissioners, memoranda and a copy of the treaty (3 vols).
William L Clements Library, University of Michigan, Ann Arbor. Presented 1941 by Lawrence Reynolds following purchase at

Sotheby's 29 July 1940, lot 568. *Guide to the manuscript collections,* 1978, pp50-1.

See also *Cabinet Ministers.*

GOWER, Earl, see Leveson-Gower, George Granville.

GRANTHAM, Baron, see Robinson T.

GRANVILLE, Earls, see Leveson-Gower, Granville and Granville George.

[146] **GRENVILLE, Thomas** (1755-1846)
Minister to France 1782; on an extraordinary mission to Austria 1794; on a special mission to Brunswick 1798-9; on an extraordinary mission to Prussia 1798-9.

Copies of despatches and private letters from him to his brother Lord Grenville 1798-9 (2 vols, 61 items); general letter books 1799 (2 vols); political corresp, incl some rel to his diplomatic missions 1794, 1798-9 (over 800 items).
Huntington Library, San Marino, California (Stowe Collection). Purchased 1925 following sale in 1921 by Baroness Kinloss, a descendant of his brother the 1st Marquess of Buckingham. *Guide to British historical manuscripts,* pp155, 157.

Letters from Lord Malmesbury, Prussian statesmen and others, and memoranda of conversations and negotiations, 1799 (47 items).
British Library (Add MSS 41855 ff178-276, 42058 ff192-9). Purchased from the Revd GWT Tyndale-Biscoe 1929-30.

See also *Cabinet Ministers.*

[147] **GRENVILLE, William Wyndham** (1759-1834), Baron Grenville 1790
On a special mission to France 1787-8; foreign secretary 1791-1801.

Corresp with George III and officials of the royal household 1789-1807 (9 vols); special corresp 1782-1834, incl many letters from British diplomats and foreign statesmen and diplomats (145 vols); general corresp 1784-1834, with indexes 1788-99, 1806 (57 vols); misc corresp with British diplomats, agents, travellers and Foreign Office staff 1788-1814, and with foreigners 1787-1828 (11 vols); précis books, mainly as foreign secretary, 1789-1801 (145 vols); corresp and papers rel to foreign affairs, arranged by country 1764-1816 (23 vols); papers rel to the slave trade 1788-1817 (1 vol); cabinet minutes 1791-1806 (1 vol).
British Library (Add MSS 58855-63, 58906-59229, 59305-6, 59354-59410). Purchased 1970 from the executors of GG Fortescue, a descendant of Grenville's nephew GM Fortescue.

Copies of despatches to him from British diplomats in Prussia 1791-2 (1 vol).

Public Record Office (PRO 30/8/338).
Bequeathed among the Pitt papers by Rear-
Admiral JE Pringle 1888.

See also *Cabinet Ministers.*

[148] **GREY, Charles** (1764-1845), styled
Viscount Howick 1806-7, 2nd Earl Grey 1807
Foreign secretary 1806-7.

Political corresp 1787-1843, incl letters from
British and foreign diplomats and statesmen 1806-
7 (*c*14,500 items); papers rel to foreign affairs,
mainly arranged by country (*c*24 bundles); copies
of Lord Durham's despatches to Lord Palmerston
1835-7 (2 vols).
*Durham University Department of Palaeography
and Diplomatic* (Grey of Howick Collection).
Deposited by the 5th Earl Grey 1955-63. NRA
6228.

See also *Cabinet Ministers.*

[149] **GREY, Sir Edward** (1862-1933), 3rd Bt
1882, Viscount Grey of Fallodon 1916
Parliamentary under secretary for foreign affairs
1892-5, foreign secretary 1905-16.

Papers 1892-5 (5 vols); papers arranged by
country 1905-16 (48 vols); Foreign Office
memoranda and corresp with other departments
1905-16 (16 vols); corresp with George V and
Queen Alexandra 1906-16 (1 vol); misc corresp
and papers 1906-16 (9 vols); index 1905-16 (1
vol).
Public Record Office (FO 800/35-113). Left at the
Foreign Office on his resignation. NRA 23627.

[150] **GREY, Hon William George** (1819-1865)
Secretary of legation in Sweden 1853-8
(intermittently in charge), secretary of embassy in
France 1859-65 (intermittently in charge 1860-5).

Letters to him and copies of despatches and
letters from him 1841-64, incl corresp with Sir
Andrew Buchanan 1854-6, Lord Clarendon
1853-7, General Charles Grey 1854-64, Lord
Ponsonby 1841-53, Lord Russell 1861-4 and
others (333 items).
*Durham University Department of Palaeography
and Diplomatic* (Grey of Howick Collection).
Deposited by the 5th Earl Grey 1955. NRA 6228.

[151] **HAGGARD, John George** (1850-1908)
Vice-consul in Zanzibar 1883-6; consul at
Tamatave 1886-8, at Brest 1888-92, at Trieste
1892-8, at Nouméa 1898-1904, at Malaga 1904-8.

Corresp and papers, incl letters from him at Lamu
and Zanzibar to his family 1883-5, official papers
and receipts 1883-*c*1885, and related material;
journals of his travels between Lamu and Kipini
and elsewhere in Africa 1884.
Rhodes House Library, Oxford (MSS Brit. Emp.
s.465). Presented by JVA Haggard 1982.

[152] **HAMILTON, Sir William** (1730-1803)
Envoy to the Two Sicilies 1764-7, envoy and
plenipotentiary 1767-1800.

The bulk of his papers descended through his
Greville nephews to his great-niece Lady Louisa
Finch-Hatton, whose son EH Finch-Hatton sold
the majority at Sotheby's 3 Mar 1886. Some were
purchased by the British Museum, and others by
the collector Alfred Morrison. The unsold portion
was acquired by the British Museum from Lady
Louisa Finch-Hatton's granddaughter Lady Capel
Cure in 1922 and 1930.
Other papers remained in the possession of Lady
Hamilton, and were acquired with her own papers
and some of Lord Nelson's by TJ Pettigrew. Most
of these were purchased by the British Museum
in 1853. Others came into the hands of Joseph
Mayer of Liverpool, from whom most were
purchased by Alfred Morrison at Sotheby's 19
July 1887.
Morrison's Hamilton-Nelson collection was sold
at Sotheby's 9 Dec 1918, lot 2671 and 5 May
1919, lots 3125-3313. Part was purchased by the
British Museum, and part subsequently acquired
by the Bodleian Library in 1921.
Further papers of Nelson and the Hamiltons were
purchased in 1817 by JW Croker, on whose death
they were sold to Sir Thomas Phillipps. In 1946
Sir James Caird purchased them for the National
Maritime Museum.

Letters from secretaries of state, diplomats and
others, with a few drafts of despatches and letters
from him and misc papers 1761-1803 (4 vols);
corresp with British diplomats and officers serving
in Italy and the Mediterranean 1767-1800 (2
vols); letters from Sir Joseph Banks and Sir
Horace Mann 1765-98 (1 vol); corresp with Sir
JFE Acton 1781-1800 (2 vols); letters from
various correspondents to him and his wife
1793-1812 (1 vol); drafts and copies of despatches
from him 1764-81, 1798-1800, with some misc
corresp and papers 1758-1800 (5 vols); misc
corresp and papers 1754-1802 (2 vols); papers rel
to the abortive Anglo-Sicilian treaty 1790 (1 vol);
memorials from Neapolitan subjects to the
Hamiltons and to King Ferdinand and Queen
Caroline of Naples 1799-1800, and intercepted
French corresp 1798-1800 (1 vol); household and
misc accounts 1764-1801 (1 vol); letters, accounts
and other papers of Hamilton and his nephews
1764-1815 (3 vols).
British Library (Add MSS 37077, 39793,
40714-16, 41197-41200, 42069-42070B, 51315;
Egerton MSS 1621-2, 2634-41). Acquired by gift
and purchase 1853-1963.

Copies of the orderly books of his regiment in the
Netherlands 1747-8 (2 vols); extracts from Sir
James Gray's corresp with secretaries of state as
envoy to Naples 1754-64 (9 vols); copies of
deciphered letters from Lord Halifax, the Duke of
Richmond and Lord Shelburne 1765-8 (1 vol);
memoranda 1783, 1789-93, and notes rel to
Naples 1783 and to art purchases (2 vols).
Bodleian Library, Oxford (MSS Eng. hist. g.3-16).

Purchased 1921. Formerly Sotheby's 5 May 1919, lot 3125.

Corresp with diplomats, naval officers, the Neapolitan secretary of state and others 1791-1800, and letters to Sir JFE Acton 1795-1800 (2 boxes).
National Maritime Museum (HML/1-21). Purchased from M Breslauer and Maggs Bros Ltd 1939. *Guide to the manuscripts,* i, p79.

Letters from Lords Hood and Nelson and others to him and his wife 1787-1810 (c427 items).
National Maritime Museum (Croker Collection). *Guide to the manuscripts,* i, p134.

Corresp with his nephew CF Greville 1769-1801 (87 items).
Huntington Library, San Marino, California. Formerly Sotheby's 5 May 1919, lot 3129. *Guide to British historical manuscripts,* p310.

Letters from the 4th Earl of Bristol 1778-1800 (30 items).
National Library of Ireland (MS 2262). *Manuscript sources for the history of Irish civilisation,* ed RJ Hayes, ii, Boston 1965, p398.

[153] **HAMILTON-GORDON** (formerly **GORDON**), **George** (1784-1860), styled Lord Haddo 1791-1801, 4th Earl of Aberdeen 1801
Ambassador to Austria 1813-14; foreign secretary 1828-30, 1841-6.

Official and private corresp with Lord Castlereagh, Prince Metternich and others, Austria 1813-14, and papers rel to the congress of Châtillon 1814 (7 vols); corresp mainly with British and foreign diplomats 1828-30, 1841-6, and papers rel to the slave trade 1825-46 (40 vols); copies of despatches to and from him 1828-30, 1841-6 (68 vols); copies and abstracts of corresp, Austria 1813-14, as foreign secretary 1828-9, 1841-6, and rel to foreign affairs 1846-50 (37 vols); printed cabinet papers mainly rel to foreign affairs 1824-66 (4 vols).
British Library (Add MSS 43073-43187, 43257-67, 43274-7, 43279-43300, 43344, 43355-8). Presented by the 1st Marquess of Aberdeen 1932.

See also *Cabinet Ministers.*

[154] **HAMILTON-TEMPLE-BLACKWOOD, Frederick Temple** (1826-1902), 5th Baron Dufferin 1841, 1st Earl of Dufferin 1871, 1st Marquess of Dufferin and Ava 1888
Special commissioner to Syria 1860-1; ambassador to Russia 1879-81, to Turkey 1881-4; special commissioner to Egypt 1882; ambassador to Italy 1888-91, to France 1891-6.

Corresp and papers, Syria 1860-3 (1 box); as under secretary for India, and for War, and as chancellor of the Duchy of Lancaster and paymaster-general 1864-72 (4 boxes, etc); as governor-general of Canada 1871-8 (7 boxes); as viceroy of India 1884-8, incl printed corresp

(11 vols and c16 boxes); rel to Turkey 1878-85 (4 vols, etc) and to Italy and France 1888-96 (1 box, etc); misc corresp and papers rel to his political, colonial and diplomatic career 1842-1902 (15 boxes, etc); to Irish local and national affairs c1860-1900 (5 boxes, etc); private letters to him 1869-1902 (143 bundles); personal, family, household and estate corresp and papers (59 boxes, etc); journals and diaries 1839-1900 (38 vols).
Public Record Office of Northern Ireland (D1071, 1231). Mostly deposited by the Marchioness of Dufferin and Ava 1957, with a later deposit by Lady Hermione Blackwood. NRA 5700; *Deputy keeper's report 1954-9,* pp41-2, *1960-5,* p60.

Printed private corresp as viceroy 1884-8 (54 vols).
India Office Library and Records (MSS Eur F 130). Transferred from the Public Record Office of Northern Ireland 1965. NRA 20537.

Private corresp as viceroy, partly printed, 1884-8 (91 vols); notes, minutes, copies of official papers, etc rel to Indian affairs 1879-88 (17 vols); private corresp 1857-64 (9 vols).
The Dowager Marchioness of Dufferin and Ava. NRA 5700. Microfilms are held by the Public Record Office of Northern Ireland and the India Office Library and Records.

[155] **HAMMOND, Edmund** (1802-1890), Baron Hammond 1874
Entered the Foreign Office 1824; chief clerk 1841-54; permanent under secretary for foreign affairs 1854-73.

Private corresp with diplomats, statesmen and others 1854-85, incl Sir Rutherford Alcock, the 4th Earl of Clarendon, the 1st Earl Cowley, Sir HG Elliot, Sir HS Parkes, the 1st Earl Russell, Sir Edward Thornton and Sir TF Wade (23 vols, 5 bundles); letters to his parents from Turkey, Spain and Germany 1831-4 (1 vol); corresp with his wife 1854-5 (1 vol, 1 bundle).
Public Record Office (FO 391). Presented to the Foreign Office in 1941 by his great-nephew Sir GS Barnes and transferred in 1942. NRA 23468.

Letters from diplomats, statesmen and others 1854-84 (2 bundles); letters from his family 1830-3 (2 bundles); letters of condolence on the death of his wife 1884 (1 bundle); misc letters and papers 1832, 1854-73, 1890 (22 items); travel journals, Europe 1817-45 (4 vols).
Mrs PJ Sisam (granddaughter of Sir GS Barnes). NRA 0566.

[156] **HAMMOND, George** (1763-1853)
Chargé d'affaires in Austria 1788-9, in Denmark 1790; minister to the United States 1791-5; under secretary for foreign affairs 1795-1806, 1807-9; on extraordinary missions to Prussia 1796, 1805, to Austria 1797.

Corresp and accounts rel to his diplomatic

missions 1789-91, 1796-7 (1 box); letter books, Prussia and Austria 1796-7 (2 vols).
Public Record Office (FO 95/502, 508-9).

Letters to him and his wife from their son Edmund 1831-4 (1 vol).
Public Record Office (FO 391/28). Presented to the Foreign Office with Edmund Hammond's papers 1941. NRA 23468.

Misc diplomatic and other corresp and papers mainly 1786-1814 (2 bundles, 16 items).
Mrs PJ Sisam. NRA 0566.

[157] **HARDINGE, Charles** (1858-1944), 1st Baron Hardinge of Penshurst 1910
Second secretary in the United States 1885-7 (in charge 1886); acting agent and consul-general in Bulgaria 1887-91; chargé d'affaires in Romania 1892-3; secretary of legation in Persia 1896-8 (in charge 1897-8), in Russia 1898-1903 (in charge 1899-1902); assistant under secretary for foreign affairs 1903-4; ambassador to Russia 1904-6; permanent under secretary for foreign affairs 1906-10, 1916-20; ambassador to France 1920-2.

Corresp and misc papers rel to his early diplomatic career and his assistant under secretaryship 1880-1903 (4 vols); corresp and papers, Russia 1903-6 (2 vols) and diary 1904-5 (1 vol); confidential print of his despatches 1904-6 (2 vols); royal corresp and related papers 1905-16 (6 vols); corresp and misc papers as under secretary 1906-10 (11 vols) and 1916-20 (22 vols); corresp with Lord Curzon 1920-2 (2 vols); corresp, memoranda, speeches and other papers, many printed, as viceroy of India 1910-16 (81 vols); indexes (3 vols).
Cambridge University Library (Hardinge Papers). Mostly purchased from the 2nd Baron Hardinge 1954, with some later gifts and purchases.
Handlist of the Hardinge papers.

Foreign Office reports and memoranda, copies of treaties, speeches, etc mainly rel to his under secretaryship and to France 1906-24 (23 vols, c25 items); corresp, mainly France 1920-3 (c105 items); corresp, reports, proceedings, memoranda, speeches, etc as viceroy 1910-16 (62 vols, c66 items); scrapbooks, photograph albums and misc papers rel to India c1905-39 (61 vols, 36 items); corresp and reports as Indian representative at the League of Nations 1923-4 (4 vols); misc corresp and papers c1871-1941, incl material rel to foreign affairs and the outbreak of the First World War.
Kent AO (U 927, 2348). Deposited by the Dowager Lady Hardinge 1962 and JA Hardinge 1980. NRA 8909 (partial list).

Press cuttings and other papers rel to the Delhi durbar 1911, addresses presented to Lady Hardinge, and misc papers 1910-16 (4 vols, 48 items).
India Office Library and Records (MSS Eur E 389). Deposited by JA Hardinge 1980.

Papers as under secretary 1906-11 (1 vol).
Public Record Office (FO 800/192).

Diaries 1895-1931 (9 vols).
Hon JA Hardinge. Not open for research.

[158] **HARRIS, Admiral Sir Edward Alfred John** (1808-1888)
Consul at Elsinore 1852; chargé d'affaires and consul-general in Peru 1852-3, in Chile 1853-8; minister to Switzerland 1858-67, to the Netherlands 1867-77.

Letters from statesmen 1811, 1855-77, and misc papers 1846-8, 1870-2 (19 items).
Hampshire RO (9M73). Deposited 1973 by Viscount FitzHarris, whose permission to consult the papers must be obtained through the record office. NRA 6589.

[159] **HARRIS, James** (1746-1820), 1st Baron Malmesbury 1788, 1st Earl of Malmesbury 1800
Secretary of embassy in Spain 1768-71 (in charge 1769-71), minister 1771-2; envoy to Prussia 1772-6, to Russia 1777-83, to the Netherlands 1784-8; ambassador to the Netherlands 1788-9; on an extraordinary mission to Prussia and the Netherlands 1793-4; plenipotentiary to France 1796, 1797.

Letters from his wife 1815 (1 vol); misc papers rel to Frederick the Great 1752, 1786 (1 bundle); his memoirs of the Harris family 1800, and of his father 1801, with other genealogical papers (1 file).
Public Record Office (PRO 30/43/1, 29, 45). Deposited with papers of his wife and other relations by his great-granddaughter Miss Mabel Lowry Cole 1936-8. NRA 8661.

Household accounts, Prussia 1775-6 (1 vol); corresp with Arthur Paget 1794-5, 1800 (14 items).
Hampshire RO (25M56/2, 9M73). Deposited 1956 by AR Martin and 1973 by Viscount FitzHarris, whose permission to consult the letters must be obtained through the record office. NRA 6589.

Letters from Lord and Lady Minto 1777-1804 and nd (1 vol).
National Library of Scotland (MS 11111). Purchased from the 5th Earl of Minto 1958. NRA 10476.

[160] **HARRIS, James Howard** (1807-1889), styled Viscount FitzHarris 1820-41, 3rd Earl of Malmesbury 1841
Foreign secretary 1852, 1858-9.

Corresp mainly with British and foreign diplomats and statesmen, letter books, memoranda, telegrams, confidential print, etc, mainly 1852, 1858-9 (72 vols, 4 bundles); political and cabinet diary kept irregularly 1852-75 (1 vol).
Hampshire RO (9M73). Deposited 1973 by Viscount FitzHarris, whose permission to consult the papers must be obtained through the record office. NRA 6589.

HARROWBY, Earl of, see Ryder.

[161] **HARTLEY, David** (1732-1813)
Minister to treat with United States envoys in
Paris 1783-4.

Corresp, speech notes, draft proposals and other
papers rel to the American colonies, treatment
and exchange of prisoners of war, and the peace
negotiations, 1766-88 (7 bundles); corresp,
speeches, memoranda and pamphlets mainly rel to
trade and commercial policy c1750-90 (3 vols, 9
bundles, 65 items); corresp, election addresses and
other political papers 1761-89 (10 bundles);
general corresp 1761-95 (23 bundles); personal,
business and scientific papers 1757-91 (16
bundles, 7 items).
Berkshire RO (D/EHy). Deposited by members
of the Hartley Russell family 1950-60. NRA 0844.

Corresp with Lord Carmarthen and CJ Fox and
misc letters from others 1783-5 (5 vols).
*William L Clements Library, University of
Michigan, Ann Arbor.* Purchased by Clements
1933, after passing through the hands of several
American collectors. *Guide to the English
manuscripts,* 1942, p136.

[162] **HASTIE, James** (1786-1826)
Agent in Madagascar 1817-26.

Letters from King Radama I of Madagascar
1823-5.
Public Record Office (PRO 30/43/89). Presented
among the papers of Sir GL Cole (governor of
Mauritius 1822-8) by Miss Mabel Lowry Cole
1936-8. NRA 8661.

Copy of journal, with papers rel to slave trade
negotiations, 1817 (1 vol).
Public Record Office (CO 167/34).

Journal 1821.
Untraced. Offered for sale at Sotheby's 8 Dec
1983, lot 347.

HAWKESBURY, Baron, see Jenkinson.

[163] **HAWKINS, General Sir John
Summerfield** (1816-1895)
Commissioner for the delimitation of the
boundary between the United States and British
N America 1856-69.

Letter book 1859-62, incl copies of letters to the
War Office (1 vol); letters from RW Haig and
WF Tomline 1859 (7 items).
Royal Engineers Museum, Chatham (4501-128).

HAY-DRUMMOND-HAY, see Drummond-Hay
R.

[164] **HAYNE, Henry** (fl 1790-1860)
Secretary to Lord Amherst's embassy to China
1816-17.

Journal 1816-17 (4 vols).
*William R Perkins Library, Duke University,
Durham, N Carolina.* Acquired 1980. NRA 25901.

[165] **HELY-HUTCHINSON, General John**
(1757-1832), Baron Hutchinson 1801, 2nd Earl of
Donoughmore 1825
Plenipotentiary to Prussia 1806-7.

Corresp with George Canning and Lord Howick,
Robert Adair, Benjamin Garlike and other British
diplomats, Baron Hardenberg, Count Zastrow and
other Prussian ministers and generals, and misc
reports, memoranda, etc 1806-7 (277 items); misc
corresp and papers 1793-1805, 1808-32, mainly rel
to his military and political career, incl papers rel
to the trial of Queen Caroline (113 items).
Trinity College, Dublin (Donoughmore E).
Deposited by the 7th Earl of Donoughmore 1980.
NRA 22331.

Letters from Henry Brougham rel to Queen
Caroline 1819-20, and notes of a conversation
between Brougham and Hutchinson 1820 (12
items).
British Library (Add MS 40344, ff15-40).
Presented among the papers of Sir Robert Peel
1917.

[166] **HELY-HUTCHINSON, John Luke
George** (1848-1900), styled Viscount Suirdale
1851-66, 5th Earl of Donoughmore 1866
Assistant commissioner for the organisation of the
province of Eastern Roumelia 1878-9.

Travel journals, Switzerland 1869, India, Ceylon
and Australia 1871-3 (5 vols); notebook kept
while on the Eastern Roumelia commission 1878;
copy of Sir HD Wolff's confidential *Notes taken in
Paris, Vienna, Pesth and Berlin* (1878); letters to
him and his wife from their son Lord Suirdale
1883-1900 (512 items); corresp rel to Suirdale's
education 1885-93 (75 items); letter books, some
rel to the claims of Peruvian bondholders in
Britain against the Peruvian government, 1888-96
(8 vols); bank book 1866-74.
Trinity College, Dublin (Donoughmore J,K).
Deposited by the 7th Earl of Donoughmore 1980.
NRA 22331.

[167] **HENDERSON, James** (c1783-1848)
Consul-general in Colombia 1823-33, consul at
Bogotá 1833-6.

Corresp and papers 1812-31, incl corresp rel to his
search for a consular post 1818-23, and with
British diplomats and consuls in S America
c1824-31, draft despatches 1824-31, letter books
1814-17, 1822-9, abstracts of letters from the
Foreign Office 1823-30, personal accounts 1812-
19, accounts and papers rel to consular fees and

allowances 1822-30, and essays and memoranda
rel to S American commerce, mining, geography,
history, etc (12 boxes); maps and plans 1824-6
(6 items).
Public Record Office (FO 357; MPK 7-10).

HENLEY, Baron, see Eden MF.

[168] **HERBERT, General George Augustus**
(1759-1827), styled Lord Herbert 1759-94, 11th
Earl of Pembroke 1794
On a special mission to Austria 1807.

Military, political, family and estate corresp
1783-1827, incl copies of his despatches to George
Canning 1807 (7 boxes); travel journals 1779-80,
1783 and engagement diaries 1789, 1791-2 (7
vols).
Wiltshire RO (WRO 2057). Deposited by the
17th Earl of Pembroke 1984. NRA 22080 (partial
list).

[169] **HERBERT, Sir Michael Henry**
(1857-1903)
Second secretary in the United States 1888-92 (in
charge 1888-9, 1892), secretary of legation 1892-3;
chargé d'affaires in the Netherlands 1893-4;
secretary of embassy in Turkey 1894-7 (in charge
1895, 1896), in Italy 1897-8, in France 1898-1902
(intermittently minister *ad interim*); ambassador
to the United States 1902-3.

Diplomatic and general corresp with Lords
Curzon and Lansdowne, Sir Wilfrid Laurier,
Theodore Roosevelt, Lords Rosebery and
Salisbury and others c1879-1903 (2 boxes); family
corresp c1882-1903 (3 boxes); journals 1883,
1885, 1894-5 (2 vols).
Wiltshire RO (WRO 2057). Deposited by the
17th Earl of Pembroke 1984. NRA 22080 (partial
list).

[170] **HERRIES, Edward** (1821-1911)
Attaché in charge in Switzerland 1850-1; attaché
in the Netherlands 1851-4 (in charge 1851);
secretary of legation in Switzerland 1854-8 (in
charge 1856), in Portugal 1858, 1861-4 (in charge
1862), in Belgium 1858-61, in Italy 1864-75
(intermittently in charge at Florence 1865-71 and
Rome 1874).

Corresp 1874-1906 and nd (1 vol).
British Library (Add MS 57469). Presented 1963
by NM Rothschild & Sons Ltd who had bought
it in 1956 from Lieutenant-Colonel GAG
Spottiswoode, a nephew of Mrs RS Herries.

Corresp and papers mainly rel to his Kent estate
1896-1905.
Kent AO (U543/E21). Deposited by Lieutenant-
Colonel Spottiswoode 1956. NRA 4798.

Corresp 1844-1908 (8 bundles, etc);
appointments, bills, etc 1854-1911.
Untraced. NRA 4798.

HERTFORD, Marquesses of, see Seymour-
Conway.

[171] **HERTSLET, Sir Edward** (1824-1902)
Foreign Office librarian and keeper of the papers
1857-96; attached to the special mission to the
congress of Berlin 1878; delegate to discuss the
boundary between British and Dutch territories in
Borneo 1889.

Letters to him from CT Beke, Lord Bessborough,
CD Cameron and others rel to Cameron's private
affairs and imprisonment at Magdala 1867-8 (1
vol).
Royal Geographical Society.

[172] **HERTSLET, Lewis** (1787-1870)
Foreign Office sub-librarian 1801-10, librarian
1810-57.

Accounts, vouchers, registers and other papers rel
to diplomatic messengers 1730-1824 (51 vols).
Public Record Office (FO 351). NRA 23627.

[173] **HERVEY, Frederick William**
(1769-1859), styled Lord Hervey 1796-1803, 5th
Earl of Bristol 1803, 1st Marquess of Bristol 1826
Under secretary for foreign affairs 1801-3.

Corresp with statesmen, diplomats and others incl
Charles Arbuthnot, the 1st Earl of Liverpool and
Sir JB Warren, 1801-9 (120 items); letters to him
rel to Lord Hervey's parliamentary candidature
for Cambridge University 1822 (47 items);
personal and family corresp 1793-1851, incl many
letters from Lord William Hervey, the Countess
of Jersey, the 2nd Earl of Liverpool and French
correspondents (10 bundles, c715 items); journal
rel to foreign affairs 1803; notes mainly rel to
French affairs c1795-1814 (8 items); legal
notebook.
Suffolk RO, Bury St Edmunds (Ac 941/1, 11A,
56). Deposited by the National Trust 1958-9.
NRA 6892.

[174] **HERVEY, Herbert Arthur Robert**
(1870-1960), 5th Marquess of Bristol 1951
Consul at Iquique 1892-9, at Montevideo 1899-
1903 (in charge in Uruguay 1900-1); consul at
Guatemala 1903-7 (in charge in Guatemala 1904,
in Central America 1905-6); consul at Addis
Ababa 1907-10 (in charge in Abyssinia 1908-9);
consul-general at Bilbao 1910-14; minister and
consul-general in Colombia 1919-23, in Ecuador
and Peru 1923-9.

Diaries, photographs, press cuttings and letters of
appointment.
The Marquess of Bristol.

[175] **HERVEY, Captain John Augustus**
(1757-1796), styled Lord Hervey 1779-96
Envoy to Tuscany 1787-91, minister 1791-4.

Draft despatches from him 1790-3 and despatches to him 1787-94 (3 bundles); official letters from Tuscan secretaries of state 1788-94 (1 bundle); corresp with Tuscan ministers, British consuls in N Italy, British and foreign diplomats and others 1787-94 (8 bundles); corresp, memoranda, intelligence reports, etc 1788-94, mainly rel to the Toulon expedition 1793-4 (5 bundles); misc corresp and papers 1778-94, incl instructions 1787, 1792 (5 bundles).
Public Record Office (FO 528). Mostly presented to the Foreign Office by the Dowager Marchioness of Bristol 1952, with additions 1960. NRA 23470.

Letters from naval officers and others 1782-94 (66 items); corresp and papers rel to settling the affairs of the 3rd Earl Cowper 1789-90 (30 items); papers rel to a scheme for a lottery 1789-90 (1 bundle); journal 1793-4.
Suffolk RO, Bury St Edmunds (Ac 941/55, HA 507/5142). Deposited by the National Trust 1958-9, 1975. NRA 6892.

[176] **HERVEY, Lord William** (1805-1850)
Secretary of legation in Spain 1830-9 (in charge 1838); secretary of embassy in France 1843-50 (intermittently minister *ad interim* 1845-7).

Private corresp with the 4th Earl of Clarendon, Lord John Hay, Colonel William Wylde and others 1831-40 (*c*108 items); misc diplomatic papers 1830-9, incl draft memoranda on the state of Portugal 1833 and draft treaty between Spain and Portugal 1834 (8 bundles and items).
Public Record Office (FO 528). Presented to the Foreign Office by the Dowager Marchioness of Bristol 1952. NRA 23470.

Travel journal, France, Italy and Belgium 1817; letters to Henry Reeve mainly rel to French and English politics, 1846-8 (67 items).
Suffolk RO, Bury St Edmunds (Ac 941/61/1,3). Deposited by the National Trust 1958-9. NRA 6892.

HEYTESBURY, Baron, see A'Court.

[177] **HILL, Sir Clement Lloyd** (1845-1913)
Entered the Foreign Office 1867; secretary to Sir HBE Frere's mission to Zanzibar 1872-3; acting chargé d'affaires in Bavaria 1876; commissioner to revise the slave trade instructions 1881; commissioner to Haiti 1886-7; superintendent of African protectorates under the Foreign Office 1900-5.

Corresp, incl letters from the 2nd Earl Granville, Sir TV Lister and the 3rd Marquess of Salisbury, commissions, papers rel to his honours, press cuttings and photographs, 1867-1905 (1 vol).
Rhodes House Library, Oxford (MSS Afr. s.703). Deposited by Major Clement Hill 1966.

HILL, William, see Noel-Hill.

[178] **HIPPISLEY, Sir John Coxe** (1748-1825), 1st Bt 1796
Agent for the British government in Italy 1779-80, 1792-6.

Letters and papers received, mainly rel to his diplomatic career 1790-1822 (1 vol).
British Library (Egerton MS 2401). Purchased 1876.

Corresp and papers 1788-1814, mainly rel to India and to the British occupation of Corsica, incl letters from Sir Gilbert Elliot and Sir John Macpherson (*c*150 items).
National Library of Scotland (Acc 6820). Purchased at Sotheby's 7 Dec 1976, lot 400.

Corresp rel to India, mainly letters from Colonel William Fullarton 1782-7 (1 vol).
British Library (Add MSS 41622). Presented 1928 by Lady Horner, widow of his great-grandson Sir JFF Horner.

Corresp, accounts, addresses and other papers as recorder and MP for Sudbury 1789-1814 (2 vols and 211 items).
Suffolk RO, Bury St Edmunds (HD 744). Transferred 1977 from the Museum of the History of Science, Oxford. NRA 21530.

HOCHEPIED LARPENT, Baron de, see Larpent.

[179] **HOHLER, Sir Thomas Beaumont** (1871-1946)
Third secretary in Turkey 1897, in Russia 1897-9, in Egypt 1899-1901 (acting agent and consul-general 1900, 1901); second secretary in Japan 1901-6, in Egypt 1906-7, in Abyssinia 1907-8 (in charge); first secretary in Turkey 1908-10; first secretary in Mexico 1910-15, counsellor of embassy 1915-17 (intermittently in charge 1911-16); counsellor of embassy in the United States 1917-18; on a special mission to Turkey 1918; high commissioner in Hungary 1919-21, minister 1921-22, consul-general at Budapest 1922-4; minister to Chile 1924-7, to Denmark 1928-33.

Letters, telegrams, and press cuttings 1898-1932 (66 vols); diaries *c*1898-1932; unpublished autobiography.
GA Hohler Esq.

HOLLAND, Baron, see Fox HE (1802-1859).

[180] **HOPE, General Sir Alexander** (1769-1837)
Plenipotentiary to Denmark and Sweden 1813.

Corresp, letter books, notebooks, reports, returns, etc rel to his military career 1791-1812 (21 vols,

173 bundles); private letter and memorandum books 1804-19 (7 vols); corresp, letter book, notebooks, copies of despatches and treaties, Denmark and Sweden 1812-13 (5 vols, 17 bundles); corresp and papers mainly rel to military, political and personal affairs 1813-37 (3 vols, 82 bundles).
Scottish Record Office (GD 364). Deposited by Colonel AJG Hope 1979. NRA 10172.

[181] **HOTHAM, Captain Sir Charles** (1806-1855)
On a special mission to the Argentine Republic and Paraguay 1852-3.

Corresp with the 5th Duke of Newcastle and others, memoranda and misc papers 1846-55, mainly as lieutenant-governor and governor of Victoria 1853-5, but incl a copy of the navigation treaty with the Argentine Republic 1853 (*c*170 items); letter and order book as captain of HMS *Gorgon* in S American waters 1842-6 (1 vol); copies of official corresp with the secretary of state for the colonies 1854-6 (2 vols).
Brynmor Jones Library, Hull University (DDHO 10). Transferred in 1974 from the East Riding RO, where they had been deposited by the 7th Baron Hotham in 1954. NRA 5408; P Mander-Jones, *Manuscripts in the British Isles relating to Australia, New Zealand, and the Pacific*, Canberra 1972, p540; *Guide to manuscript sources for the history of Latin America and the Caribbean in the British Isles*, ed P Walne, 1973, pp356-7.

[182] **HOWARD, George** (1773-1848), styled Viscount Morpeth 1773-1825, 6th Earl of Carlisle 1825
Plenipotentiary to Prussia 1806.

Corresp and papers, Prussia 1806 (1 bundle); political and personal corresp, incl letters from the 1st Baron Dunfermline, the 3rd Baron Holland and his wife, and the 1st Earl of Morley (13 bundles); papers rel to Foreign Office business 1832-3, 1848 (1 bundle).
In family possession. NRA 24681.

[183] **HOWARD, Sir Henry** (1843-1921)
Chargé d'affaires in Guatemala 1883-4; secretary of legation in Greece 1885, in Denmark 1885-7, in China 1887-90; secretary of embassy in Russia 1890-4 (intermittently in charge), in France 1894-6 (intermittently minister *ad interim* 1895-6); minister to the Netherlands and Luxemburg 1896-1908; on a special mission to the Vatican 1914-16.

Family corresp 1857, 1878-1921 (10 boxes, 1 vol); diaries 1881-1921 (47 vols).
Library of Congress, Washington. Presented by his grandson Franz von Recum 1975. NRA 25957.

HOWARD DE WALDEN, Baron, see Ellis CA.

HOWDEN, Baron, see Caradoc.

HOWICK, Viscount, see Grey C.

HUTCHINSON, Baron, see Hely-Hutchinson.

IDDESLEIGH, Earl of, see Northcote.

ILCHESTER, Earl of, see Fox-Strangways.

[184] **JACKSON, Francis James** (1770-1814)
Secretary of legation in Prussia 1789-91 (in charge 1790-1); secretary of embassy in Spain 1791-5 (minister *ad interim* 1792-3, 1794-5); on a special mission to Austria 1795; minister *ad interim* to France 1801-2; minister to Prussia 1802-6; minister *ad interim* to Denmark 1807; minister to the United States 1809-10.

Private diplomatic corresp and intelligence reports 1790-1807 (24 vols and bundles); corresp and papers rel to Spain 1792-6 (4 bundles); official letters received by successive ministers and chargés d'affaires in Prussia 1777-1806 (14 bundles); official letter books of the legation in Prussia 1772-1806, and of his mission to Denmark 1807 (29 vols); consular corresp, Prussia and Bucharest 1803-6 (2 bundles); notes on the Danish expedition 1807 (1 bundle); corresp, draft despatches and papers, United States 1807-11 (5 bundles); notes from foreign ministers 1790-1805 (1 bundle); misc official and other papers 1790-1806 (2 bundles); corresp and papers from the archive of the legation in Poland 1763-8, 1786-92 (2 bundles); copies and extracts 1801-2 (1 bundle); copies of corresp between Sir Francis Baring and the E India Co 1807-9 (1 bundle).
Public Record Office (FO 353). His papers, with the official records of the Berlin legation, removed when diplomatic relations were broken off in 1806, passed to his brother Sir George Jackson. They were claimed by the Foreign Office from the latter's widow in 1864, and transferred to the PRO in 1904. NRA 23624.

Letters from William Cavendish MP 1804-6 (11 items); corresp with George Canning 1807 (10 items); letters from and rel to General JV Moreau 1811-13 (7 items).
The Trustees of the Chatsworth Settlement.
Enquiries to the Librarian and Keeper of the Devonshire Collections, Chatsworth, Bakewell, Derbyshire DE4 1PP. NRA 20594/3.

[185] **JACKSON, Sir George** (1785-1861)
Attaché in France 1801-2, in Prussia 1802-6; chargé d'affaires in Prussia 1806-7, 1807; secretary of legation in Spain 1808-9, in Prussia 1813-15 (in charge 1814-15); secretary of embassy in Russia 1816-22; commissioner in the United States under the treaty of Ghent 1823-7; commissary judge at

Sierra Leone 1828-32; commissioner for the abolition of the slave trade at Rio de Janeiro 1832-41, Surinam 1841-5, Luanda 1845-59.

Draft letters, memoranda and a journal, Prussia 1806-7 (1 bundle); draft despatches, letters to Sir Charles Stewart, and other papers 1812-15 (2 bundles); corresp and papers rel to the United States 1823-7, and to the slave trade 1822-56 (8 vols and bundles).
Public Record Office (FO 353). Claimed by the Foreign Office from his widow 1864 and transferred to the PRO 1904. NRA 23624. (Further papers used by Lady Jackson in her editions of her husband's papers have not been traced).

Letters from William Cavendish MP 1803-5 (15 items) and from Friedrich von Gentz 1813 (9 items).
The Trustees of the Chatsworth Settlement. Enquiries to the Librarian and Keeper of the Devonshire Collections, Chatsworth, Bakewell, Derbyshire DE4 1PP. NRA 20594/3.

[186] **JAMES, George Payne Rainsford** (1801-1860)
Consul in Virginia 1852-8; consul-general at Venice 1858-60.

Letters from him and others to Francis Scott MP with misc related papers 1846-54 (44 items); papers rel to agreements with publishers 1836-50 (66 items); MS of part of his *Castle of Ehrenstein* (1845); misc personal and family corresp and papers, mainly legal and financial, 1705-1853.
Greater London RO (Acc 976/1-255). Deposited by Mackarness & Lunt, solicitors, Petersfield. NRA 16333.

Letters to him mainly from statesmen and authors 1826-52 (33 items); letters from him 1832-40 (3 items); MS poems (2 items).
Boston Public Library, Massachusetts (Chamberlain Autograph Collection). Bequeathed by Mellon Chamberlain 1900. NRA 26054.

Letters to various correspondents 1826-56 (48 items); MS of part of his *Life and Times of Louis XIV* (1838) (19pp).
Huntington Library, San Marino, California.

[187] **JENKINSON, Robert Banks** (1770-1828), styled Lord Hawkesbury 1796-1808, 2nd Earl of Liverpool 1808
Foreign secretary 1801-4.

Official corresp mainly as foreign secretary 1801-4, incl many despatches from Francis Drake 1803-4 (6 vols); copies of corresp rel to the congress of Amiens 1801-2 (8 vols); papers mainly rel to foreign affairs 1801-4, incl enclosures from official corresp (2 vols); account for secret service money 1802-5 (1 roll); letters from George Canning 1797-1827, many rel to foreign affairs (2 vols).
British Library (Add MSS 38193, 38237-40, 38312-19, 38357-8, 38489B, 38568-9, 38571).

Presented 1911-12 by HB Portman, great-grandson of the 3rd Earl of Liverpool.

Political and general corresp of the Earls of Liverpool c1763-1857, incl letters to the 2nd Earl from Lord Bloomfield, George Canning, Lords Castlereagh and Clancarty, Francis Drake, Lord Whitworth and other diplomats and statesmen c1798-1827 (39 vols).
British Library (MS Loan 72). Deposited 1977. NRA 21672.

Misc corresp and papers, incl memoranda c1801-4 rel to Central America, Minorca and Anglo-Russian negotiations over Malta (1 vol).
William R Perkins Library, Duke University, Durham, N Carolina. Purchased 1965. NRA 22308.

See also *Cabinet Ministers.*

[188] **JERNINGHAM, Hon George Sulyarde Stafford** (1806-1874)
Chargé d'affaires in the Netherlands 1832-6; secretary of legation in Sardinia 1836-7, in Portugal 1837-9 (in charge 1838), in Spain 1839-49 (intermittently in charge); secretary of embassy in Turkey 1849-50, in France 1850-4 (intermittently in charge 1851-2); minister to Württemberg and Baden 1854-9, to Spain 1859-72.

Diplomatic and personal corresp 1823-72 (2 bundles, 12 items); drafts and copies of letters and reports, mainly to Lord Palmerston, Netherlands and Portugal 1832-8 (1 bundle); copies of his despatches from Württemberg 1854-9 (1 vol); journals 1828-44 (3 vols); commissions, expenses, etc 1832-65 (c16 items).
Staffordshire RO (D641/3). Deposited by his great-great-nephew, the 14th Baron Stafford 1961.

[189] **JOEL, Lewis** (d 1899)
Vice-consul at Bolivar 1866-69, consul-general 1869-70 (in charge in Venezuela 1867, 1869); consul at Rosario 1870-7, at Brindisi 1877-80, at Savannah 1880-3, at Cadiz 1883-8, at Panama 1888-91, at Valparaiso 1891-4.

Official papers, commissions and personal corresp mainly rel to his consular service in S America 1861-99 (22 items).
William R Perkins Library, Duke University, Durham, N Carolina.

See also *Molyneux.*

[190] **JOHNSON, John Mordaunt** (c1776-1815)
Employed by the Foreign Office in confidential missions to Europe 1809-14; chargé d'affaires in the Southern Netherlands 1814; consul at Genoa 1814-15.

Copies of official letters to Lords Castlereagh, Clancarty and Lynedoch, Sir Charles Stuart and others 1814 (2 vols), with separate indexes; misc

papers 1809-14, incl an entry book of private letters sent 1814 (1 bundle).
Public Record Office (PRO 30/26/70). Bequeathed to Robert Mitford, and presented by Major-General BR Mitford 1929.

Misc corresp and papers 1804-15, incl private letters from Robert Mitford and DR Morier, and official corresp rel to his mission to the Netherlands 1814 (*c*70 items).
Dr APW Malcomson. Photocopies are in the Public Record Office of Northern Ireland (T2762). *Deputy keeper's report 1966-72*, p158.

Journal of his mission to the British fleet in the Adriatic 1812.
Beinecke Library, Yale University, New Haven, Connecticut (Osborn Collection: MS f d 48). Purchased at Sotheby's 23 Feb 1953, lot 152, by Myers & Co (Booksellers) Ltd; Myers catalogue 377, item 221.

[191] JOHNSTON, Sir Harry Hamilton (1858-1927)
Vice-consul in the Cameroons and Niger delta 1885-9 (acting consul at Old Calabar 1887-8); consul at Mozambique 1889-91; commissioner and consul-general in British Central Africa 1891-7; consul-general at Tunis 1897-9; special commissioner, commander-in-chief and consul-general in Uganda and adjoining territories 1899-1901.

Corresp and papers 1871-1927, incl letters from CJ Rhodes, Theodore Roosevelt, the 3rd Marquess of Salisbury, HM Stanley and others (866ff); family and misc corresp 1892-1932 (*c*162ff); diaries and travel journals, Europe and Africa 1878-89, incl notes, Old Calabar 1887-8 (8 vols); notes for published works, sketches, photographs, press cuttings, etc *c*1880-1927 (21 vols).
National Archives of Zimbabwe, Harare (JO 1-2). *Guide to the historical manuscripts in the National Archives of Rhodesia*, pp226-31.

Sketch book and diary of an expedition to Rio-del-Rey 1887.
Royal Geographical Society.

Notes on and vocabularies of African languages (97pp).
Royal Commonwealth Society. Presented by the Royal African Society 1972.

[192] JONES (afterwards JONES BRYDGES), Sir Harford (1764-1847), 1st Bt 1807
E India Co assistant and factor at Basra 1783-94; resident and consul at Baghdad 1798-1806; minister to Persia 1807-11.

Letter books, Persia 1791-2, 1804-11 (2 vols); misc personal, literary and legal papers 1799-1847 (9 vols).
National Library of Wales, Aberystwyth (MSS 4901-2, 4904-12). Acquired on the death of Lady Jones-Brydges 1923. *Handlist of manuscripts*, ii, pp52-3.

Private corresp incl letters from E India Co officials, foreign secretaries, diplomats, consuls, business partners, his family and others *c*1784-1843 (*c*2,650 items); letter books, Persia 1788-91, 1798-1804 (5 vols); draft despatches to London and Calcutta 1808-9 (112 items); account books of the residencies at Basra 1793-4 and Baghdad 1801-3 (2 vols); personal account books 1803, 1807-16 (4 vols); misc memoranda, notes and accounts rel to his business concerns, Persian affairs, etc *c*1761-1843 (*c*320 items); journal of his travels from Bushire to Shiraz 1787 (1 vol); estate corresp and papers 18th-19th cent (*c*1,160 items).
Hereford RO (Kentchurch Court Papers). Transferred 1984 from the National Library of Wales where they had been deposited 1942-3 and 1966 by members of the Lucas-Scudamore family, descendants of his eldest daughter. NRA 23683.

Copies of despatches and letters to Lord Minto as governor-general of India 1808-9 (1 vol).
In private possession. A microfilm is in Leicestershire RO (MF 133-4).

[193] KEITH, Lieutenant-General Sir Robert Murray (1730-1795)
Envoy to Saxony 1769-71, to Denmark 1771-2; minister to Austria 1772-92; plenipotentiary to the congress of Sistova 1790-1.

His papers were inherited by his daughter Amelia, whose guardian entrusted them to the 3rd Earl of Hardwicke, a trust later converted into ownership. The bulk was purchased from the 6th Earl of Hardwicke by the British Museum in 1899, and other groups passed to the families of Elizabeth, Countess of Hardwicke, sister of the 23rd Earl of Crawford, and of her daughter Catherine, Countess of Caledon.

Corresp, mainly diplomatic, with secretaries and under secretaries of state, British and Austrian diplomats and others 1752-92 (44 vols); copies of letters to successive secretaries of state 1772-92, and to British diplomats at Constantinople 1772-88 and elsewhere 1772-90 (37 vols).
British Library (Add MSS 35503-83).

Political, diplomatic and personal corresp and papers 1768-92 (96 items).
John Rylands University Library of Manchester (Crawford and Balcarres 72/2). Deposited by the 28th Earl of Crawford 1946. *Hand-list of personal papers from the muniments of the Earl of Crawford and Balcarres*, pp92-3.

Letters to him 1776-7, mainly from his family and British diplomats (203 items); paper rel to the alleged infidelity of the Queen of Denmark 1772 (25pp).
Public Record Office of Northern Ireland (D2433/D/1). Deposited by the Trustees of the Caledon Estates 1969. NRA 13276.

[194] **KENNEDY, Sir Charles Malcolm** (1831-1908)
Head of the commercial department of the Foreign Office 1872-93; commissioner in the Levant 1870-1 and intermittently at Paris 1872-87; delegate to the North Sea fishery conference at The Hague 1881, and plenipotentiary for signing the North Sea fishery convention 1882.

Corresp rel to the commercial department 1873-93, incl corresp while at Paris 1874-5 (2 vols).
Public Record Office (FO 800/4-5).

KIMBERLEY, Earl of, see Wodehouse.

[195] **KINNEIR** (formerly **MACDONALD**), **Sir John Macdonald** (1782-1830)
E India Co envoy to Persia 1824-30.

Official letter book 1829-30 (1 vol); commission as envoy to Persia 1824; Persian diplomatic notes, narrative in Persian of Mirza Saleh's mission to Russia, misc letters, translations and Indian newspapers 1827-30 (1 bundle); European newspapers 1828-30 (22 items).
Edinburgh University Library (Df 1.53, Dk 2.37-8, S R Ft). Presented by J Forbes Mackay 1955.

[196] **KIRK, Sir John** (1832-1922)
Vice-consul at Zanzibar 1866-73 (assistant political agent from 1868), consul-general 1873-80, agent and consul-general 1880-7; plenipotentiary to the Brussels slave trade conference 1889; commissioner to revise the slave trade instructions 1891.

Corresp with Charles Allen 1885-1920, David Livingstone 1858-69, HW Wylde 1867-86, African rulers c1856-1905 and others 1858-c1922 (c300 items); corresp of Kirk and other members of his family 1858-1918 (c80 items); register of several hundred telegrams sent and received at Zanzibar 1884-6; his and Lady Kirk's diaries 1851-84 (17 vols); papers rel to honours and appointments 1858-1902; printed papers mainly rel to Zanzibar 1866-93 (15 vols); memoranda on the slave trade, etc.
Mrs Daphne Foskett (his granddaughter).

Letters to him from David Livingstone and others 1858-80 (9 items), and from him to his brother Alexander 1859-63 (19 items); journals, Zambezi expedition 1858-63 (15 vols).
Untraced. Sold by Mrs Foskett at Sotheby's 21 Mar 1966, lots 175-7, 179-85, 188. Lots 186-7 (2 letters from Livingstone to Kirk 1863) were purchased by Rhodes House Library, Oxford.

Misc letters to him 1867-1903 and nd (17 items).
National Library of Scotland (Acc 4084). Sold by Mrs Foskett at Sotheby's 21 Mar 1966, lot 178.
Accessions of manuscripts 1965-1970, p48.

[197] **LAIDLAW, James** (1847-1915)
Vice-consul at Portland 1874-95, consul 1895-1913.

Misc corresp and papers as consul rel to his dealings with Portland hospitals, fund raising bodies, etc 1886-1912 (1 vol, 55 items).
Oregon Historical Society, Portland. See *National union catalog,* MS 74-668.

[198] **LAMB, Frederick James** (1782-1853), Baron Beauvale 1839, 3rd Viscount Melbourne 1848
Secretary of legation in the Two Sicilies 1811-13; secretary of embassy in Austria 1813-15 (minister *ad interim* 1814); minister to Bavaria 1815-20; on a special mission to the Germanic Confederation 1817, minister 1817-24; minister to Spain 1825-8; ambassador to Portugal 1827-8, to Austria 1831-41.

Drafts and copies of despatches from him, originals and copies of those to him, private corresp, letter books, memoranda, etc rel to his early diplomatic career 1812-15 (1 vol), to Bavaria and the Germanic Confederation 1813-23 incl papers concerning the territorial commission of Frankfurt (24 vols), to Spain 1825-7 incl notebooks (22 vols), to Portugal 1827-9 incl protocols of the Vienna conference (9 vols), to Austria 1832-41 (24 vols); personal corresp and misc papers, partly his wife's, 1814-53 (5 vols).
British Library (Add MSS 60399-60483). Presented 1978 by HM the Queen to whom they had been presented in 1954 by Lady Salmond, great-great-granddaughter of his sister Emily, Countess Cowper, afterwards Viscountess Palmerston. NRA 23026.

Misc diplomatic corresp and papers 1825-41, incl letters from Friedrich von Gentz and Prince Metternich (c3 bundles); family and misc corresp 1805-45 (1 bundle); draft despatches from him 1841 (1 bundle); rough journal with notes of conversations, Spain 1825-6 (1 vol); accounts and misc papers 1824-53 (1 vol and 3 bundles).
Hertfordshire RO (D/EP). Deposited by Lady Salmond and JJW Salmond 1952.

Corresp with his sister Lady Palmerston 1802-51 (3 vols), his mother Lady Melbourne, his brother the 2nd Viscount Melbourne and others 1805-51 (c118 ff).
British Library (Add MSS 45546-52, 45911). Presented 1940, 1944 by Mabell, Countess of Airlie, great-granddaughter of Lady Palmerston.

Letters to him from Lady Palmerston 1817-52 (c165 items).
Hampshire RO (27M60). Deposited 1960 by the Broadlands Archives Trust.

Letters to him from Prince Metternich, Lord Ponsonby and others 1832-41 (49 items).
Broadlands Archives Trust (GC/BE/5-407). Enclosed in his letters to Viscount Palmerston. Enquiries to the Historical Manuscripts Commission. NRA 12889.

[199] **LAMBTON, John George** (1792-1840),
1st Baron Durham 1828, 1st Earl of Durham 1833
On an extraordinary mission to Russia and
Prussia 1832; ambassador to Russia 1835-7.

Corresp and papers rel to foreign affairs 1830-7,
mainly Russia 1835-7, incl corresp with Lord
Palmerston and with British consuls in Russia,
copies of despatches, register of despatches
received 1832, 1835, official diary and
appointments books 1835-7, papers rel to Poland
1831-2, and travel journals, Russia, Turkey and
Greece 1832-5 (3 boxes, 6 vols, *c*24 bundles).
Viscount Lambton. Not open for research. NRA
11184.

See also *Cabinet Ministers.*

[200] **LANGLEY, Sir Walter Louis Frederick
Goltz** (1855-1918)
Entered the Foreign Office 1878; private secretary
to successive parliamentary under secretaries
1887-98; assistant clerk 1898-1902; senior clerk
1902-7; assistant under secretary 1907-18.

Private corresp, Foreign Office 1886-1918 (2
vols); misc corresp rel to the Far East 1908-15
(1 vol).
Public Record Office (FO 800/29-31).

[201] **LARPENT, John James de Hochepied**
(1783-1860), Baron de Hochepied Larpent
Consul at Antwerp 1825-39.

Letter book as consul 1831-2.
Bodleian Library, Oxford (MS Eng. hist. c.195).
Purchased 1923.

[202] **LASCELLES, Sir Frank Cavendish**
(1841-1920)
Acting agent and consul-general in Egypt 1878,
1879; agent and consul-general in Bulgaria
1879-87; minister to Romania 1887-91, to Persia
1891-4; ambassador to Russia 1894-5, to Germany
1895-1908.

Corresp and papers, Bulgaria 1880-6 (1 vol),
Romania, Russia, etc 1886-1908 (2 vols), Persia
1892-1908 (1 vol), Russia and Germany
1894-1900 (1 vol), Germany 1895-1908 (7 vols)
and various countries 1874-1908 (2 vols); index to
the principal subjects in the corresp 1874-1908 (1
vol).
Public Record Office (FO 800/6-20). Presented to
the Foreign Office by his daughter Lady Spring-
Rice 1924.

LAUDERDALE, Earl of, see Maitland.

[203] **LAYARD, Sir Austen Henry** (1817-1894)
Attaché in Turkey 1847-52; parliamentary under
secretary for foreign affairs 1852, 1861-6; minister
to Spain 1869-77; ambassador to Turkey 1877-80.

Special corresp with Lord Hammond, the 1st Earl
of Lytton, Lord Stratford de Redcliffe, Sir Henry
Thompson and others 1835-94 (37 vols); general
corresp 1838-52 (6 vols), 1852-69 (16 vols),
1869-77 (15 vols), 1877-80 (22 vols), 1880-94 (18
vols); political corresp, Turkey and Spain 1857-85
(6 vols); corresp as under secretary 1861-6 (20
vols); copies of his despatches and letters mainly
to successive foreign secretaries and to British
diplomats and consuls 1869-80 (14 vols); papers
mainly rel to Turkey and the Balkans 1806-88 (5
vols); papers as MP and as first commissioner of
works 1849-69 (1 vol); journals, notebooks,
sketches, etc rel to his travels and archaeological
excavations 1835-51 (43 vols); misc papers
1829-92, incl literary MSS and lecture notes (15
vols); memoirs 1817-47, 1869-80 (8 vols);
confidential print, mainly rel to the Ottoman
empire 1855-80 (21 vols).
British Library (Add MSS 38931-39164).
Bequeathed by his widow 1912.

Corresp, partly his wife's, 1828-1911, incl corresp
rel to Turkey and Spain (16 vols); notebooks,
Italy 1837-9, 1859, India 1857-8 and Spain
*c*1869-77 (7 vols); accounts 1833-9, 1877-83 (5
vols); misc papers incl diary 1854, press cuttings
and other printed material 1834-1902 (14 vols).
British Library (Add MSS 58149-53, 58159-72,
58174-96). Presented 1970 by Gordon Waterfield,
a great-nephew of his wife.

Letters mainly to him and his wife 1843-96 (2
vols).
British Library (Add MSS 58222-3). Purchased at
Sotheby's 22 July 1974, lots 537, 539.

Letters from Henry Ross mainly to him
1847-60 (30 items).
Middle East Centre, St Antony's College, Oxford.
Presented by Gordon Waterfield 1969.

LEEDS, Duke of, see Osborne.

[204] **LENOX-CONYNGHAM, George**
(d 1866)
Clerk at the Foreign Office from 1812, senior
clerk 1834-41, chief clerk 1841-66.

Corresp with Foreign Office officials, British
consuls and others, with related papers 1816-*c*1866
(*c*5 bundles, 25 items, etc); corresp with his
family *c*1820-66 (1 box, etc); personal, financial
and household papers 1819-*c*1866 (3 boxes,
1 bundle); corresp and papers of his son George,
incl material rel to his diplomatic career in
Europe and S America, *c*1840-66 (1 box, 1
bundle); misc papers rel to family history, etc.
GH Lenox-Conyngham Esq. Photocopies are in the
Public Record Office of Northern Ireland
(T3161). NRA 25889.

[205] **LEVER, Charles James** (1806-1872)
Vice-consul at Spezzia 1858-67; consul at Trieste
1867-72.

Letters to his family and others 1835-70 (321 items); notebooks 1849-64, 1867-72 (5 vols); post book 1864-7 (1 vol).
Huntington Library, San Marino, California (HM 240-1, 269-72).

Journal, commonplace and sketch book kept as a student at Göttingen University 1828 (1 vol).
Royal Irish Academy, Dublin (MS SR 3 B 52). Presented 1903 by C Litton Falkiner. RIA, *Abstracts of minutes 1902-30*, p22.

Letters to various correspondents (60 items); MS of his *Lord Kilgobbin* (1872).
Princeton University Library, New Jersey (Parrish Collection).

[206] **LEVESON GOWER, Arthur Francis Gresham** (1851-1922)
Second secretary in Switzerland 1887-9 (in charge 1888-9), in Serbia 1893-5 (in charge 1894, 1895); secretary of legation in Greece 1895-8 (in charge 1898), in the Netherlands 1898-1905 (intermittently in charge 1899-1905).

Diaries 1870-1922 (35 vols); letters to him from Count Leckendorff rel to social matters 1887-99; misc corresp, telegrams and press cuttings, Greece and the Netherlands 1895-1905; household account book 1892-6; family corresp, photographs, etc.
Surrey RO (Acc 498). Deposited 1969 by Miss Victoria Leveson Gower.

[207] **LEVESON-GOWER, George Granville** (1758-1833), styled Viscount Trentham 1758-86 and Earl Gower 1786-1803, 2nd Marquess of Stafford 1803, 1st Duke of Sutherland 1833
Ambassador to France 1790-2.

Corresp with Lord Grenville, Thomas Grenville, William Pitt and others 1785-1826 (c80 items); patronage corresp 1814-29 (1 bundle); letters from James Loch rel to the Sutherland estates 1816-32 (1 bundle); bank books 1792-1834 (8 vols).
Staffordshire RO (D593, D868). Deposited by the Trustees of the Will of the 4th Duke of Sutherland 1959, 1966. NRA 10699.

Corresp and papers rel to the Sutherland militia and volunteers 1794-1813 (3 boxes, 1 vol); letters from his wife 1805-20 (1 box), from James Loch 1813-33 (2 boxes); misc corresp 1807-28, accounts and bills 1787-99, 1829, and papers 1814-33 (1 box).
National Library of Scotland (Deposit 313). Deposited by the Countess of Sutherland 1980. NRA 11006.

[208] **LEVESON-GOWER, Granville** (1773-1846), 1st Viscount Granville 1815, 1st Earl Granville 1833
On a special mission to Prussia 1798; ambassador to Russia 1804-7, 1807, to the Netherlands 1824;

on a special mission to France 1824, ambassador 1824-8, 1830-5, 1835-41.

Despatches, corresp with the Foreign Office and British representatives abroad, intelligence reports and other papers rel to his early diplomatic career and to Prussia 1796-8 (1 bundle, etc), Russia 1804-7 (c8 boxes), the Netherlands 1824 (1 box, 1 bundle) and France 1824-41 (c40 boxes); general corresp, incl letters from FG Byng, George Canning, Lord Stuart de Rothesay and other diplomats 1789-1844 (3 boxes, 4 bundles); political and diplomatic notes and memoranda, verses, accounts, etc 1790-1842 (5 vols, 9 bundles); diaries as attaché to Lord Malmesbury 1796-7 and in Russia 1805 (3 vols).
Public Record Office (PRO 30/29). Deposited by Castalia, Countess Granville 1927 and by the 3rd Earl Granville 1938. NRA 8654.

Copies of despatches from him 1824-39 (5 boxes); misc papers, incl trade agreements, draft despatches and speeches, etc 1807-34 (2 boxes).
Christ Church, Oxford. Presented 1923 by the 3rd Earl Granville.

See also *Cabinet Ministers.*

[209] **LEVESON-GOWER, Granville George** (1815-1891), styled Lord Leveson 1833-46, 2nd Earl Granville 1846
Parliamentary under secretary for foreign affairs 1840-1; foreign secretary 1851-2, 1870-4, 1880-5; special ambassador to Russia 1856.

Royal corresp 1851-85 (19 vols, 1 box, 1 bundle); corresp with Cabinet colleagues 1868-74, 1880-5 (44 vols); Cabinet papers 1869-74, 1880-5 (5 vols); political corresp, memoranda and other papers, incl material rel to foreign affairs 1846-90 (c46 bundles); corresp and papers as foreign secretary 1851-2 (c11 bundles), 1870-4 (c45 vols), 1880-5 (c71 vols); as ambassador to Russia 1856 (4 bundles); Foreign Office confidential print 1819-88 (c180 vols, 2 boxes).
Public Record Office (PRO 30/29). Deposited by Castalia, Countess Granville 1927 and by the 3rd Earl Granville 1938. NRA 8654.

Corresp with British representatives in France 1870-1, Austria 1870-3 and the United States 1870-4 (5 vols).
Public Record Office (FO 362). Transferred from the Foreign Office 1921.

See also *Cabinet Ministers.*

[210] **LISTER, Sir Thomas Villiers** (1832-1902)
Entered the Foreign Office 1853; attached to special missions to the peace congresses at Vienna and Paris 1855-6, and to special embassies to Russia and Prussia 1856, 1861; private secretary to the foreign secretary 1857-8, 1865-6, 1868-70; senior clerk 1872-3, assistant under secretary 1873-94.

Corresp and papers 1845-92, mainly Foreign
Office memoranda for and from Lords Clarendon,
Derby, Granville and Salisbury (250ff); Villiers
and Lister family corresp 1831-65 and nd (87ff);
journals, Austria, Russia and Prussia 1855-6, 1861
(211ff).
Bodleian Library, Oxford (MSS Eng. hist. c.1034,
d.483). Purchased at Sotheby's 29 June 1982, lot
66.

Letters to him and his family from Lord and
Lady Russell 1837-64 (c100 items); corresp with
WM Thackeray 1860 (8 items).
Untraced. Sold at Sotheby's 29 June 1982, lots 81,
83.

[211] **LISTON, Sir Robert** (1742-1836)
Chargé d'affaires in Bavaria intermittently 1774-7,
at Ratisbon 1776-7, in Prussia 1779-80, in
Sardinia 1782-3; secretary of embassy in Spain
1783, minister 1783-8; minister to Sweden
1789-93; ambassador to Turkey 1794-5; minister
to the United States 1796-1800, to the Batavian
Republic 1802-3; on an extraordinary mission to
Denmark 1803-4; ambassador to Turkey 1812-20.

Private corresp, copies of despatches and other
official papers, memoranda, etc rel to his early
career, Bavaria and Ratisbon 1756-76 (8 vols),
Prussia 1777-82 (6 vols), Sardinia 1782-3 (4
vols), Spain 1783-8 (34 vols), Sweden 1789-92 (6
vols), Turkey 1794-5 (13 vols), the United States
1796-1801 (11 vols), the Netherlands 1802-3 (8
vols), Denmark 1803-4 (6 vols), and Turkey and
the Ionian Islands 1812-20 (39 vols); private
corresp at home 1793, 1804-11, 1821-32 and nd
(41 vols); travel journals, 1769-76 and nd (9
vols); misc estate plans, MSS of German and
Spanish literary and historical works, etc 18th-
19th cent (3 vols, etc); passports and misc papers
1749-1819 (c22 items).
National Library of Scotland (MSS 5510-5695,
5713-21, 9819, Ch 5780-5795A, 5839-42).
Purchased 1936, 1948, 1965. *Catalogue of
manuscripts*, iv, pp59-73, 153-5, 156; *Accessions of
manuscripts 1965-1970*, p24.

Letter book of Louis Dutens and Liston as
chargés d'affaires in Sardinia 1780-3 (1 vol).
British Library (Add MS 36805). Purchased at
Sotheby's 9 May 1903, lot 34 among papers of the
1st Marquess of Bute.

LIVERPOOL, Earl of, see Jenkinson.

[212] **LIVINGSTONE, Charles** (1821-1873)
Consul at Fernando Po and in the Bight of Biafra
1864-7, in the Bights of Biafra and Benin 1867-73.

Journals of Zambezi expedition 1864 (3 vols).
*Seeley G Mudd Learning Center, Oberlin College
Library, Ohio* (091.916.L763). GW Clendennen
and IC Cunningham, *David Livingstone: a
catalogue of documents*, Edinburgh 1979, p268.

[213] **LIVINGSTONE, David** (1813-1873)
Consul at Quelimane 1858-64, in the independent
territories of central Africa 1865-73.

Corresp and papers 1840-73, incl letters from the
Foreign Office, Sir Thomas Maclear, Sir RI
Murchison and others (c2,800ff); maps,
astronomical observations, linguistic notes and
misc papers 1853-72; diaries and journals 1851-3,
1858-9 (4 vols); notebook 1858.
National Archives of Zimbabwe, Harare (LI 1-2).
Presented by Miss Diana Livingstone Bruce.
*Guide to the historical manuscripts in the National
Archives of Rhodesia*, pp249-63.

Corresp of and rel to him c1837-1959; field diaries
and journals 1861-73 (18 vols); astronomical and
other notes 1852-72 (5 vols); financial accounts of
the Zambezi expedition 1858-64 (68pp); maps,
sketches, literary and misc papers.
National Library of Scotland. See *Annual reports,
passim;* GW Clendennen and IC Cunningham,
David Livingstone: a catalogue of documents,
Edinburgh 1979, *passim;* N Matthews and MD
Wainwright, *Guide to manuscripts and documents in
the British Isles relating to Africa*, 1971, pp245-6,
250-1.

Corresp 1841-72; field diaries 1860, 1868 (3 vols);
notebooks 1854-69 (6 vols).
National Museum, Livingstone, Zambia.
Clendennen and Cunningham, *passim.*

Corresp and papers of and rel to him 1850-73,
incl astronomical observations 1872-3, maps, etc.
Royal Geographical Society. C Kelly, *RGS
Archives. A handlist*, pp103-4.

Corresp 1857-65; journals and field diaries
1853-66 (13 vols).
Executors of Dr HF Wilson (his grandson).
Clendennen and Cunningham, *passim.*

Astronomical observations and other notes
1855-60 (6 vols).
South African Library, Cape Town. Clendennen
and Cunningham, pp7, 280.

Astronomical observations 1866-8 (1 vol).
*Educational Resource Service Headquarters,
Hamilton, Lanarkshire.* Clendennen and
Cunningham, p280.

Field diaries 1863-71 (5 vols); notebooks 1850-4
(2 vols).
In private possession (various owners). Microfilms
are in the National Library of Scotland.
Clendennen and Cunningham, pp275–8.

[214] **LOFTUS, Lord Augustus William
Frederick Spencer** (1817-1904)
Secretary of legation in Prussia 1853-8
(intermittently in charge 1853-7); minister to
Austria 1858-60, to Prussia 1860-2, to Bavaria
1863-6; ambassador to Prussia 1866-8, to the
North German Confederation 1868-71, to Russia
1871-9.

Entry books of despatches to him 1871-7 (7 vols);

private letters to him and his wife from various correspondents 1853-96 (1 bundle).
Public Record Office (FO 519/274-80, 284). Presented by his grandson Sir VAAH Wellesley 1952. NRA 23469.

Letters to him and his wife from various correspondents 1848-1903, and misc passports and commissions (93 items); travel journal, Europe 1842, with extracts from Chateaubriand 1845 (1 vol).
Edinburgh University Library (Dk 6.19⁶⁻⁷, Gen 715/7, Gen 2148D). Purchased from a bookseller 1958, 1960, and at Phillips's 10 June 1982, lot 473.

Letters mainly from diplomats 1858-92 (15 items).
William R Perkins Library, Duke University, Durham, N Carolina. See *Guide to the cataloged collections,* p328.

Letters mainly from WB Dalley 1879-86 (26 items).
Mitchell Library, Sydney (A 3057). Acquired 1949. *Catalogue of manuscripts of Australasia and the Pacific. Series A,* p141.

Copies of his despatches as governor of New South Wales to Lord Derby 1882-3 (1 vol).
National Library of Australia, Canberra (MS 589). Presented by the 3rd Earl of Iddesleigh 1959.

LONDONDERRY, Marquesses of, see Stewart; Vane CW.

[215] **LOWTHER, James William** (1855-1949), 1st Viscount Ullswater 1921
Parliamentary under secretary for foreign affairs 1891-2.

Corresp, mainly as under secretary, *c*1891-4, with misc corresp of Sir James Fergusson and GN Curzon 1886-97 (2 vols).
Public Record Office (FO 800/28, 34).

[216] **LUMSDEN, General Sir Peter Stark** (1829-1918)
Commissioner for the delimitation of the Russo-Afghan boundary 1884-5.

Papers and water colours, some rel to the Afghan boundary commission.
In family possession.

[217] **LYALL, Robert** (1790-1831)
Agent in Madagascar 1826-8.

Journal 1827.
British Library (Add MS 34408). Presented by the family of Sir Richard Owen 1893.

[218] **LYONS, Admiral Sir Edmund** (1790-1858), 1st Bt 1840, 1st Baron Lyons 1856
Minister to Greece 1835-49, to Switzerland 1849-51, to Sweden 1851-3.

Corresp 1811-58 (102 boxes); letter books, Greece 1844, 1850 (3 vols) and copies of his despatches 1835-47 (5 vols); letter book, Sweden 1851-2 (1 vol); copies of his corresp and sailing orders in the Mediterranean 1853-8 (37 vols); diaries 1819-20, 1842-4, 1853 (6 vols); engagement books 1837-9, 1842-8, 1850-7 (16 vols); logs as captain of HMS *Blonde* 1828, 1831 (4 vols).
West Sussex RO. The papers passed to his grandson the 15th Duke of Norfolk and were deposited in 1975 by the 17th Duke. Access restricted.

[219] **LYONS, Richard Bickerton Pemell** (1817-1887), 2nd Baron Lyons 1858, Viscount Lyons 1881
Secretary of legation in Tuscany, residing at Rome, 1856-8 (in charge 1857); on a mission to the Two Sicilies 1858; minister to Tuscany 1858, to the United States 1858-65; ambassador to Turkey 1865-7, to France 1867-87.

Letters to him 1858-87 (55 boxes); copies of despatches and letters from him 1854-87 (85 vols); diaries 1827-8, 1837, 1845, 1851-85 (39 vols) and draft diaries from 1845 (6 vols).
West Sussex RO. The papers passed to his nephew the 15th Duke of Norfolk and were deposited in 1975 by the 17th Duke. Access restricted.

LYTTON, Earl of, see Bulwer-Lytton.

[220] **MACARTNEY, George** (1737-1806), Baron Macartney 1776, Viscount Macartney 1792, Earl Macartney 1794
Envoy to Russia 1764-7, ambassador 1767 (did not proceed); ambassador to China 1792-4; on a mission to Louis XVIII at Verona 1795-6.

His papers were inherited mainly by his niece Elizabeth Hume, whose eldest son assumed the name Macartney. The family sold part of the papers to George Hyndman in 1850 (*HMC Ninth Report, Appendix II,* 1884, pp330-40), and most of the remainder at Puttick & Simpson's in 1854. Some were purchased by the British Museum, and many others by Sir Thomas Phillipps (Phillipps MSS 13351-13438, 14177-99, 18995-19002, 20642-3, 21644-8, etc, mainly dispersed at Sotheby's 19 May 1913, lots 884-955). Further papers remained in the Macartney family until sold at Sotheby's 7 July 1915, lots 280-318. Many of the items in the 1913 and 1915 sales have not been traced.
Other papers descended through the family of Macartney's widow, a daughter of the 3rd Earl of Bute, and were presented to the Bodleian Library by WD Clark 1954-60.

Copies of corresp as governor of the Caribbee

Islands with Lord George Germain 1776-9 (2 vols); copies of official and private corresp as governor of Madras 1781-5 (24 vols); copies of proceedings of the select committee of Fort St George 1781-5 (24 vols); copies of corresp rel to Tanjore 1777-80 and to an embassy to Mysore 1783-4 (3 vols); daily registers of official business at the Cape of Good Hope 1797-1800 (2 vols); letter book 1762-1801 (1 vol); copies of papers rel to the commercial treaty with Russia 1766 (1 vol); corresp and papers rel to his mission to Louis XVIII 1795-6 (1 vol); maps, charts and sketches, India, China, S Africa, etc 1762-99 (4 vols, 14 rolls); heraldic and genealogical MSS 16th-18th cent (6 vols).
British Library (Add MSS 19814-25, 22415-64, 38717-18, 39856-8, 51389, 58834, 62665). Acquired by purchase 1854-1983.

MSS of his published *Account of Russia, 1767* and *Account of Ireland in 1773* (4 vols).
British Library (King's MSS 106-7, 189-90). Presented by George IV 1823.

Corresp and papers, India 1778-87, incl letters from Sir Eyre Coote, Sir Edward Hughes and others rel to the war against Hyder Ali (7 vols, *c*220 items); narrative of the war against Hyder Ali 1779-82 (3 vols); account of Dutch possessions in E Indies 1801 (1 vol).
India Office Library and Records (MSS Eur C 22, C 229, E 87-9, E 273, E 291, F 190). Acquired by gift and purchase *c*1913-1980.

Draft of parts of his *Account of Russia, 1767* (1 vol).
School of Slavonic and East European Studies, London. Formerly Sotheby's 24 June 1935, lot 363. NRA 24277.

Copy *c*1805 of his journal of his voyage to China 1792-3 (1 vol).
Wellcome Historical Medical Library, London. Purchased 1930. Formerly Sotheby's 19 May 1913, lot 911. *Catalogue of western manuscripts,* ii, pp651-2.

Copies of official and private corresp, India 1780-5 (36 vols); private general letter books 1781-5 (14 vols); papers rel to native rulers 1778-81 (2 vols); private accounts 1784-5 (1 vol).
Bodleian Library, Oxford (MSS Eng. hist. c.66-118). Purchased 1916 from Francis Edwards, bookseller, who had bought them at Sotheby's 1913, 1915. NRA 23419.

Official corresp, misc papers and accounts 1775-86, mainly India 1780-5 (9 vols); public accounts, Madras 1737-90 (6 vols).
Bodleian Library, Oxford (MSS Eng. hist. b.173-85, d.142-3). Purchased at Sotheby's 28 July 1931, lot 639, from Colonel RG Berry who had acquired them from the Hyndman family. NRA 23419.

Private general letter book 1784.
Bodleian Library, Oxford (MS Eng. hist. c.399). Presented by Dr LS Sutherland 1964. NRA 23419.

Corresp 1763-1805, incl letters of recommendation, Madras (1 vol); letter books *c*1766-79, mainly copies of private letters to an unidentified correspondent (2 vols); observations on Russia (1 vol); commonplace books *c*1760-94, incl autobiographical memoranda and notes rel to China (3 vols); misc papers incl accounts with Coutts & Co 1803-6 (4 vols).
Bodleian Library, Oxford (MSS Eng. lett. b.23, d.373-4; MSS Eng. misc. b.162, c.625, d.938-9, e.879, f.533-5). Presented by WD Clark 1954-60. NRA 21249.

Official corresp 1767-1806, mainly with military and naval officers, W Indies 1778-9 (1 vol); copies of corresp, proclamations and public papers as governor of the Cape of Good Hope 1797-8 (4 vols).
Rhodes House Library, Oxford (MS W.Ind. s.9; MSS Afr. t.2-4*). Purchased from Maggs Bros Ltd 1930, Bernard Quaritch Ltd 1934, and Francis Edwards Ltd 1937. Cape volumes formerly Sotheby's 19 May 1913, lots 888, 891-3.

Corresp and papers 1760-1806, as chief secretary for Ireland 1769-72, and rel to his Irish estates and political and personal affairs, with letters from diplomats concerning his mission to Louis XVIII 1795, and misc corresp rel to the W Indies, India, China and the Cape of Good Hope (17 vols, *c*550 items).
Public Record Office of Northern Ireland (D572). Purchased at a sale of his papers formerly in the possession of Colonel RG Berry, held by John Ross & Co, Belfast 26 June 1947. NRA 6465. See also T Bartlett, *Macartney in Ireland 1768-72,* Belfast 1978.

Corresp and papers, India 1778-87 (5 vols, 82 items); misc corresp, speech notes and papers *c*1767-98 (45 items); Irish estate corresp and papers 1664-1853 (*c*120 items).
Public Record Office of Northern Ireland (D2225). Presented by Colonel JVO Macartney-Filgate 1961. NRA 6465.

Despatches to him, Russia 1765-6 (2 vols).
University College Library, Cork. Presented by WH Crawford 1879-80.

Letter books 1777-9 (4 vols); entry book of proclamations, administrative papers, etc, Caribbee Islands 1653-1772 (1 vol).
Library of Congress, Washington (Phillipps Collection). Formerly Sotheby's 19 May 1913, lot 905. NRA 22523.

Papers 1774-1807, mainly corresp with Major-General James Grant 1779 (32 items).
Boston Public Library, Massachusetts (MS Eng. 461.1-32). Purchased 1972.

Copies of corresp with Admirals Barrington and Byron and Major-General Grant 1778-9 (1 vol).
Boston University Library, Massachusetts (Bortman MSS YZ 1207, F481). Formerly Sotheby's 19 May 1913, lot 907. KE Ingram, *Manuscripts relating to Commonwealth Caribbean countries in United States and Canadian repositories,* St Lawrence 1975, pp104-5.

Papers rel to E India Co affairs in China 1622-1791 (21 vols); corresp and papers, China 1791-5, incl corresp with Francis Baring, Henry Dundas, Chinese officials and others, instructions from the court of directors, etc (10 vols).
Cornell University Libraries, Ithaca, New York (Wason Collection). Purchased at Sotheby's 19 May 1913, lot 915 and 7 July 1915, lot 283. See EH Pritchard, *The crucial years of early Anglo-Chinese relations 1750-1800*, Washington 1936, pp408-10.

Corresp 1779-98, mainly Madras 1780-5 (158 items).
William R Perkins Library, Duke University, Durham, N Carolina. Purchased at various dates from 1963. *Guide to the cataloged collections*, p336.

Commonplace book *c*1767-78, incl observations on Russia, Canada and Trinidad.
Huntington Library, San Marino, California (HM 686).

Papers 1765, 1776-1800, mainly rel to the war in the W Indies 1778-9, and the administration of his W Indian estates after his departure (57 items).
William L Clements Library, University of Michigan, Ann Arbor. Purchased 1925. *Guide to the manuscript collections*, 1978, pp79-80.

Copies of corresp between Sir Hector Munro and commanders of the forces south of Madras 1781-2 (3 vols).
Ames Library of South Asia, University of Minnesota, Minneapolis. Formerly Sotheby's 19 May 1913, lot 929.

Proclamations issued by WL Leyborne and William Young as governors of the Caribbees 1771-6, with a list of new commissions issued following Macartney's arrival 1776.
New York Public Library. Ingram, p219.

Corresp with E India Co administrators and soldiers, and papers rel to E India Co commercial interests 1781-5 (21 boxes).
University of Pennsylvania Library, Philadelphia. Purchased 1954. See H Furber, 'Preliminary report on the Macartney manuscripts', *Library Chronicle of the Friends of the University of Pennsylvania Library*, xxi, 1955, pp43-50.

Instructions, etc received on appointment as ambassador to China 1792 (34 items).
Washington State University Library, Pullman. Presented by EH Pritchard, who had purchased them from Bernard Halliday, bookseller, in 1931. *National union catalog*, MS 70-1392.

Letters mainly to him from various correspondents 1765-1806 (*c*200 items); papers rel to Russia 1764-7, incl notes, memoranda, accounts of travel and the court, and a copy of the commercial treaty 1766 (2 boxes); visitors' book 1765 (1 vol); copy of his account of the embassy to China 1792-4 (1 vol).
Beinecke Library, Yale University, New Haven, Connecticut (Osborn Collection). NRA 18661.

Papers 1776-98 (115 items).
National Archives of India, New Delhi. Purchased 1954 from Mohammed Hussain, bookseller, Bhopal.

Corresp and papers, mainly Madras 1780-5 (over 3,000 items).
Deccan College Postgraduate and Research Institute, Poona. Formerly in the Historical Museum, Satara. See *Studies in the history of the British in India*, ed AP Dasgupta, Calcutta 1942, pp74-129.

Letters from Alexander Davidson, William Hodges, John Macpherson and others 1781-5.
Tamil Nadu Archives, Madras. Purchased from Francis Edwards, bookseller.

Journal of his embassy to China 1793-4 (3 vols).
Tôyô Bunko (Oriental Library), Tokyo. Purchased 1917 by Baron Iwasaki from GE Morrison, who had bought them at Sotheby's 19 May 1913, lot 913. JL Cranmer-Byng, *An embassy to China*, 1962, p332.

Letters mainly to him from John Barrow, General Francis Dundas, Acheson Maxwell, John Pringle and others 1798-1804, and misc papers 1795-1800 (2 vols, a few loose items).
Kimberley Public Library, Cape Province. Purchased 1919. NRA 26032.

Letters from Robert Brooke, governor of St Helena, 1795-8 (1 vol); copies of letters to Lord Melville 1795-1806 (2 vols); notebook 1798-9 (1 vol); 'Account of the Cape of Good Hope' by Sir JH Craig 1798 (1 vol); 'Sketches of the political and commercial history of the Cape of Good Hope' by John Bruce 1798 (1 vol).
HF Oppenheimer Esq (Nos 4050 (I-IV), 5324, 6085). Microfilms are in the University of the Witwatersrand (MIC A732-7). *University of the Witwatersrand Library: guide to the archives and papers*, pp9-10, 45-7.

Corresp, letter books, memoranda, returns, etc 1779-1803, mainly Cape of Good Hope 1796-9 (2 vols, 514 items).
University of the Witwatersrand, Johannesburg (A88). Purchased from Francis Edwards Ltd by Dr JG Gubbins 1931, and presented by him 1932. *Historical and literary papers: inventories of collections, 5: Earl Macartney papers*.

MACDONALD, see Kinneir.

[221] **MACDONELL, Hugh** (fl 1792-1837)
Consul-general at Algiers 1814-27.

Corresp and papers of Macdonell and members of his family *c*1773-1915, incl material rel to Algiers, and to the career of his son Sir HG Macdonell (several hundred pages).
Untraced. Sold at Sotheby's 23 Mar 1981, lot 107.

[222] **MACDONELL, Sir Hugh Guion** (1832-1904)
Secretary of legation in the Argentine Republic 1869-72, in Spain 1872-5; secretary of embassy in Germany 1875-8, in Italy 1878-82; chargé d'affaires in Bavaria 1882-5; minister to Brazil 1885-8, to Denmark 1888-93, to Portugal 1893-1902.

See Macdonell H.

[223] **MacLEOD, Sir James MacIver** (1866-1944)
Vice-consul at Fez 1892-1907, consul 1907-17; consul-general at Valparaiso 1919-23, at Tunis 1923-30.

Letters from Sir EM Satow 1895-1929 (2 vols); drafts of letters to Satow 1897, 1899, with MacLeod's notes on the corresp 1937 (1 vol).
Public Record Office (PRO 30/26/85). Presented by him 1937.

[224] **McNEILL, Sir John** (1795-1883)
Attached to the E India Co legation in Persia 1824-35; secretary to a special mission to Persia 1835-6, minister 1836-42.

Corresp with foreign secretaries, British diplomats and consuls, E India Co employees and soldiers, Board of Control officials and others rel to Persia 1819-43 (c1,500 items); memoranda, notes, draft reports, 'anecdotes', etc rel to Persia 1802-43 (3 vols, c250 items); corresp and misc printed material rel to Scottish emigration to Australia and Tasmania 1851-7 (c50 items); corresp, memoranda, notes, etc concerning the commission of enquiry into the British commissariat in the Crimea 1854-7 (c200 items); misc corresp and papers rel to Persia, the Scottish poor law, his literary work, etc 1843-78 (3 vols, c220 items); diaries and journals of his service in Persia, and of other travels by him and his wife 1816-51 and nd (14 vols); additional papers 1808-82, mainly rel to Persia 1823-42 (56 bundles, etc).
Scottish Record Office (GD 371). Deposited by John McNeill of Druimavuie 1980 and by Jane (née McNeill), Duchess of Buccleuch 1982. NRA 24144; *Keeper's report 1980*, pp12, 22 and *1982*, pp23, 27.

Corresp and papers rel to the commission of enquiry into the commissariat in the Crimea 1855-7 (14 bundles, etc).
Scottish Record Office (GD 1/928). Deposited 1981 by Major-General JM McNeill. *Keeper's report 1981*, pp19, 25.

[225] **McTAVISH, John** (1788-1852)
Consul at Baltimore 1834-52.

Notebooks 1840-52, bank book 1839-43, cash book 1844-6 (5 vols); papers mainly rel to estate administration 1820-49, with misc papers of his wife and brother Alexander 1812-67 (1 box).

Maryland Historical Society, Baltimore (MS 220, boxes 16-17). Purchased from CB Carroll 1949.

[226] **MAGENIS, Sir Arthur Charles** (1801-1867)
Attaché in Russia 1830-8 (in charge 1832); secretary of legation in Switzerland 1838-44 (in charge 1839, 1839-40); secretary of embassy in Austria 1844-51 (intermittently minister *ad interim* 1845-51); minister to the Swiss Confederation 1851-2, to Württemberg 1852-4, to Sweden 1854-9, to the Two Sicilies 1859 (did not proceed), to Portugal 1859-66.

Corresp mainly with the Foreign Office rel to Switzerland 1838-9, and draft despatches 1839-40 (1 bundle, 60 items); corresp incl letters from HF Howard and Lord Westmorland, mainly Austria, 1848-52 (91 items); corresp with Andrew Buchanan, Lord Clarendon and others, and memoranda and misc papers, Sweden 1854-9 (2 bundles, 127 items); corresp and papers rel to the Two Sicilies 1859 and Portugal 1859-66 (2 bundles, 77 items); letters from his sister Elizabeth c1855-66 (2 bundles); travel journals, Switzerland and Italy 1823-4 (5 vols); sketches 1831 (1 vol); misc papers 1838-65 (1 file, 17 items).
In private possession. NRA 23648.

[227] **MAGRA, Perkins** (d 1826)
Consul at Tunis c1791-1804.

Corresp as commander of Dover Castle 1768-9, letters from Admiral Sir GC Berkeley, Lord George Lennox and others on personal and military matters, events in Portugal, etc 1782-1809, papers as consul 1791-1804, incl material rel to negotiations with the bey of Tunis, piracy, provisions for the Mediterranean fleet, etc, and archaeological and historical notes on Tunis, Carthage and Zaghouan (155 items).
William R Perkins Library, Duke University, Durham, N Carolina. Purchased 1969. *Guide to the cataloged collections*, pp353-4; *National union catalog*, MS 71-1661.

MAHON, Viscount, see Stanhope.

[228] **MAITLAND, James** (1759-1839), styled Viscount Maitland 1759-89, 8th Earl of Lauderdale 1789
Plenipotentiary to France 1806.

Copies of despatches from him 1806 (2 vols); copies of private letters to CJ Fox and others 1806 (1 vol); misc letters to him and his family 1756-1863 (3 bundles); corresp, notes and press cuttings rel to the abolition of local token currency 1812-14 (1 vol); corresp, papers and pamphlets rel to the corn laws 1814-28 (2 vols); parliamentary diary 1827-8, with misc letters 1775-1808 (1 vol); essay on the public wealth

1804 (1 vol); list of office holders in Scotland 1806 (1 vol).
In private possession. Enquiries to NRA (Scotland). NRA 10211.

Letters from CJ Fox 1796-1806 (1 vol).
British Library (Add MS 47564). Presented among Fox's papers by Professor GM Trevelyan 1951.

[229] **MALCOLM, Sir Ian Zachary** (1868-1944)
Attaché in Germany 1891-3, in France 1893-6, in Russia 1896; assistant parliamentary private secretary to Lord Salisbury as foreign secretary 1895-8; private secretary to AJ Balfour as foreign secretary 1916-19.

Diaries of foreign travel 1895-1900, political events in England 1910 and the Paris peace conference 1918-19 (3 vols); albums of press cuttings rel to his political speeches, social engagements, etc 1887-1940 (5 vols); corresp, papers, diary extracts, etc mainly rel to his work for the British Red Cross 1914-18 (4 vols); misc writings, personal and estate papers (5 vols, etc).
RNL Malcolm Esq. Enquiries to NRA (Scotland). NRA 15645.

Travel diaries 1890-1902 (4 vols); photograph albums, India and Burma 1901-2 (3 vols).
National Library of Scotland (Acc 4304). Purchased 1967.

Corresp with the Foreign Office, the Treasury and other government departments as senior British director of the Suez Canal Co 1924-30 (8 vols).
Public Record Office (T 206). Presented by him to the Treasury 1939.

[230] **MALCOLM, Sir John** (1769-1833)
Envoy from the governor-general of India to Persia 1799-1801, 1808-9, 1810.

Private corresp and misc papers, India and Persia 1796-1832 (2 vols); corresp rel to Persia 1809-10, bound with a private letter book 1818 (1 vol); private letter book as governor of Bombay 1827-30 (1 vol); private letter book 1831-2, bound with other papers incl a journal of travel from Alnwick to London 1831 (1 vol).
India Office Library and Records (Home Misc Series 733-7). *Catalogue of the Home Miscellaneous Series*, pp491-7.

Private letter book 1799-1801, mainly copies of letters to Lord Wellesley (1 vol).
National Library of Wales, Aberystwyth (MS 4903). Acquired among papers of Sir Harford Jones Brydges 1923. *Handlist of manuscripts*, ii, p52.

Translations of Persian works for his *History of Persia* (1815) (2 vols).
Bodleian Library, Oxford (MSS Eng. hist. b.151-2). Purchased 1925.

[231] **MALET, Sir Alexander** (1800-1886), 2nd Bt 1815
Attaché in Russia 1824-7, in France 1827-33, in Portugal 1833-5; secretary of legation in Sardinia 1835-6, in the Netherlands 1836-43 (intermittently in charge); secretary of embassy in Austria 1843-4; minister to Württemberg 1844-52, to the Germanic Confederation 1852-66.

Copies of despatches sent 1852-66 (5 vols); letters from diplomats and others 1827-84 (67 items); draft despatches, letters and papers rel to appointments, and miscellanea 1827-83 (76 items); letters from him to his mother 1822-45 (362 items); letters to his wife from Queen Sophia of the Netherlands 1842-77 (916 items); corresp of his wife with him, with Lord and Lady Brougham, the 15th Earl of Derby and others 1833-c1871, and misc papers (c450 items); letters to him and his wife from their elder son Henry in the Crimea 1855-6, with an album of his sketches (1 vol, 80 items); letters to them from their younger son Edward 1854-90 (1,644 items); MS and proofs of *The overthrow of the Germanic Confederation by Prussia in 1866* (1870) (3 bundles).
William R Perkins Library, Duke University, Durham, N Carolina. Purchased from Sir EWStL Malet Bt 1970-3. NRA 25904.

Letters mainly to him from British and foreign diplomats and statesmen 1815-84 (104 items); misc letters and papers 1833-81, incl letters from him to Lady Brougham 1833-4 (20 items).
In private possession. NRA 18542.

[232] **MALET, Sir Edward Baldwin** (1837-1908), 4th Bt 1904
Second secretary in the United States 1862-5, in Portugal 1865, in France 1867-71 (in charge 1871); secretary of legation in China 1871-3, in Greece 1873-5 (in charge 1874, 1875), in Italy 1875-6; secretary of embassy in Italy 1876-8 (in charge 1876), in Turkey 1878-9 (minister *ad interim* 1879); agent and consul-general in Egypt 1879-83; minister to Belgium 1883-4; ambassador to Germany 1884-95; member of the international court of arbitration at The Hague 1899-1906.

Diplomatic corresp 1861-95, incl letters from Lords Dufferin, Granville, Lyons and Salisbury, and copies of despatches (1,195 items); letters from diplomats, relatives and friends 1860-95 (846 items); from British statesmen and British and foreign royalty 1880-1908 (c100 items); from Sir JR Rodd 1888-1906 and EW Howard 1891-5 (209 items); copies of despatches from him 1881-3, notes on the rebellion and trial of Arabi Pasha 1882, and confidential print rel to Egypt 1882-4, 1905 (7 vols); papers rel to the court of arbitration at The Hague 1900-6 (1 vol, 35 items); rel to his controversy with WS Blunt 1907 about the British occupation of Egypt (1 vol, 31 items); letters and papers rel to his memoirs *Shifting scenes* (1901) (2 bundles, 114 items).

William R Perkins Library, Duke University, Durham, N Carolina. Purchased from Sir EWStL Malet Bt 1970-3. NRA 25904.

Private corresp with Queen Victoria, members of the royal family and household, foreign secretaries and Foreign Office staff, the Emperor Wilhelm II and members of the German government, King Leopold II of the Belgians and others 1884-95 (14 vols).
Public Record Office (FO 343). Presented to the Foreign Office 1936 by his former private secretary the 1st Baron Rennell, and transferred to the Public Record Office 1938. NRA 23621.

[233] **MALLET, Sir Claude Coventry** (1860-1941)
Vice-consul at Panama 1884-5; vice-consul at Colón 1885-8, consul 1888-91; consul at Panama 1891-1908, consul-general 1908-19 (in charge in Peru 1894, in Ecuador 1894-5, in Colombia 1902-3); minister resident in Panama and Costa Rica 1908-14, minister 1914-19; minister to the Argentine Republic 1919-20, 1922, to Uruguay 1919-25.

Corresp, Ecuador 1894, letters from him to Rear-Admiral LS Beaumont and GE Welby 1899-1900, corresp 1909-12, letters to his wife, etc (1 box); MS memoir; press cuttings rel to his career.
Mrs Dita Mallet.

[234] **MALLET, Sir Louis** (1823-1890)
Assistant commissioner for tariff negotiations with France 1860; commissioner for tariff negotiations with Austria 1865-7; commissioner for commercial treaty negotiations with France 1877.

Corresp and papers rel to his work at the Board of Trade 1847-72 and the India Office 1872-83 (2 boxes).
PLV Mallet Esq.

Draft treaties, protocols, tariff schedules, memoranda, etc mainly rel to the Anglo-Austrian tariff negotiations 1865-9 (2 vols).
British Library (Add MSS 38814-15). Purchased 1914.

Letters from Sir RBD Morier 1863-89 (1 box, 1 bundle).
Balliol College, Oxford. Lent to Morier's daughter by Sir Bernard Mallet c1910, and deposited among Morier's papers. NRA 26599.

Letters to him 1876-88, mainly from Lord Lytton 1876-8, with a few draft replies (2 vols).
India Office Library and Records (MSS Eur E 218/48). Deposited among Lytton's papers by Lady Hermione Cobbold 1956.

MALMESBURY, Earl of, see Harris J and JH.

MANCHESTER, Duke of, see Montagu.

[235] **MARTIN LEAKE, Lieutenant-Colonel William** (1777-1860)
On a military mission to Turkey 1799-1801; on missions to the governors of European Turkey 1804-7, 1808-10; resident at the Swiss army headquarters 1815.

Corresp, memoranda and reports 1800-12, mainly rel to European Turkey, and incl letters from Sir Robert Adair, Ali Pasha and Sir AJ Ball (80 items); corresp and letter book while in Switzerland 1815 (1 vol, 13 items); corresp, notebooks, pamphlets, etc mainly rel to his archaeological and topographical studies 1800-60 (150 vols, bundles and items).
Hertfordshire RO (85483-85584, 85593-85719, 85769-85). Deposited by JR Martin-Leake 1955. NRA 9367.

MATHEW, see Buckley-Mathew.

[236] **MATTHEWS, James Robert** (fl 1806-39)
Consul at Cadiz 1816-22; consul-general at Lisbon 1822-34, chargé d'affaires in Portugal 1828-9.

Journal 1828-9, incl a draft report on the Portuguese government and people, an address presented to him by the British residents of Lisbon, and a copy of his reply (1 vol).
British Library (Add MS 61972). Purchased 1981 from Henry Bristow, catalogue 272, item 169.

Memorandum book 1806-16; letters and papers 1816-39 (8 items); copies of his despatches 1822-8 (1 vol); travel journal, Italy 1839.
Untraced. Henry Bristow, catalogue 269, 1981, items 16, 50, 76, 98, 109.

[237] **MAYCOCK, Sir Willoughby Robert Dottin** (1849-1922)
Entered the Foreign Office 1872; attached to the royal commission for negotiation of a commercial treaty with France 1881, and to Joseph Chamberlain's special mission to the United States 1887-8; assistant in the treaty department 1896-1903, superintendent 1903-13.

Corresp and papers mainly rel to his career 1879-1913 (118 items); corresp and press cuttings rel to his indexes of diplomatic and consular reports 1889-96 (1 vol).
Greater London RO (F/MCK). Deposited by Mrs B Billson 1963. NRA 10887.

[238] **MEADE, Richard Charles Francis Christian** (1795-1879), 3rd Earl of Clanwilliam 1805
Acting under secretary for foreign affairs 1820-1, under secretary 1822-3; minister to Prussia 1823-8.

Letters from his family and others 1820-77, with some typescript copies of political and diplomatic corresp 1815-52 (97 items); letter book containing copies of letters and despatches to Count

Bernstorff, George Canning and Lord Dudley 1823-8 (2 vols); copies of letters from him mainly rel to the reform bills 1831-2 (1 vol); diaries 1812-14, 1819-54, 1858-71, 1873-9 (12 vols); reminiscences 1795-1850 (1 vol); commissions, philosophical reflections, a commonplace book and misc papers 1818-79 (2 vols, 35 items).
Public Record Office of Northern Ireland (D3044/F). Deposited by the 6th Earl of Clanwilliam 1973, and by SRJ Meade 1975. NRA 21971.

[239] **MEADE, Sir Robert Henry** (1835-1898)
Clerk in the Foreign Office 1859-71; secretary to Lord Dufferin's mission to Syria 1860-1; delegate at the Berlin conference 1884-5.

Official and personal letters to him 1860-2 (4 vols); letter books, Syria 1860-1 (2 vols); corresp, Berlin 1884-5 (1 vol); family corresp 1849-87 (335 items); misc corresp and papers 1852-97, incl letters from the Prince of Wales 1863-8 (83 items); diaries 1854-8, 1860, 1862, 1864, 1895-7 (9 vols); visitors' book 1872-97, anecdote books 1878-94, genealogical notes 1886-90 (6 vols).
Public Record Office of Northern Ireland (D3044/J). Deposited by SRJ Meade 1975. NRA 21971.

Personal and family corresp and misc papers 1830-98, incl many letters of condolence from members of the royal family, statesmen, Colonial Office officials and others on the deaths of his wife 1881, his daughter Mary 1897 and himself 1898 (*c*640 items).
University College of Swansea (Grenfell MSS L-N). Deposited by his niece Viscountess Gage 1953. NRA 26521.

MELBOURNE, Viscount, see Lamb.

[240] **MERRY, Anthony** (fl 1783-1835)
Consul at Malaga 1783-6, at Madrid 1786-90 (in charge in Spain 1789-90); consul-general at Madrid 1790-6; chargé d'affaires in Denmark 1799-1800; secretary of embassy at the congress of Amiens 1801-2; minister *ad interim* to France 1802; minister to the United States 1803-6, to Denmark 1807, to Sweden 1808-9.

Letters from Lord Hawkesbury 1802 (70 items); letters from Joseph Bonaparte, CM de Talleyrand and French officials 1802 (2 bundles); copies of despatches from him 1802 (1 vol); papers rel to the imprisonment of William Girod 1802 (1 bundle).
Kent AO (U269/O200). Deposited among the papers of Earl Whitworth by the 4th Baron Sackville 1950. NRA 8575.

[241] **MIDDLETON, Robert Thomas Charles** (d 1902)
Secretary of legation in Mexico 1864-8 (in charge 1866-7), in Brazil 1868-9; chargé d'affaires and consul-general in Venezuela 1869-72, minister resident and consul-general 1872-8.

Papers rel to the shooting of Emperor Maximilian and the withdrawal of the British mission from Mexico 1867-8 (11 items); diplomatic appointments, etc 1862-70 (8 items).
Dorset RO (MZ). Presented by Major HF Middleton 1951. NRA 5597.

Scrapbook containing copies of letters, reports, news cuttings, photographs, etc, Venezuela 1872-8 (1 vol).
Untraced. Henry Bristow Ltd, catalogue xi (new series), 1974, item 145.

MIDLETON, Earl of, see Brodrick.

[242] **MIÉVILLE, Sir Walter Frederick** (1855-1929)
Second clerk in the consular court at Alexandria 1874-81; acting consul at Suez 1881-2; acting vice-consul at Alexandria 1882-3.

Misc personal papers, press cuttings, photographs, and some letters 1871-*c*1929 (5 vols); material rel to family history (4 vols).
Hove Central Library. NRA 10102.

[243] **MILLER, William** (1795-1861)
Consul-general at Honolulu 1843-55, commissioner and consul-general 1855-61.

Misc papers *c*1821-1862, incl descriptions of his part in battles in Peru 1822, 1824 (38 items).
Hawaii Public Archives, Honolulu. See *National union catalog*, MS 70-554.

MINTO, Earls of, see Elliot-Murray-Kynynmound.

[244] **MOLYNEUX, Edmund** (d 1864)
Secretary to the consulate at Savannah 1826-31, consul 1831-64.

Corresp and papers 1816-75, incl letters and instructions from Lord Lyons 1857-62, and corresp with British subjects in Georgia during the American civil war (531 items).
William R Perkins Library, Duke University, Durham, N Carolina. Acquired 1950-8. NRA 25907.

Official and personal corresp, instructions and circulars from the Foreign Office, maritime and customs papers, and other records of the consulate, incl some rel to Lewis Joel and James Wallace, 1821-95 (120 items).

Georgia Historical Society, Savannah (Collection 648). Presented by the estate of KM Read 1956 and later. NRA 25907.

Letters 1859-69, mainly to him or to the vice-consul Allan Fullarton rel to the conscription of British subjects and other matters arising from the American civil war (62 items).
Robert W Woodruff Library, Emory University, Atlanta, Georgia. Acquired from KM Read 1938. NRA 25907.

MONK BRETTON, Baron, see Dodson.

[245] **MONSON, Sir Edmund John**
(1834-1909), 1st Bt 1905
Consul in the Azores 1869-72; consul-general at Budapest 1871-9; on a special mission to Montenegro 1876-7; minister resident and consul-general in Uruguay 1879-84; minister to the Argentine Republic and Paraguay 1884, to Denmark 1884-8, to Greece 1888-92, to Belgium 1892-3; ambassador to Austria-Hungary 1893-6, to France 1896-1904.

Private corresp with the Foreign Office, British and foreign diplomats, his wife, brothers and others, commissions, instructions, accounts, etc, Uruguay 1879-83 (*c*50 items), the Argentine Republic and Paraguay 1884-5 (*c*150 items), Denmark 1884-8 (*c*1,750 items), Greece 1888-91 (*c*1,000 items), Belgium 1892-3 (*c*100 items), Austria-Hungary 1893-6 (*c*1,500 items) and France 1896-1904 (*c*3,000 items).
In private possession.

Corresp with Queen Victoria, foreign secretaries, British diplomats, consuls and others 1876-1905 (5 vols); corresp with his wife and brother Lord Oxenbridge 1875-85 (1 vol, *c*60 items); misc corresp and papers 1841-1903 (1 vol, etc); diaries 1888-9 (2 vols).
Bodleian Library, Oxford (MSS Eng. hist. c.589-95, d.358, b.172 ff117-19, e.341-2; MSS Don. d.178-9, c.154). Purchased 1972 from George Greer and 1978 from Henry Bristow Ltd, catalogue 238, item 57, and presented 1982 by John Wilson (Autographs) Ltd. NRA 23418 (partial list).

Copies of private letters and despatches to Queen Victoria, King George of Greece, King Leopold of the Belgians, foreign secretaries and others 1891-1903 (4 vols); travel diary, Antwerp and elsewhere 1853 (1 vol).
Ohio University Library, Athens. Purchased from Peter Eaton (Booksellers) Ltd 1970. NRA 23417.

[246] **MONTAGU, George** (1737-1788), styled Viscount Mandeville 1739-62, 4th Duke of Manchester 1762
Ambassador to France 1783-4.

The papers of the Dukes of Manchester, deposited in the Public Record Office in 1880 and listed in· *HMC Eighth Report, Appendix II*, 1881,

were withdrawn in 1969 and a large quantity, including the papers of the 4th Duke, sold at auction in 1970. Other family and estate papers were deposited in Huntingdonshire RO in 1948 and 1954.

Diplomatic corresp, instructions, memoranda and treaty papers 1783-4, and intelligence reports 1779-88 (295 items); copies of corresp between Alleyne Fitzherbert, CJ Fox and Lord Grantham 1782-3 (2 vols); copies of corresp between Fox, Thomas Grenville, Manchester and others 1782-3 (2 vols).
William L Clements Library, University of Michigan, Ann Arbor. Purchased at Sotheby's 20 July 1970, lots 606-10, and 26 Oct 1970, lots 357-8. *Guide to the manuscript collections*, 1978, p83; *HMC Eighth Report, Appendix II*, pp120-37.

Copies of reports by British agents in France rel to the strength and disposition of French warships 1781 (1 vol).
Bodleian Library, Oxford (MS Eng. misc. d.704). Purchased 1971 after sale at Sotheby's 26 Oct 1970, lot 366. *HMC Eighth Report, Appendix II*, p121, item 922.

Notebook containing copies of secret corresp, notes of movements of British and enemy fleets and other intelligence 1778-9 (1 vol).
Portsmouth City RO. Purchased at Sotheby's 26 Oct 1970, lot 362. *HMC Eighth Report, Appendix II*, p120, item 909.

Letters from his wife *c*1783 (20 items); letters and papers rel to the Huntingdonshire lieutenancy 1743-1800 (31 items).
Cambridgeshire RO, Huntingdon (DDM 21B/6, 85/11-12). NRA 0902.

[247] **MORIER, David Richard** (1784-1877)
Second secretary in Turkey 1810-12; attaché in Austria 1813-15; consul-general in Paris 1815-32; minister to the Swiss Confederation 1832-47.

Letters from Stratford Canning, Bartholomew Frere, Terrick Hamilton, Sir Harford Jones, EM Ward, Sir Henry Willock and other diplomats, Ottoman empire and Persia 1809-59 (11 bundles); memoranda, notes, drawings and other papers, Ottoman empire and Persia *c*1804-10 (4 vols, 4 bundles); official, personal and family corresp and papers, Austria, France and Switzerland 1813-42 (24 bundles); corresp with his family 1801-34 (18 bundles); letters from Sir TD Acland 1833-55 (1 bundle); letters from Edward Lear 1872-4 (1 bundle); accounts 1807-15 (2 vols); misc corresp and papers (1 vol, 4 bundles).
Hon Mrs FH Cunnack (his great-granddaughter). NRA 26039.

Letters from his son Sir RBD Morier and other members of his family 1848-77; notebooks *c*1870 (2 vols).
Balliol College, Oxford. Presented by Mrs Cunnack. NRA 26599.

[248] **MORIER, Isaac** (1750-1817)
Consul-general at Constantinople 1804-6, consul
1806-17.

Corresp mainly with his wife and sons 1787-1817
(14 bundles); corresp with his partner at Smyrna
Robert Wilkinson 1801-3, and related papers (1
bundle); account and memorandum book
1794-1815 (1 vol); register of family births,
deaths and marriages 1778-1816 (1 vol).
Hon Mrs FH Cunnack (his great-great-
granddaughter). NRA 26039.

[249] **MORIER, James Justinian** (1782-1849)
Secretary of legation in Persia 1808-9, secretary of
embassy 1810-15 (in charge 1814, minister *ad
interim* 1814-15); commissioner and
plenipotentiary to Mexico 1824-5.

Journal of his voyage from England to the Persian
Gulf and of his travels in Persia 1810-15 (6 vols).
British Library (Add MSS 33839-44). Purchased
1890.

Family corresp of JJ and DR Morier 1801-6 (1
bundle); drawings made in Persia *c*1811-15 (1
vol); exercises of JJ and DR Morier and other
papers in Greek, Persian and Turkish (2
bundles); letters from him to his family 1799-1842
(27 bundles).
Hon Mrs FH Cunnack (his great-great-niece).
NRA 26039.

[250] **MORIER, John Philip** (1778-1853)
Consul-general in Albania and the Morea
1803-10; secretary of legation in the United States
1810-12 (in charge 1810-11); acting under
secretary for foreign affairs 1815-16; minister to
Saxony 1816-24.

Corresp in Greek, Italian and Turkish of JP and
DR Morier 1806-21 (1 bundle); papers rel to the
expenses of his mission to Norway 1814 (1
bundle); letters from him to his family 1787-1831
(14 bundles).
Hon Mrs FH Cunnack (his great-great-niece).
NRA 26039.

[251] **MORIER, Sir Robert Burnett David**
(1826-1893)
Attaché in Austria 1853-8; attaché in Prussia
1858-62, second secretary 1862-5; commissioner
for tariff negotiations with Austria 1865, 1866,
1867; secretary of legation in Greece 1865, to the
Germanic Confederation 1865-6, in Hesse-
Darmstadt 1866-71; chargé d'affaires in
Württemberg 1871-2, in Bavaria 1872-6; minister
to Portugal 1876-81, to Spain 1881-4; ambassador
to Russia 1884-93.

Corresp and papers, mainly Austria and Germany
1850-76, rel to tariff negotiations, the Franco-
Prussian war, Schleswig-Holstein, etc (5 boxes,
2 vols); Portugal and Spain 1874-85, incl corresp
with successive foreign secretaries, Lord Edmond
Fitzmaurice, CM Kennedy, the Marqués de la

Vega de Armijo and others, and papers rel to
commercial negotiations, Gibraltar and the Goa
and Lourenço Marques treaties (14 boxes,
9 vols); Russia 1885-93, incl corresp with the
Foreign Office and members of the Russian
government, and papers rel to British trade with
eastern Siberia (7 boxes, 3 vols); corresp and
press cuttings mainly 1888-9 rel to German
allegations that he had passed confidential
military information to France in 1870 (5 boxes);
general corresp with the 15th Earl and Countess
of Derby, Sir CW Dilke, WE Gladstone, AHG
Grey, Charles Grey, CL Hill, Benjamin Jowett,
Sir AH Layard, Sir Louis Mallet, DR Morier, Sir
HF Ponsonby and others 1853-93 (18 boxes);
family and personal corresp and papers 1850-93,
incl letters from the Stockmar family 1870-93,
guest lists of the British embassy St Petersburg
1886-9, condolences to Lady Morier 1893, and
misc papers of DR Morier (17 boxes);
engagement diaries and journals 1863-93
(incomplete series), notebooks 1846-77 and nd,
press cuttings 1858-80, misc papers rel to Austria,
Russia, Schleswig-Holstein, etc (6 boxes, 1 vol);
typescript copies of his corresp made by his
daughter, and draft chapters of her *Memoirs and
letters of the Right Hon Sir Robert Morier* (1911)
(6 boxes).
Balliol College, Oxford. Presented by his
granddaughter Mrs FH Cunnack 1965 and 1973.
NRA 26599.

Caricatures drawn by him 1861-2 (1 vol).
Hon Mrs FH Cunnack. NRA 26039.

MOUNTSTUART, Viscount, see Stuart J.

[252] **MURRAY, Sir Charles Augustus**
(1806-1895)
Agent and consul-general in Egypt 1846-53;
minister to Switzerland 1853-4, to Persia 1854-9,
to Saxony 1859-66, to Denmark 1866-7, to
Portugal 1867-74.

Papers as master of the royal household, incl
letters from Queen Victoria, the Duchess of Kent,
Lord Liverpool and others 1837-44 (*c*4 bundles),
and journals 1837, 1844 (3 vols); corresp with
Lords Canning and Elphinstone, Sir James
Outram, Sir HJ Rawlinson, the Shah and others,
and misc papers, Persia *c*1856-60 (*c*5 bundles);
letter book 1857 (1 vol), précis of despatches
from Herat 1858 (1 vol), memoranda (1 vol),
instructions and journals, Persia 1855-9 (5 vols);
other diplomatic papers, incl corresp with Lord
Westmorland on Swiss-Austrian relations 1853-4
and letters rel to Egypt, Portugal and Spain
1848-74 (*c*9 bundles); literary MSS, papers rel to
Near Eastern languages and culture,
autobiographical notes, corresp with his family,
Samuel Rogers, Sir CR Vaughan and others,
papers of his brother Rear Admiral HA Murray
and other members of his family, etc *c*1807-89 (4
vols, 30 bundles, etc).

Scottish Record Office (GD 261). Mainly deposited in 1970 by Mrs E Murray, who has retained some of the personal and family correspondence. NRA 14153.

Letters from his uncle the 10th Duke of Hamilton and others mainly rel to financial matters 1836-7 and the Lanarkshire elections 1837, 1841 (60 items).
The Duke of Hamilton. Enquiries to NRA (Scotland). NRA 10979 (C4, pp70-3, 85, 87).

[253] **NEVILLE-ROLFE, Eustace** (1845-1908) Consul at Naples 1895-1903, consul-general 1903-8.
Letters from the royal family from 1888 (1 vol), Lord Dufferin 1890-1902 (1 vol), Lord Rosebery from 1895 (1 vol), and his family and others 1877-1908 (4 vols); estate and financial corresp 1868-95 (12 vols), with other personal, family, legal, business and estate papers; letter books 1871-9 (2 vols); diaries of his residences at Naples and of his travels, Europe and S Africa 1857-93 (6 vols); memoir of his father 1879; biographical material 1845-1908.
Norfolk RO (NRS 27114). Deposited by his grandson AE Gunther 1968-71. NRA 17981.

[254] **NEWTON, Sir Charles Thomas** (1816-1894)
Vice-consul at Mytilene 1852-9; acting consul at Rhodes 1852-3; consul at Rome 1859-61.

Copies of letters and despatches to the Foreign Office 1856-9 and to Lord Stratford de Redcliffe 1856-7 rel to his excavations at Halicarnassus, Cnidus and Branchidae (2 vols); plans, drawings and photographs of the excavations 1856-9 (3 vols); misc corresp as keeper of Greek and Roman antiquities at the British Museum with WE Gladstone, EW Hamilton and others 1877-84 (11 items).
British Library (Add MSS 31980, 46889-90, 50850I). Add MS 31980 purchased 1882, Add MSS 46889-90 transferred from the office of the director of the British Museum 1949, Add MS 50850I transferred from the Department of Greek and Roman Antiquities 1962.

[255] **NICOLSON, Sir Arthur** (1849-1928), 11th Bt 1899, 1st Baron Carnock 1916
Second secretary in Turkey 1879-84; chargé d'affaires in Greece 1884-5, in Persia 1885-8; consul-general at Budapest 1888-93; chargé d'affaires in Turkey 1893-4; agent and consul-general in Bulgaria 1894-5; minister to Morocco 1895-1904; ambassador to Spain 1904-6, to Russia 1906-10; permanent under secretary for foreign affairs 1910-16.

Corresp 1889-1916, mainly 1901-16 but incl some corresp and papers, Budapest 1889-93 (49 vols).
Public Record Office (FO 800/336-81). Deposited by him in the Foreign Office Library 1925. NRA 23627.

Letters to him, Persia 1885-7 (2 vols); letter books, Greece and Persia 1885-8 (5 vols), Turkey 1893-4 (2 vols), Bulgaria 1894-5, incl household accounts 1897-1902 (1 vol), Morocco 1895-6 (1 vol); journals, Persia 1885-8 (1 vol), Russia 1906-10 (3 vols) and from 1916 (1 vol); copies of his letters to Sir WA White 1874-c1891, with related papers 1916-33.
Public Record Office (PRO 30/81). Presented by Nigel Nicolson 1980.

[256] **NOEL-HILL** (formerly **HILL**), **William** (1773-1842), 3rd Baron Berwick 1832
Minister to Sardinia 1807-24, to the Two Sicilies 1824-32.

Official letters to Joseph Brame, John Collet and other British consuls and vice-consuls at Genoa, with a few copies of replies, 1764-1800 (c800 items); official letter books of the British consulate at Genoa 1782-1804 (6 vols); receipts for provisions 1789, 1796 (6 bundles, 103 items); letters to the British consul at Cagliari from 1800, and to Hill in Sardinia and the Two Sicilies 1807-30 (c2,000 items); copies of despatches from him 1808-32 (7 vols); copies of diplomatic, personal and estate corresp 1816-33 (7 vols); letters from members of the Stanhope family 1806-11 (95 items); other personal corresp and accounts (c400 items); accounts and vouchers rel to the Shrewsbury election 1796 (4 boxes); private accounts 1808-9 (1 vol); household accounts, Cagliari 1812-15 (3 vols); letters and papers rel to his English estates c1800-42 (c140 items).
Shropshire RO (SRO 112). Deposited by the Dowager Lady Berwick 1947 and by the National Trust 1973. NRA 26124.

NORMANBY, Marquess of, see Phipps.

[257] **NORTHCOTE, Sir Stafford Henry** (1818-1887), 8th Bt 1851, 1st Earl of Iddesleigh 1885
Commissioner to the United States to settle the *Alabama* claims 1871; foreign secretary 1886-7.

Corresp with WE Gladstone, Lord Granville, HS Northcote and others rel to the *Alabama* claims and the treaty of Washington 1871-2, misc corresp with Lord Salisbury rel to foreign affairs and his resignation 1886-7, and a brief journal kept while foreign secretary 1886.
British Library (Add MSS 50014, 50020, 50022, 50032, 50038-9, 50044, 50051). Presented by the 3rd Earl of Iddesleigh 1959. NRA 5873.

See also *Cabinet Ministers.*

[258] **O'LEARY, General Daniel Florence** (d 1854)
Consul at Puerto Cabello 1841-3; chargé d'affaires and consul-general in New Granada 1843-54.

Corresp with General Simón Bolívar, General Carlos Soublette, Sir BH Wilson and other S American politicians and soldiers 1814-42; diaries 1825-6, 1834, 1836 (4 vols); 'Detached Recollections' (1 vol); misc papers, incl biography of Bolívar to 1810, appointments 1841, 1843, later family papers, etc.
PT O'Leary Esq.

[259] **OSBORNE, Francis Godolphin**
(1751-1799), styled Marquess of Carmarthen 1761-89, 5th Duke of Leeds 1789
Ambassador to France 1783 (did not proceed); foreign secretary 1783-91.

Corresp mainly with George III, statesmen and diplomats 1783-98 (13 vols); copies of letters, memoranda etc, formerly enclosed in despatches from diplomats 1782-94 (1 vol); précis of corresp between the Foreign Office and diplomats in Prussia and the United Provinces 1789-90 (1 vol); political and diplomatic memoranda 1774-96 (2 vols); misc corresp and papers mainly rel to foreign affairs 1769-97 (1 vol); copy and translation of Russian naval regulations 1788 (1 vol).
British Library (Add MSS 27914, 27918, 28059-68; Egerton MSS 3498-3504). Purchased at Sotheby's 11 July 1868 and 5 Apr 1869, and from the 11th Duke of Leeds 1947.

See also *Cabinet Ministers.*

[260] **PAGET, Sir Arthur** (1771-1840)
Secretary of legation in Prussia 1794-5 (in charge); envoy to Bavaria 1798-9; minister to the Two Sicilies 1800-1, to Austria 1801-6; ambassador on a special mission to Turkey 1807.

Royal corresp, credentials and instructions 1796-1819 (1 vol); corresp with Queen Caroline of Naples 1801-7 (1 vol); corresp mainly with the Foreign Office 1794-1823 (9 vols); corresp with diplomats, naval officers and foreign statesmen and officials 1794-1823 (11 vols); corresp with Friedrich von Gentz 1803-10 (1 vol); copy of Gentz's diary 1806 (1 vol); general corresp 1792-1840 (9 vols); family and personal corresp 1794-1835 (7 vols).
British Library (Add MSS 48383-48416). Presented 1954 by his great-granddaughter Lady Phyllis Benton and her family.

Copies of intercepted French diplomatic corresp 1803-4 (1 vol); copies of despatches from him 1804-5 (1 vol); misc letters and papers 1804-6 (8 items).
Trustees of the Bedford Estates. Enquiries to the Archivist, Bedford Office, 29A Montague Street, London WC1B 5BL. The papers passed from Sir Robert Adair, his successor at Vienna, to the Dukes of Bedford. NRA 26179.

Letters from and copies of letters to Lord Malmesbury 1794-5, 1800 (14 items).
Hampshire RO (9M73). Deposited 1973 by Viscount FitzHarris, whose permission to consult the letters must be obtained through the record office. NRA 6589.

Letters from Lord Minto 1800-3 (1 vol).
National Library of Scotland (MS 11227). Purchased 1958 from the 5th Earl of Minto, to whom they had been returned in 1915 by Lady Walburga Paget. NRA 10476.

[261] **PAGET, Sir Augustus Berkeley**
(1823-1896)
Attaché in Spain 1843-6 (in charge 1844), in France 1846-52; secretary of legation in Greece 1852-4, in the Netherlands 1854-7 (in charge 1855, 1856), in Portugal 1857-8 (in charge), in Prussia 1858 (in charge); minister to Saxony 1858-9, to Denmark 1859-66, to Portugal 1866-7, to Italy 1867-76; ambassador to Italy 1876-83, to Austria-Hungary 1884-93.

Royal corresp (1 vol); corresp with Lord Lyons 1867-83, Lord Lytton 1883-9, and Sir WA White 1885-9 (1 vol); letters to Lord Wharncliffe 1876-93 (2 vols); corresp with the Foreign Office, mainly copies of despatches to successive foreign secretaries, 1852-93 (25 vols); general corresp 1844-96 (1 vol); literary MSS (2 vols).
British Library (Add MSS 51205-36). Presented 1960 by his granddaughter Lady Phyllis Benton.

[262] **PAGET, Sir Ralph Spencer** (1864-1940)
Third secretary in Japan 1893-5 (in charge 1894), second secretary 1895-9; second secretary in Egypt 1899-1900, in Bavaria 1900-1, in Turkey 1901; chargé d'affaires in Guatemala 1901-2; chargé d'affaires in Siam 1902-4, minister and consul-general 1904-9; minister resident in Bavaria and Württemberg 1909-10; minister to Serbia 1910-13; assistant under secretary for foreign affairs 1913-15; minister to Denmark 1916-19; ambassador to Brazil 1919-20.

Corresp with the royal family, the Foreign Office and others 1894-1921 (6 vols), letter book 1901-7 (1 vol) and a card index of corresp as minister to Denmark.
British Library (Add MSS 51252-9). Bequeathed by Dame Leila Paget 1962.

PALMERSTON, Viscount, see Temple HJ.

[263] **PARISH, Frank** (1824-1906)
On consular service in China 1844-52; vice-consul at Buenos Aires 1852-60 (acting consul-general 1854-60), consul 1860-74 (in charge in the Argentine Republic 1872-3).

Corresp 1844-52, mainly letters to his father Sir Woodbine Parish (97pp); journal of his travels from London to Naples 1840-3.
University of British Columbia Library, Vancouver.

[264] **PARISH, Sir Woodbine** (1796-1882)
Consul-general in the Argentine Republic 1824-32
(plenipotentiary 1824-5, chargé d'affaires 1825-6,
1828-31); commissioner to examine French port
dues on British shipping *c*1833; commissioner to
the Two Sicilies 1840-2, plenipotentiary 1842-5.

Copies of corresp 1823-32 (5 vols); official papers,
Buenos Aires 1813-25 (1 bundle); commercial and
other reports 1824-31 (2 bundles); corresp
1832-55 (1 bundle); reports and papers rel to the
French port dues commission 1833 (1 vol);
corresp, papers and instructions rel to the sulphur
dispute and commercial negotiations, Two Sicilies
1823-46 (6 vols).
Public Record Office (FO 354). Partly presented
to the Foreign Office by CW Parish 1885 and
transferred 1910. The remainder was acquired in
1951. NRA 23630.

Corresp, papers and transcripts collected by him
rel to the history of S America, especially Spanish
and British rule in the Argentine Republic,
Falkland Islands, etc 1692-1834 (13 vols).
British Library (Add MSS 19571-6, 32603-9).
Purchased from him 1853 and from CW Parish
1885.

Corresp, papers and printed works rel to
S American history and geography collected
or written by him 1612-1855.
Royal Geographical Society. See C Kelly, *RGS
Archives. A handlist,* pp127-8.

[265] **PARKES, Sir Harry Smith** (1828-1885)
Consul at Amoy 1854-5; secretary to special
mission to Siam 1855; acting consul at Canton
1856-8; commissioner at Canton 1858-61; consul
at Shanghai 1864-5; minister to Japan 1865-83, to
China 1883-5, to Korea 1884-5.

Corresp mainly with British and foreign
diplomats, consuls, merchants and others
1849-*c*1885 (*c*740 items); official letters of
approval of his services 1852-61 (28 items);
despatches to him 1858-61 (1 bundle); copies of
despatches from him 1857-65 (4 bundles);
memoranda rel to China and Japan *c*1860-79 (15
items); subject files *c*1848-83, rel to China, Hong
Kong, Japan, Korea and the Straits Settlements
(23 bundles); misc draft despatches, telegrams,
memoranda, reports, maps, translations, etc (*c*44
bundles and items).
Cambridge University Library (Sir Harry Parkes
Papers). Deposited by Jardine Matheson & Co
Ltd. Permission to consult the papers must be
obtained from their London subsidiary Matheson
& Co Ltd. NRA 25705.

[266] **PAUNCEFOTE, Julian** (1828-1902),
Baron Pauncefote 1899
Under secretary for foreign affairs 1876-89;
minister to the United States 1889-93, ambassador
1893-1902.

Letters and telegrams to him and his wife mainly
from Lords Carnarvon, Rosebery, Salisbury and
other statesmen 1855, 1875-1902 (41 items).
In private possession. Photocopies are in the
University of Virginia Library, Charlottesville.
NRA 4779. Most of his papers were destroyed by
his widow.

[267] **PELLY, General Sir Lewis** (1825-1892)
Secretary of legation in Persia 1859-60 (in charge
1860); political agent and consul at Zanzibar
1861-2; political resident in the Persian Gulf
1862-72; attached to Sir HBE Frere's mission to
Zanzibar 1872-3; envoy from the government of
India to Afghanistan 1876-7.

General corresp and papers, incl letters from
Frere and papers rel to India and Persia, 1838-92
(1 box); corresp rel to the Persian Gulf and his
expedition to Riyadh, incl letters to Charles
Alison and Lord Canning 1860-74 (1 box, 29
bundles); letter books, Persian Gulf 1863-73 (2
vols); corresp and papers as agent in Rajputana
*c*1873-7 (1 vol, 8 bundles); corresp and papers as
special commissioner to investigate the condition
of Baroda 1874-5 (8 bundles, 2 items); journals
1842, 1853-4, 1860, 1862, 1864-6 (7 vols).
India Office Library and Records (MSS Eur F
126). Presented by his widow 1923.

Corresp and papers rel to Persia, incl letters from
Sir HC Rawlinson, memoranda and draft
despatches, mainly 1860 (1 vol); corresp and
memoranda rel to Zanzibar and the slave trade
1861-3 (1 vol).
Public Record Office (FO 800/233-4). Transferred
from the India Office to the Foreign Office
Library in accordance with Lady Pelly's wishes
1927.

PEMBROKE, Earl of, see Herbert GA.

[268] **PETHERICK, John** (1813-1882)
Vice-consul at Khartoum 1850-60, consul 1860-4.

Travel journal, Sudan 1862-3 (1 vol); journal of
his wife 1862-3 (1 vol); sketches of Sudanese
weapons, tools, musical instruments, etc (1 vol);
cuttings from the *Morning Advertiser* 1864
defending him against attacks by JH Speke
(1 vol).
Wellcome Historical Medical Library, London (Acc
78231-3). Purchased at Sotheby's 16 Mar 1931,
lot 445. NRA 25910.

[269] **PETTY-FITZMAURICE, Lord Edmond
George** (1846-1935), Baron Fitzmaurice 1906
Member of the international commission to
reorganise the European provinces of Turkey
1880-1; plenipotentiary to the Danube Navigation
conference 1882-3; parliamentary under secretary
for foreign affairs 1882-5, 1905-8.

Special corresp with Lord Bryce 1900-21, Sir

Henry Campbell-Bannerman 1900-7, Sir CW Dilke 1876-1908, WE Gladstone 1874-98, Lord Granville 1880-9 and others (7 boxes); general corresp (1 box); subject files, incl corresp with FH Hill 1876-7, drafts and printed copies of Foreign Office letters and memoranda, and corresp rel to Congo reform 1907-8 (3 boxes). *In family possession.* Not open for research in 1983.

Letters from Sir RBD Morier 1883-5 (1 bundle). *Balliol College, Oxford.* Returned by Fitzmaurice to Morier's daughter, and deposited among Morier's papers. NRA 26599.

[270] **PHIPPS, Constantine Henry** (1797-1863), styled Viscount Normanby 1812-31, 2nd Earl of Mulgrave 1831, 1st Marquess of Normanby 1838
Ambassador to France 1846-52; minister to Tuscany 1854-8.

Corresp and papers rel to his embassy to France and other aspects of his career.
The Marquess of Normanby.

[271] **PIERREPONT, Hon Henry Manvers** (1780-1851)
Minister to Sweden 1804-7; on a special mission to Sweden 1807.

Despatches to him 1804-7 (2 vols); drafts and copies of despatches from him 1804-7, incl copies of notes from the Swedish government 1804-5 (5 vols); copies of despatches received and sent by Benjamin Bathurst and Alexander Straton 1807 (1 vol); corresp with the Foreign Office and other departments 1804-7 (1 vol); with British diplomats, consuls, naval and military officers 1804-7, incl Lord Cathcart, Benjamin Garlike, FJ Jackson, Lord Granville Leveson Gower, Edward Thornton and HWW Wynn (5 vols, 1 bundle); with the Swedish government and other foreign correspondents 1804-7 (1 vol); misc official and private corresp and papers (mainly copies) 1791-1807, incl papers rel to the detention of Swedish convoys 1798 and the Anglo-Swedish convention 1805 (4 vols).
Public Record Office (FO 334). Presented to the Foreign Office by his great-grandson the 7th Duke of Wellington 1934 and 1958. NRA 23465.

Journal while attached to Lord St Helens's mission to Russia, Denmark and Sweden 1801-2 (1 vol); travel journals, France and Italy 1814, 1823-5 (2 vols).
The Duke of Wellington.

[272] **PONSONBY, Arthur Augustus William Harry** (1871-1946), 1st Baron Ponsonby of Shulbrede 1930
Third secretary in Turkey 1896-8; third secretary in Denmark 1898-1900 (in charge 1899), second secretary 1900; employed at the Foreign Office 1900-2; parliamentary under secretary for foreign affairs 1924.

Corresp and papers 1890-1905, incl his 'Suggestions for reform in the Diplomatic Service' 1900 and corresp rel to his resignation from the Foreign Office 1902 (475ff); corresp and papers as private secretary to the prime minister 1906-7 (646ff), rel to parliamentary and constituency affairs 1908-23 (2,287ff), to foreign affairs 1924-8 (255ff), to the formation of the Labour government and to his peerage 1929-30 (223ff), as chancellor of the Duchy of Lancaster 1931 (144ff), rel to disarmament, the Peace Pledge Union, etc 1932-7 (1,411ff), to his war activities 1940-1 (176ff), to his writings 1899-1941 (641ff); undated corresp and papers (202ff).
Bodleian Library, Oxford (MSS Eng. hist. a.20, c.561-85, d.363). Presented by the 2nd Baron Ponsonby of Shulbrede 1971. NRA 18634.

Memoir 1871-90 (1 vol); diaries 1893-1943 (20 vols); letters to his wife 1894-1941 (*c*1,500 items) and to other members of his family *c*1890-1915 (*c*350 items); literary MSS.
Lord Ponsonby of Shulbrede. Access to the diaries is restricted.

Corresp, memoranda and other papers as under secretary for foreign affairs 1924, mainly rel to Anglo-Soviet relations, incl minutes of his conversations with the Soviet chargé d'affaires KG Rakovsky (22 items).
Public Record Office (FO 800/227).

[273] **PONSONBY, John** (*c*1770-1855), 2nd Baron Ponsonby 1806, Viscount Ponsonby 1839
On a special mission to Brazil 1826; minister to the Argentine Republic 1826-8, to Brazil 1828-9; joint commissioner from the conference of London to Belgium 1830-1; minister to the Two Sicilies 1832-3; ambassador to Turkey 1832-41, to Austria 1846-50.

Corresp, despatches and papers *c*1808-50 mainly rel to Turkey 1834-41, but incl material rel to S America, Belgium and Austria (50 boxes).
Durham University Department of Palaeography and Diplomatic (Grey of Howick Collection). Deposited 1955 by his great-great-nephew the 5th Earl Grey.

[274] **PORTAL, Sir Gerald Herbert** (1858-1894)
Third secretary in Italy 1881-4, in Egypt 1884-5; second secretary in Egypt 1885-91 (intermittently in charge 1886-8); on a special mission to Abyssinia 1887; acting consul-general at Zanzibar 1889, agent and consul-general 1891-3; special commissioner to Uganda 1892-3.

Misc letters from Lord Salisbury and others with papers rel to appointments and honours 1881-92, and letters from him to his wife 1889-93 (2 vols); copies of letters to Sir HP Anderson, EJL Berkeley, Lords Rosebery and Salisbury and others 1891-3 (5 vols); diaries 1884, 1892-3 (3 vols); drawings of Abyssinian scenes with notes 1887 (1 vol); letters of condolence on his death, and papers rel to his estate 1894-5 (1 vol).

Rhodes House Library, Oxford (MSS Afr. s.103-14). Presented by Priscilla, Lady Norman 1951. NRA 19041.

Papers rel to his entry into the diplomatic service 1879 and to his marriage settlement 1889 (24 items).
Hampshire RO (5M52/F15,19). Deposited by FS Portal 1952. NRA 15311.

[275] **PORTER, Sir Robert Ker** (1777-1842)
Consul at Caracas 1826-35; chargé d'affaires and consul-general in Venezuela 1835-42.

His papers passed to his sister Jane Porter. She sold a manuscript of her brother's *Travels* to the British Museum in 1844, and at the sale of her library in 1850 the Museum acquired four volumes of his sketches. Most of his papers, with those of his sisters, were sold at Sotheby's 19 Mar 1852, lots 413-29, to Sir Thomas Phillipps (Phillipps MSS 14524-14778, 15546-86). These were dispersed with the Phillipps collection. Many were purchased privately by Sir David Eccles, who resold them at Sotheby's 4 Nov 1957, lots 168-83. Others were included in Phillipps sales at Sotheby's 27 June 1966, lots 432-94 and 26 June 1974, lot 3016. The present locations of some papers have not been traced.

Letters to him from the Foreign Office, letters from him to his family, and other corresp and misc papers 1794-1842 (11 vols); copies of letters to and from him 1824-9 (1 vol); index of letters from him 1825-41 (1 vol); letters to him and his sister Jane from diplomats, painters, military and naval officers and others 1800-40 (15 vols); corresp mainly with Princess Mary Scherbatov 1805-26 (11 vols); letters to him mainly from his sister Jane 1830-40 (14 vols); letters from Maria Roche 1830-41 (5 vols); travel journal, Flanders, Denmark, Prussia and Austria 1801 (1 vol); journal, Russia and England 1824-5 (1 vol).
Kenneth Spencer Research Library, University of Kansas, Lawrence. Purchased from WP Wreden, who had acquired them at Sotheby's 4 Nov 1957, lots 176-7 and from Francis Edwards Ltd after sale at Sotheby's 27 June 1966, lots 432-3, 440, 465, 475, 480, 484, 486, 488.

Letters to him from Patrick Campbell 1826-30 (69 items), from BH Wilson 1827-38 (43 items), from British naval officers, consuls and residents in Venezuela c1826-40 (over 120 items); letters from him to his family 1825-40 (408 items); copies of letters sent 1826-8 (1 vol); copies of letters received 1830-40 (1 vol); engagement diaries 1832-4, 1836-9, 1841-2 (9 vols); MS and printed proclamations and misc papers rel to Venezuela c1825-42.
Fundación John Boulton, Caracas. Purchased at Sotheby's 4 Nov 1957, lots 171, 178, 182-3, and 27 June 1966, lot 478.

Letter books 1828-40, containing drafts of letters to statesmen, diplomats and others (2 vols); letters to him and his sister Jane from BH Wilson 1829-43 (16 items).

Lilly Library, Indiana University, Bloomington. Purchased at Sotheby's 27 June 1966, lots 479, 493. NRA 23228.

Letters to him and his sister Jane from DF O'Leary 1834-42 (17 items); journals 1825-42 (9 vols).
Untraced. Sold at Sotheby's 4 Nov 1957, lot 173 and 12 Feb 1968, lot 497, and exported to Henrik Blohm, Caracas. Microfilms are in the British Library (RP 273, 597).

Family corresp 1805-49, mainly letters from him to his mother and sisters 1805-25 (276 items); journals, notes and sketches, Russia and Sweden 1805-8 (4 vols, 2 files).
Houghton Library, Harvard University, Cambridge, Massachusetts (bMS Eng 1256). Purchased at Sotheby's 27 June 1966, lots 472-3. NRA 26791.

Travel journal, N Wales, Cheshire and Derbyshire 1799 (1 vol).
National Library of Wales, Aberystwyth (MS 12651). Purchased at Sotheby's 27 June 1966, lot 464.

Diary and personal accounts 1801-3 (1 vol).
RG Searight Esq. Purchased from Winifred Myers (Autographs) Ltd after sale at Sotheby's 27 June 1966, lot 466.

Travel journals and notebooks, Russia, the Caucasus, Persia and Mesopotamia, 1817-20, and a draft of his *Travels in Georgia, Persia, Armenia...* (1821-2) (10 vols).
British Library (Add MSS 53791-9, 58217). Purchased at Sotheby's 27 June 1966, lot 476, and 26 June 1974, lot 3016.

MS of his *Travels* (1821-2), incl many drawings not in the published version, four letters from Prince Abbas Mirza 1819-21, and a military sketch of Russia 1812 (1 vol).
British Library (Add MS 14758). Purchased from Jane Porter 1844.

Views and sketches made during his travels in Europe, Asia and S America (4 vols).
British Library (Add MSS 18280-3). Purchased 1850.

Misc notes and drafts c1820-36, mainly rel to military colonisation in Russia, the death of Alexander I and the state of Persia in 1820 (c90pp).
Bodleian Library, Oxford (MSS Eng. hist. c.369 ff 9-11, c.409, d.263). Purchased at Sotheby's 27 June 1966, lot 485.

His draft of a dramatic version of Sir Walter Scott's *Marmion*, and Sir Thomas Phillipps's index to the Porter papers (1 vol).
National Library of Scotland (Acc 4155). Purchased at Sotheby's 27 June 1966, lot 463.

[276] **POTTINGER, Lieutenant-General Sir Henry** (1789-1856), 1st Bt 1840
Plenipotentiary and superintendent of trade in China 1841-4.

Corresp with Lords Auckland and Clare, Mountstuart Elphinstone, Charles Masson and others 1817-40, 1844 (14 bundles); reports, memoranda, copies of despatches, etc, Kutch and Sind 1809-44 (20 vols and bundles); journals 1829-36, memoir on Sind 1832, sketches of Sind (11 vols); corresp with Lord Auckland, Sir TJ Cochrane, Sir Hugh Gough, Lord Palmerston, Sir William Parker and others as plenipotentiary to China and governor of Hong Kong 1841-4 (*c*24 bundles); register of letters to him 1841-3 (1 vol); indexes of despatches and letters from him 1841-4 (4 vols); memoranda rel to the treaty of Nankin and the administration and finances of Hong Kong 1841-4 (5 bundles); accounts and related corresp, misc reports, commissions and printed papers 1840-6 (12 bundles); letters of appointment, commissions and instructions as governor of the Cape of Good Hope 1846 (1 bundle); corresp with Lord Grey 1847-9 (1 bundle); printed official corresp, Cape 1847-8 and Orange River Territory 1851 (4 vols); private letter books 1844-50 (3 vols); reports, memoranda, accounts, etc as governor of Madras 1848-54 (5 vols, several dozen bundles); misc personal and family corresp and papers 1768-1879, incl commissions 1810-51 and memorandum and address book 1844-54 (18 vols, bundles and items).
Public Record Office (FO 705). Presented to the Foreign Office 1950 by his great-granddaughter's husband Sir Algar Howard. NRA 23471.

[277] **POWELL, Wilfred** (1853-1942)
Consul in Samoa and deputy commissioner for the Western Pacific 1885-8; consul at Stettin 1888-98; adviser to the British plenipotentiaries to the Samoa conference at Berlin 1889; consul at Philadelphia 1898-1913, consul-general 1913-15.

Papers rel to his travels 1873-83, incl material on New Guinea and his *Wanderings in a wild country; or, three years amongst the cannibals of New Britain* (1883) (1 vol, etc); papers rel to Samoa 1884-9, incl corresp, reports, notes and accounts as consul, other writings and photographs (2 vols, etc); papers rel to his consular appointments 1885-98 (12 items); drafts of his articles, stories, speeches and letters (1 vol); corresp with Evans Lewin and Commander AB Campbell 1934-40; misc papers and biographical material.
Royal Commonwealth Society. Presented by Miss Powell 1942. *Manuscript catalogue,* pp152-3, 178-9; P Mander-Jones, *Manuscripts in the British Isles relating to Australia, New Zealand, and the Pacific,* Canberra 1972, p332.

[278] **PRIMROSE, Archibald Philip**
(1847-1929), styled Lord Dalmeny 1851-68, 5th Earl of Rosebery 1868
Foreign secretary 1886, 1892-4.

Special and general corresp 1859-1927, incl many letters from cabinet colleagues and others during his terms as foreign secretary (132 vols); corresp,

telegrams and papers, mainly printed, rel to foreign affairs 1884-7, 1892-5 (13 vols).
National Library of Scotland (MSS 10001-10144, 10250). Presented by Lord Primrose 1966, except MS 10250, purchased 1970. NRA 22490.

See also *Cabinet Ministers.*

[279] **PROBY, John Joshua** (1751-1828), 2nd Baron Carysfort 1772, 1st Earl of Carysfort 1789
Envoy to Prussia 1800-2.

Copies of letters to Lords Grenville and Minto and others 1800 (1 vol); copies of despatches to and from him 1800-1 (2 vols), with copies of enclosures 1800 (1 vol); copies of letters from him rel to his English and Irish estates 1800 (2 vols); accounts 1777-1828 (2 vols); library catalogues by him and notes on authors (7 vols); drawings made in Russia and elsewhere (2 vols).
WH Proby Esq. Access restricted.

RADSTOCK, Baron, see Waldegrave.

RAGLAN, Baron, see Somerset.

[280] **RAWLINSON, Sir Henry Creswicke** (1810-1895), 1st Bt 1891
Political agent in Lower Afghanistan 1840-2, in Turkish Arabia 1843-55; consul at Baghdad 1844-51, consul-general 1851-5; minister to Persia 1859-60.

Misc official and personal corresp 1837-44, mainly rel to the first Afghan war, incl letters from Sir Alexander Burnes, Sir Willoughby Cotton, Sir WH Macnaghten and Major-General William Nott; journals 1831, 1834, 1836, 1839, 1841-3, 1860; notes and sketches mainly rel to the antiquities of Central Asia and the Middle East 1843-50, nd; parliamentary and confidential India Office papers rel to relations with Russia on the Afghan and Persian frontiers 1869-93 (*c*300 items).
Royal Geographical Society. Deposited by Meredith, Lady Rawlinson.

Letters from Sir WH Macnaghten, Major-General William Nott and Major James Outram rel to the Afghan war 1840-1 (1 vol); travel journals, mainly Middle East 1849 (2 vols); notes for publications *c*1839-88, with letters from Sir AH Layard and others 1838-*c*1860 (4 vols); notebooks rel to Assyrian and Old Persian cuneiform inscriptions *c*1835-73 (37 vols).
British Library (Add MSS 47619-62). Presented 1951 by Miss Elmira Wade, executrix of Meredith, Lady Rawlinson.

Misc corresp rel to the Syrian excavation fund 1845-51 (1 bundle); corresp rel to his appointments to Persia 1859 (1 bundle) and to the council of India 1863-8 (3 bundles); social letters to him and his wife from statesmen, soldiers, explorers and others 1871-81 (1 bundle);

condolences on his wife's death 1889 (1 bundle); abstract of private corresp 1838 (1 vol); journals 1827-8, 1841 (4 vols, 1 bundle); notes on his life dictated to his wife 1884 (1 vol); notes and drafts of memoranda and speeches mainly rel to Afghanistan, Persia, Russian expansion and Middle Eastern archaeology *c*1833-60 and nd (2 bundles); accounts of the political agency at Baghdad 1848-53 (1 vol); personal accounts 1853-5, 1879-90 (2 vols); family and misc personal corresp, incl letters from him to his sister Maria 1828-54 (75 items), to his wife 1862-87 (1 box), and to his son Henry 1888-9 (1 bundle).
Royal Asiatic Society. Deposited by Miss Elmira Wade *c*1951 and 1973.

RENNELL, Baron, see Rodd.

[281] RIDGEWAY, Colonel Sir Joseph West (1844-1930)
Commissioner for the delimitation of the Russo-Afghan boundary 1884-6 (continued negotiations in Russia 1887); on a special mission to Morocco 1893.

Corresp with Sir Peter Lumsden and others, memoranda, maps and confidential print rel to the Afghan boundary 1884-7 (*c*215 items); corresp mainly with AJ Balfour and misc papers as under secretary for Ireland 1887-92 (32 items); personal and misc corresp 1881-1930 (50 items); commissions, letters of appointment, autobiographical notes and drafts of memoirs, press cuttings and miscellanea rel to India, Morocco, the Isle of Man and Ceylon 1862-1919 (1 vol, *c*50 items).
Lord Tollemache (his great-grandson). NRA 6957.

RIPON, Marquess of, see Robinson GFS.

[282] ROBINSON, George Frederick Samuel (1827-1909), styled Viscount Goderich 1833-59, 2nd Earl of Ripon and 3rd Earl De Grey 1859, 1st Marquess of Ripon 1871
First commissioner to the United States to settle the *Alabama* claims 1871.

Corresp with WE Gladstone, Lords Granville and Tenterden and others, memoranda, speech notes and misc papers rel to the *Alabama* claims and the treaty of Washington 1871-2.
British Library (Add MSS 43514, 43520-1, 43528, 43623-5). Presented by the executors of the 2nd Marquess of Ripon 1923.

See also *Cabinet Ministers.*

[283] ROBINSON, Thomas (1738-1786), 2nd Baron Grantham 1770
Ambassador to Spain 1771-9; foreign secretary 1782-3.

Corresp 1771-9, mainly with members of the British and Spanish governments, British diplomats in Europe, and British consuls in Spain (22 vols).
British Library (Add MSS 24157-78). Presented 1861 by his granddaughter Countess Cowper.

Corresp and papers rel to Spain 1757-79 (1 vol, 204 items); corresp as foreign secretary with Alleyne Fitzherbert, Sir James Harris, Sir RM Keith and other diplomats 1782-3 (368 items); reports, notes and other papers mainly rel to the peace negotiations 1782-3 (*c*130 items); cabinet minutes 1782-3 (27 items); general corresp 1758-86, incl letters from British and foreign diplomats (*c*2,500 items).
Bedfordshire RO (L 29-30). Deposited 1961 by Baroness Lucas, great-granddaughter of Countess Cowper. NRA 6283.

See also *Cabinet Ministers.*

[284] RODD, James Rennell (1858-1941), 1st Baron Rennell 1933
Acting agent and consul-general in Zanzibar 1893-4; secretary of legation in Egypt 1894-1901 (intermittently acting agent and consul-general); on a special mission to Ethiopia 1897; secretary of embassy in Italy 1901-4 (intermittently chargé d'affaires 1902-4); minister to Sweden 1904-8; ambassador to Italy 1908-19.

Family papers 1768-20th cent, incl those of the 1st and 2nd Barons Rennell.
Bodleian Library, Oxford. Bequeathed by the 2nd Baron Rennell 1978. Not available until 2000, except with the written permission of the trustees of Lord Rennell's estate, which must be sought through Allen & Overy, solicitors, 9 Cheapside, London EC2V 6AD.

Letters from Sir Edward Grey 1894-1916 (15 items) and from Benjamin Jowett 1876-91 (8 items).
Bodleian Library, Oxford. Purchased at Bloomsbury Book Auctions 14 June 1984, lots 106, 108. Further correspondence of Rodd offered in this sale (lots 103-5, 107, 112) and in those of 7 Mar 1984 (lots 82-6, 88-107) and 17 Jan 1985 (lots 105-15) has not been traced.

[285] ROSE, Sir George Henry (1771-1855)
Secretary of legation and chargé d'affaires in Prussia 1793-4; on a special mission to the United States 1807-8; minister to Bavaria 1814-15, to Prussia 1815-23.

Private corresp with George Canning, Lord Castlereagh, Foreign Office officials and Bavarian and Prussian statesmen 1814-23 (1 vol); corresp with British diplomats mainly in Austria and Russia 1814-23 (4 vols); general corresp 1814-24 (1 vol); draft despatches to Castlereagh and Canning 1814-23 (9 vols).
British Library (Add MSS 42781-95). Presented 1932 by his great-great-grandson Captain ASG Douglas.

Letters from his father and others 1794-1854
(2 vols).
National Library of Scotland (MSS 3796-7).
Purchased at Sotheby's 19 May 1947, lot 223.
Catalogue of manuscripts, ii, p295.

[286] **ROSE, Field Marshal Hugh Henry**
(1801-1885), Baron Strathnairn 1866
Consul-general at Beirut 1841-51; secretary of
embassy in Turkey 1851-4 (in charge 1852-3);
commissioner with the French army in the
Crimea 1854-6; on a military mission to Austria
1856-7.

Corresp with Lord Aberdeen, Sir Stratford
Canning, the Rt Revd Samuel Gobat and Lord
Palmerston 1840-51 (2 vols); with the Duke of
Cambridge 1854-76, and other military
commanders in the Crimea 1854-5 (2 vols); with
Lord Canning, Sir WR Mansfield and others,
India 1857-64 (2 vols); general corresp 1834-85
(1 vol); draft letters to foreign secretaries, with
related papers, 1851-7 (6 vols); letter books
1854-84 (25 vols); journals and diaries 1841-56
(4 vols); maps, Sebastapol 1855, India 1841-78
(8 items).
British Library (Add MSS 42796-42838).
Presented 1932 by his great-great-nephew Captain
ASG Douglas.

Corresp 1832-85 (1 vol); memorandum book 1832
(1 vol); commissions and warrants 1824-77 (22
items).
National Library of Scotland (MSS 3798-9, Ch
2595-2616). Purchased at Sotheby's 19 May 1947,
lot 223. *Catalogue of manuscripts,* ii, pp295, 361.

ROSEBERY, Earl of, see Primrose.

[287] **ROSS, Rear-Admiral Sir John**
(1777-1856)
Vice-consul at Karlskrona 1809; consul at
Stockholm 1839-46.

Letters from Sir JC Ross and others 1809-51 (c30
items); log book, notebooks, journal and memoirs
of his arctic voyages 1818-19, 1828-31, 1845-52
(11 vols); signal and order book as lieutenant (1
vol); misc papers 1807-50 (23 items).
Scott Polar Research Institute, Cambridge (MSS
486, 546, 550, 557, 655, 752, 1413). *Manuscripts in
the Scott Polar Research Institute,* pp573-9.

Letters from various correspondents mainly rel to
naval business, arctic exploration and his
published works 1807-54 (97 items).
McCord Museum, Montreal (Ross Collection).
NRA 25852.

Misc family and other corresp and papers 1818-56
(1 vol).
Museum of the History of Science, Oxford.
Deposited by the executors of Dr LHD Buxton.

Journal and memoirs of his arctic voyages 1818,
1829-33 (5 vols).

Huntington Library, San Marino, California.
Journal of his arctic voyage 1830-3 (1 vol).
Royal University Library, Oslo.

[288] **ROSS-OF-BLADENSBURG, Sir John
Foster George** (1848-1926)
Assistant commissioner for the delimitation of the
Serbian boundary 1878-9; secretary to the
financial commissioner in Turkey 1881; secretary
to special missions to the Vatican 1887, 1889-90.

Corresp, reports and maps rel to the Serbian
boundary commission 1878-9 (25 items); corresp,
memoranda, reports, etc mainly rel to Irish and
papal affairs, the Roman Catholic church in
Uganda and his missions to the Vatican
c1885-1920 (1 box, c140 items); journals 1874-85
covering his service on the Serbian boundary
commission (3 vols); misc personal corresp and
papers, incl his wife's, 1868-1926 (1 bundle, c20
items); estate corresp c1876-1925 (c8 bundles, c90
items); literary papers 1861-c1895 (2 vols, 8
items); notebooks kept at Staff College 1876-8 (6
vols) and others containing mathematical
calculations 1922 and nd (4 vols, 1 bundle).
Public Record Office of Northern Ireland (D2004).
Partly deposited by Mrs Penelope Campbell (née
Ross) and partly purchased 1981-2. NRA 25260.

ROSSLYN, Earl of, see St Clair-Erskine.

[289] **RUMBOLD, Sir George Berriman**
(1764-1807), 2nd Bt 1791
Chargé d'affaires in the Hanse Towns 1801-6.

Private and official corresp 1801-4 (c290 items).
Archives Nationales, Paris. Acquired by the
French government at the time of his abduction
by French troops in 1804.

Corresp with his wife, descriptions by him of his
abduction in 1804, and other papers.
Sir HJS Rumbold Bt.

[290] **RUMBOLD, Sir Horace** (1829-1913), 8th
Bt 1877
Secretary of legation in Switzerland 1864-8
(intermittently in charge in Greece 1864-7);
secretary of embassy in Russia 1868-71 (in charge
1869, 1871), in Turkey 1871-2 (in charge 1872);
minister resident and consul-general in Chile
1872-8; minister to Switzerland 1878-9, to the
Argentine Republic 1879-81, to Sweden and
Norway 1881-4, to Greece 1884-8, to the
Netherlands 1888-96; ambassador to Austria-
Hungary 1896-1900.

Copies of letters and despatches to the Foreign
Office 1856-90 (7 vols); private corresp (1 box);
misc corresp and papers among family papers
mainly collected and annotated by him 17th-20th
cent (12 vols).
Sir HJS Rumbold Bt.

Corresp 1877-1905 and nd (126ff).
Bodleian Library, Oxford (MS Rumbold dep.).
Deposited 1973 by Sir HAC Rumbold Bt. NRA
22147.

[291] **RUSSELL, Major-General Lord George
William** (1790-1846)
On a special mission to Portugal 1832-4; minister
to Württemberg 1833-5, to Prussia 1835-41.

Copies of despatches and other diplomatic corresp
1832-42 (7 vols); letters from Lord Palmerston
1832-42 (1 vol); despatches, corresp and other
papers rel to Portugal, mainly 1832-4 (54 bundles
and items), to Württemberg 1834-5 (2 bundles),
to Prussia, mainly 1835-41 (37 bundles and
items); misc diplomatic corresp and papers
1821-31 (1 bundle, 1 roll, 2 items); letters mainly
from royalty, Sir Herbert Taylor and the Duke of
Wellington *c*1824-41 (1 box); from relatives,
friends, diplomatic colleagues and others *c*1824-46
(2 vols, 5 boxes, 11 bundles); military corresp and
papers *c*1825-45 (4 bundles); letters from him to
his wife 1823 (10 items); pocket books *c*1817-40
(7 vols); misc accounts and other papers (2
boxes, 2 bundles); typescript copies of his corresp
(12 vols, *c*40 items).
Trustees of the Bedford Estates. Enquiries to the
Archivist, Bedford Office, 29A Montague Street,
London WC1B 5BL. NRA 26179.

[292] **RUSSELL, Lord John** (1792-1878), 1st
Earl Russell 1861
Foreign secretary 1852-3, 1859-65; first
commissioner to the international conference at
Vienna 1855.

Official corresp mainly with Lords Bloomfield,
Clarendon, Cowley and Stratford de Redcliffe,
memoranda, protocols and other papers rel to the
Vienna conference 1855 (2 boxes); private letters
from diplomats, drafts and memoranda as foreign
secretary 1859-65 (84 vols); corresp with cabinet
colleagues 1859-65 (10 vols); misc corresp rel to
the Foreign Office and diplomatic appointments,
and with the royal household 1859-65 (2 vols);
political and general corresp and misc papers
1804-78, incl many letters from diplomats,
statesmen and others rel to foreign affairs, and
private corresp during his mission to Vienna 1855
(114 vols); cabinet notes and memoranda mainly
rel to foreign affairs 1859-65 (1 vol).
Public Record Office (PRO 30/22). Bequeathed
by his daughter-in-law Gertrude Russell 1942.
NRA 8659.

Letters from Queen Victoria 1839-66 (9 vols);
letters and memoranda from Prince Albert
1846-61 (4 vols).
The Royal Archives, Windsor Castle. Returned to
Queen Victoria in 1878. Access restricted.

See also *Cabinet Ministers.*

[293] **RUSSELL, Lord Odo William Leopold**
(1829-1884), 1st Baron Ampthill 1881
Attaché in Austria 1849-51, in France 1852-4, in
Turkey 1854-7 (in charge 1855), in the United
States 1857-8, in Tuscany 1858-60, in the Two
Sicilies 1860; on special service at the Vatican
1860-70; assistant under secretary for foreign
affairs 1870-1; ambassador to Germany 1871-84.

Corresp with prime ministers and foreign
secretaries 1858-75 (10 bundles); corresp 1852-84,
mainly with British diplomats and Foreign Office
officials incl Lord Cowley, Sir HG Elliot and
Lord Hammond, and with foreign diplomats and
statesmen incl Prince Bismarck and Count Bülow
(55 bundles); personal and misc corresp 1859-84
(18 bundles); typescript copies of letters from
Russell to his mother and brother Arthur 1851-84
(2 vols).
Public Record Office (FO 918). Presented by the
3rd Baron Ampthill 1969. NRA 23628.

[294] **RYDER, Dudley** (1762-1847), 2nd Baron
Harrowby 1803, 1st Earl of Harrowby 1809
Under secretary for foreign affairs 1789-90;
foreign secretary 1804-5; on an extraordinary
mission to Prussia 1805-6.

Corresp with FJ Jackson, Lord Mulgrave, Arthur
Paget, Brook Taylor, Edward Thornton and other
British and foreign diplomats and statesmen
mainly 1804-6 (6 vols); general corresp
1784-1809, incl further letters rel to foreign affairs
(6 vols); misc papers 1692-1813, incl reports on
affairs in Genoa and Tuscany 1793-4, and
memoranda rel to the Foreign Office and the
diplomatic establishment 1804-5 (1 vol).
Harrowby MSS Trust (vols 8-13, 29-33, 82-3).
Enquiries to the Earl of Harrowby, Sandon Hall,
Stafford ST18 0BZ. NRA 1561.

See also *Cabinet Ministers.*

[295] **SACKVILLE, John Frederick**
(1745-1799), 3rd Duke of Dorset 1769
Ambassador to France 1784-90.

Corresp with Lord Carmarthen, mainly
despatches received and sent, 1784-9 (522 items);
corresp mainly as ambassador to France, with
diplomats, statesmen and others, incl Sir Robert
Ainslie, William Eden and Lords Hawkesbury
and Massereene, 1766-97 (*c*700 items); diplomatic
instructions, credentials, memoranda, etc 1784-9
(1 vol, 24 items); corresp and papers as lord
lieutenant of Kent and colonel of the W Kent
militia 1769-97 (2 vols, 2 bundles, 60 items);
papers as lord steward of the royal household
1789-96 (2 vols, 12 items); personal accounts
1766-9 and bank books 1769-95 (9 vols); misc
papers 1774-96 (5 items).
Kent AO (U 269). Deposited by the 4th Baron
Sackville 1950 and the 6th Baron Sackville 1973.
NRA 8575.

[296] **ST CLAIR-ERSKINE** (formerly
ERSKINE), **General Sir James** (1762-1837), 6th
Bt 1765, 2nd Earl of Rosslyn 1805
On an extraordinary mission to Portugal 1806.

Corresp rel to Portugal 1806, and with statesmen,
admirals and others c1799-c1829.
Untraced. See *HMC Second Report, Appendix,*
1871, p192.

See also *Cabinet Ministers.*

ST GERMANS, Earls of, see Eliot.

ST HELENS, Baron, see Fitzherbert.

SALISBURY, Marquess of, see Cecil.

[297] **SALT, Henry** (1780-1827)
On a mission to Abyssinia 1809-10; consul-general
at Cairo 1815-27.

Letters from Ras Waldá Selasé and others with
English translations 1810-27 (1 vol); journal of
visits to Massawa and Ariko 1805, with an
account of his travels in Egypt 1806 (1 vol);
travel notes, Abyssinia and Mozambique 1809-10,
with corrected drafts of poems (1 vol);
memorandum book, incl material on Abyssinia,
vocabularies, grammatical notes, etc (1 vol); misc
papers collected as consul-general mainly rel to
Egyptian archaeology 1818-21 (1 vol).
British Library (Add MSS 19338, 19419-20,
19343, 54195). Purchased 1853 and presented
1967.

[298] **SANDERSON, Sir Percy** (1842-1919)
Consul at Galati 1876-82, consul-general 1882-94;
consul-general at New York 1894-1907.

Corresp and papers rel to the Danube
commission, navigation, fortifications, railways,
church affairs, etc 1876-94, to his appointments at
Galati 1876 and New York 1894 and his refusal
of appointment as minister to Siam 1888, to his
inspection of the consulates at Baltimore, Boston,
Chicago and Philadelphia 1907, and to
representation of Bulgaria and Serbia on the
Danube commission 1908 (1 vol).
Public Record Office (FO 800/21).

[299] **SANDERSON, Thomas Henry**
(1841-1923), Baron Sanderson 1905
Entered the Foreign Office 1859; assistant under
secretary for foreign affairs 1889-94; permanent
under secretary 1894-1906.

Private corresp, memoranda and other papers
1860-1922, mainly corresp with Lord Cromer, Sir
HM Durand, Lords Kimberley, Rosebery and
Salisbury and others 1889-1905 (2 vols).
Public Record Office (FO 800/1-2).

[300] **SATOW, Sir Ernest Mason** (1843-1929)
Japanese secretary to the British legation in Japan
1868-84; consul-general at Bangkok 1884-5;
minister to Siam 1885-8, to Uruguay 1888-93,
to Morocco 1893-5, to Japan 1895-1900, to China
1900-6; British member of the court of arbitration
at The Hague 1906-12.

Corresp and notes, Japan 1865-84, and corresp,
mainly private, with the Foreign Office, British
authorities in Burma, India and the Straits
Settlements, the Siamese government, etc 1884-9
(5 boxes); corresp, mainly private, with the
Foreign Office, legation and consular staff, etc,
Uruguay and Morocco 1888-95 (7 boxes); with
the Foreign Office, British diplomats, consuls,
naval officers and colonial governors, officials of
the supreme court for China and Japan, the
Japanese government, etc 1895-1900 (7 boxes);
with the Foreign Office, consuls, military
authorities incl commanders of the British
contingent of the China Field Force, the Chinese
government, foreign diplomats in China, etc
1900-6, and while serving at The Hague 1906-12
(11 boxes); general and family corresp 1877-1927
(9 boxes); private letter books 1884-1906 (17
vols); diaries 1861-1926 (46 vols); notes for and
proofs of *A guide to diplomatic practice* and other
literary and misc papers 1861-1929 (7 boxes).
Public Record Office (PRO 30/33). Bequeathed
by him. NRA 8656.

[301] **SAVILE** (formerly **SAVILE-LUMLEY**),
John (1818-1896), 1st Baron Savile 1888
Secretary of legation in the United States 1854-8;
secretary of embassy in Spain 1858-9, in Russia
1859-60, in Turkey 1860, in Russia 1860-6;
minister to Saxony 1866, to Switzerland 1867-8, to
Belgium 1868-83; ambassador to Italy 1883-8.

Diplomatic and personal corresp with Sir Andrew
Buchanan, Sir JFT Crampton, William Lowther,
the 8th Earl of Scarbrough, WW Synge, and
others 1824-89 (c760 items); letters to Lord
Clarendon 1856-8 (1 bundle); letters and papers
rel to Sir WHLE Bulwer's charges against him
1860 (31 items); corresp with Major Cowell and
others, Russia 1862-4 (1 bundle); draft
despatches, corresp, etc, mainly Saxony 1866 (41
items); papers rel to the Russian tea trade 1867-8
(1 bundle); report on Franco-Belgian railways
1868-9 (1 vol); despatches rel to the Franco-
Prussian war 1870-1 (1 vol); private corresp with
Lords Derby and Tenterden and other papers rel
to the Brussels conference for regulating the
usages of war 1874 (53 items); invitation lists
c1874 (1 bundle); printed reports and corresp rel
to the Spanish vine disease 1859, the sugar
convention 1864, the Russian cotton and tea
trades 1865-7, and the international sanitary
conference 1885 (7 vols).
Nottinghamshire RO (DDSR 226). Deposited by
the 3rd Baron Savile 1957. NRA 6119.

[302] **SCHOMBURGK, Sir Robert Hermann**
(1804-1865)
Commissioner for surveying and delimiting the
boundaries of British Guiana 1840-4; consul at
Santo Domingo 1848-57, at Bangkok 1857-64.

Report, diary, notes and accounts rel to his second
expedition into Guiana 1837, with reports,
sketches, etc rel to other expeditions, mainly sent
for publication in the *Journal* of the Royal
Geographical Society 1833-60.
Royal Geographical Society.

Journal of his survey expedition from Pirara to
the upper Courantyne river and Demerara 1843
(1 vol).
British Library (Add MS 34205). Purchased 1892.

[303] **SCOTT, Charles** (1805-1841)
Entered the Foreign Office 1828; attaché in Persia
1841.

Corresp and misc papers 1820-41; letter book
1831-2; journals 1830-41 (9 vols); engagement
diary 1831; extracts by him and his brother 1832
from marginalia by Sir Walter Scott (1 vol).
National Library of Scotland (MSS 852, 917-18,
1552-6, 1558, 1571, 1614-22). Partly purchased
from and partly presented by Major-General Sir
WM Scott 1931-4. *Catalogue of manuscripts,* i,
pp110, 122, 183-4, 186.

Letters from his father 1820-31 (1 vol).
National Library of Scotland (MS 141). Presented
by Sir AJ Law 1928. *Catalogue of manuscripts,* i,
p23.

[304] **SCOTT, Sir Charles Stewart** (1838-1924)
Second secretary in Mexico 1866-8, in Portugal
1868-71, in Württemberg 1871-2 (in charge 1871,
1872), in Bavaria 1872-3, in Austria-Hungary
1873-4, in Russia 1874-7, in Hesse-Darmstadt
1877-9 (intermittently in charge); secretary of
legation in Saxe-Coburg-Gotha 1879-83
(intermittently in charge); secretary of embassy in
Germany 1883-8 (intermittently in charge);
minister to Switzerland 1888-93, to Denmark
1893-8; ambassador to Russia 1898-1904.

Royal corresp 1878-1918 (1 vol); corresp with
foreign secretaries 1866-1904 (3 vols); corresp
with Sir TH Sanderson 1867-1904 (2 vols);
general corresp 1858-1910 (3 vols); family corresp
1866-1911 (2 vols); letter books 1899-1904 (2
vols); diary 1900, 1907 (1 vol); letters of
appointment, autobiographical notes, press
cuttings and photographs (3 vols).
British Library (Add MSS 52294-52310).
Presented by his daughter Mrs John Warre 1963.

[305] **SCOTT, Sir James George** (1851-1935)
Commissioner for the delimitation of the Burmese
boundary 1889-1900; chargé d'affaires in Siam
1893-4.

Corresp, papers and confidential print rel to the
boundary commissions *c*1889-*c*1900 (7 bundles);
letters from the Siamese foreign ministry and
other corresp, Siam 1893-4 (2 bundles); letters
from local rulers and other corresp, maps,
confidential print, etc, Burma *c*1885-*c*1910 (*c*1,200
items).
Cambridge University Library. Presented 1933 by
the widow of his brother Sir RF Scott. Access by
written application to the Department of Oriental
and Other Languages.

Journals 1884-97 (13 vols).
India Office Library and Records (MSS Eur C
102-14). Presented 1942.

Letters from MWE de Bunsen, Alexander Michie,
RH Thomson and others, memoranda, drawings,
etc 1888-97, mainly Siam 1893-4 and on the
Mekong commission 1894-6 (2 vols).
*William R Perkins Library, Duke University,
Durham, N Carolina.* Acquired 1961. *Guide to the
cataloged collections,* p 497.

Letter book 1889-98, mainly 1893-4 (1 vol).
*School of Oriental and African Studies Library,
London* (MS 339679).

[306] **SEYMOUR, Sir George Hamilton**
(1797-1880)
Private secretary to Lord Londonderry 1822;
secretary of legation to the Germanic
Confederation 1823-6 (in charge 1823-5), in
Württemberg 1826-8 (in charge 1827), in Prussia
1828-9 (in charge 1828, 1829); minister to
Tuscany 1830-6, to Belgium 1836-47, to Portugal
1847-51, to Russia 1851-4, to Austria 1855-8.

Journals 1818-25, 1828-78 (23 vols).
British Library (Add MSS 60290-60312).
Purchased at Sotheby's 24 July 1978, lot 105.

Letters to him from British consuls in Portugal
and from Portuguese and other foreign politicians
and diplomats 1831-41, 1847-51 (83 items).
Broadlands Archives Trust (GC/SE/105-370).
Enclosed in his letters to Viscount Palmerston.
Enquiries to the Historical Manuscripts
Commission. NRA 12889.

Letters from GPR James, CJ Lever, Lord
Palmerston and others 1822-72 (*c*58 items).
Untraced. Sold at Sotheby's 19 Dec 1949, lot 470.

[307] **SEYMOUR-CONWAY** (afterwards
INGRAM-SEYMOUR-CONWAY), Francis
(1743-1822), styled Viscount Beauchamp 1750-93
and Earl of Yarmouth 1793-4, 2nd Marquess of
Hertford 1794
On special missions to Baden, Hesse-Cassel and
Hesse-Darmstadt 1793, to Austria 1794.

General corresp of the Marquesses of Hertford
1760-1843 (2 vols); letters to members of the
family from George IV 1784-1823, and family
corresp 1785-94, 1803-36 (2 vols); corresp and
papers of the 3rd Marquess rel to his mission to
Paris 1806, memoranda for a parliamentary speech

1807, and papers rel to legal proceedings arising from a fraud upon the 4th Marquess 1816-25 (1 vol).
British Library (Egerton MSS 3260-4). On the death of the 4th Marquess these papers were inherited by his natural son Sir Richard Wallace Bt, whose widow bequeathed them to his secretary Sir JEA Murray Scott Bt. Purchased 1942.

Accounts with Coutts & Co 1810-22 (1 vol); misc papers 1803, 1815-16 (4 items).
Warwick County RO (CR 114A/293-6). Deposited by the 8th Marquess of Hertford 1951. NRA 8482.

[308] **SEYMOUR-CONWAY, Francis Charles** (1777-1842), styled Viscount Beauchamp 1793-4 and Earl of Yarmouth 1794-1822, 3rd Marquess of Hertford 1822
Plenipotentiary to France 1806; on a special mission to Russia 1827.

See Seymour-Conway F.

[309] **SHEE, Sir George** (1785-1870) 2nd Bt 1825
Parliamentary under secretary for foreign affairs 1830-4; minister to Prussia 1834 (did not proceed), to Württemberg 1835-44, to Baden 1841-4.

Corresp with Lord and Lady Palmerston 1830-62, and misc papers 1802-37 (2 vols); corresp and papers rel to his appointment to Prussia 1834, misc corresp, Württemberg 1835-44, and despatches to and from Lord Aberdeen 1841-4 (1 vol).
British Library (Add MSS 60340-2). Purchased 1978 from his great-great-nephew Captain Richard Neall. NRA 19146.

[310] **SHERIDAN, Richard Brinsley** (1751-1816)
Under secretary for foreign affairs 1782.

Corresp, with a few letters of other members of his family, 1781-1826, and speech notes and papers rel to foreign affairs 1790-1814 (2 vols); speech notes and papers rel to domestic and colonial affairs *c*1781-1812, and misc literary papers (2 vols); misc letters to him 1770-92, with later papers rel to Drury Lane Theatre *c*1792-1827 (1 vol).
British Library (Add MSS 35118, 58274-7). Purchased at Sotheby's 17 May 1897, lot 702 and 13 May 1974, lot 222.

Misc corresp, speech notes and papers mainly rel to Drury Lane Theatre and parliamentary elections 1784-1812 (4 bundles).
William Salt Library, Stafford (S.MS 343). NRA 8254.

Family corresp (4 boxes); speech notes (1 vol).
Houghton Library, Harvard University, Cambridge, Massachusetts (MS Eng 1142, bMS Eng 1276). Acquired 1960, 1967. NRA 20129.

Corresp and memoranda mainly rel to the Prince of Wales 1781-1812 (42 items).
Beinecke Library, Yale University, New Haven, Connecticut (Osborn Collection: Sheridan Papers). NRA 18661.

Notes and memoranda rel to the impeachment of Warren Hastings *c*1788-95 (173pp).
Untraced. Sold at Sotheby's 29 Nov 1971, lot 200, and exported. Photocopies are in the British Library (RP 730).

Additional papers rel solely to his literary career and to the management of Drury Lane Theatre are in the British Library (Add MSS 25906-26036, 29709-11), the Bodleian Library, Oxford (MS Eng. lett. c.214), King's College, Cambridge (Le Fanu Papers), the Theatre Museum London, and the Houghton Library Theatre Collection, Harvard.

[311] **SIMMONS, Field Marshal Sir John Lintorn Arabin** (1821-1903)
Commissioner for the delimitation of the Russo-Turkish boundary 1857; consul-general at Warsaw 1858-60; chief technical military delegate at the congress of Berlin 1878 and the international conference on the Greek boundary 1880; on a special mission to the Vatican 1889-90.

Corresp, memoranda, reports, confidential print, etc mainly rel to the Russo-Turkish war and the Turkish boundary question 1876-80 (4 bundles); misc papers 1850-96, partly printed, rel to the Vatican 1889, Russian military intentions 1891-6, etc (2 bundles).
Public Record Office (FO 358). NRA 23627.

[312] **SKENE, James Henry** (1812-1886)
Vice-consul at Constantinople 1852-5 (in charge of the consulate at Kayseri 1852-3); consul at Aleppo 1855-78.

Misc corresp and papers incl his commission as consul 1855 and letters from his son FJH Skene 1881-7 (*c*30 items).
National Library of Scotland (Acc 7263). Purchased 1978. NRA 13753.

[313] **SMITH, John Spencer** (*c*1770-1845)
Chargé d'affaires in Turkey 1795-8, secretary of legation 1798, secretary of embassy 1798-1801 (minister *ad interim*); envoy to Württemberg 1803-4.

Misc corresp and papers 1788-1806, mainly Turkey (*c*24 items).
National Maritime Museum. Acquired among the papers of his brother Admiral Sir WS Smith.

[314] **SMITH, Joseph** (d 1813)
On a special mission to Sardinia 1806-8; secretary of legation in Sardinia 1808-13, in the Two Sicilies 1813.

Copies of his despatches to George Canning 1807-8 (1 vol); letters from the Cavaliere Rossi 1807-8 (23 items).
Shropshire RO (SRO 112). Deposited among the papers of the 3rd Baron Berwick 1947. NRA 26124.

[315] **SMITH, Admiral Sir William Sidney** (1764-1840)
Plenipotentiary to Turkey 1798-9.

Corresp and papers mainly rel to his naval and diplomatic service 1790-1814, his imprisonment in France 1796-8 and his retirement at Paris 1815-40, incl letters and despatches from British statesmen and naval officers and from agents in the eastern Mediterranean (several hundred items).
National Maritime Museum. Presented by Sir James Caird 1946, and purchased at Sotheby's 17 Dec 1975, lot 755 and 27 Oct 1981, lot 439.

Misc corresp and papers rel to naval, diplomatic and personal affairs c1745-1832, incl letters from JS Smith (63 items).
Huntington Library, San Marino, California. Presented by Mrs Hardin Craig Jr 1972.

Letters to him 1795-1817, mainly while commanding HMS *Tigre* in the Levant and during his mission to Turkey 1798-9 (22 items).
Untraced. IK Fletcher, catalogue 173, 1956, item 40.

Letters from Commander Septimus Arabin 1814-30 (22 items).
Untraced. Francis Edwards Ltd, catalogue 1038, 1982, item 556.

[316] **SMYTHE, Percy Clinton Sydney** (1780-1855), 6th Viscount Strangford 1801
Secretary of legation in Portugal 1803-8 (intermittently in charge 1804-7, minister *ad interim* 1807); minister to Brazil 1808-15, to Sweden 1817-20; ambassador to Turkey 1820-5, to Russia 1825-8; on a special mission to Brazil 1828-9.

Many of his papers passed to his granddaughter Mrs Frank Russell and were sold at Sotheby's 12 Dec 1927, lots 893-915. Most of these have not been traced.

Letters from François Chabert, dragoman of the embassy at Constantinople, containing reports of interviews with the sultan's ministers, news from other embassies, etc 1821-2 (2 vols); letters and reports from Bartolomeo Pisani, former dragoman, 1821-5 (1 vol).
British Library (Add MSS 36299-36301). Purchased 1900.

Letters from François Chabert 1823 (2 vols).
Gennadius Library, American School of Classical Studies, Athens. Purchased by Joannes Gennadius at Sotheby's 12 Dec 1927, lot 915.

[317] **SOMERSET, Field Marshal Lord Fitzroy James Henry** (1788-1855), 1st Baron Raglan 1852
Secretary of embassy in France 1814-19 (minister *ad interim* 1815); on a special mission to Spain 1823.

Corresp and papers 1808-26, incl letters from the Duke of Wellington and other papers rel to France 1815-18 and Spain 1823 (2 boxes); corresp and patronage papers 1827-54, mainly as military secretary to the commander-in-chief (2 boxes); corresp with his children 1826-55, and misc letters and papers (5 boxes).
Lord Raglan.

Letter books 1810-12 and corresp and papers 1812-14 as military secretary to the Duke of Wellington (3 vols, 52 bundles).
Southampton University Library (Wellington Papers 9/2). Among papers allocated in 1983 after acceptance for the nation in satisfaction of tax on the estate of the 7th Duke of Wellington. NRA 20085.

Corresp, despatches, letter books, intelligence reports, etc as commander-in-chief in the Crimea 1854-5 (4 vols, c4,300 items).
National Army Museum (6807/279-305). Deposited in the Royal United Service Institution by the 4th Baron Raglan 1922, and transferred 1968. NRA 20794.

[318] **SPENCER, George John** (1758-1834), styled Viscount Althorp 1765-83, 2nd Earl Spencer 1783
On an extraordinary mission to Austria 1794.

General corresp and papers 1766-1834, incl 304 letters from Thomas Grenville 1793-1834, and misc letters from other diplomats after 1794.
British Library. Purchased from the 8th Earl Spencer 1985. Not yet open for research. NRA 10410.

See also *Cabinet Ministers.*

[319] **SPENCER, Lord Henry John** (1770-1795)
Secretary of embassy in the Netherlands 1790-3 (minister *ad interim* 1791-2, 1793); on a special mission to Austria 1792; envoy to Sweden 1793-5; minister to Prussia 1794-5.

Copies of his official corresp with Lord Grenville, Sweden and Prussia 1793-5, with a list of his books sent from Stockholm (2 vols).
British Library (Add MSS 34470-1). Purchased among the Auckland papers 1893.

[320] **SPRING-RICE, Sir Cecil Arthur** (1858-1918)
Entered the Foreign Office 1882; third secretary in the United States 1886-8, second secretary 1889-91, 1891-2, 1893-5; second secretary in Belgium 1891, 1892-3, in Germany 1895-8, in Turkey 1898; secretary of legation in Persia

1898-1901 (in charge 1900-1); secretary of embassy in Russia 1903-4, counsellor 1904-6 (intermittently in charge); minister and consul-general in Persia 1906-8; minister to Sweden 1908-13; ambassador to the United States 1913-18.

Corresp with diplomats, Foreign Office officials, politicians, journalists and others incl Sir IV Chirol, Sir MWE de Bunsen, Sir AH Hardinge, LduP Mallet and Sir FH Villiers 1874-1918 (*c*3,850pp); corresp and papers, Persia 1900-1, incl letters from British consuls and agents (*c*105pp); copies of his letters to the Foreign Office, Russia 1905-6 and Persia 1906-7; travel diaries, Japan 1892-3 (2 vols); family corresp 1892-1918 (993pp); speeches, notes and other literary papers (82pp); misc papers 1886-1916.
Churchill College, Cambridge (CASR). Deposited by his daughter Lady Arthur 1972. NRA 5574.

Misc corresp, Persia, Sweden and the United States 1903-18 (2 vols).
Public Record Office (FO 800/241-2).

Corresp with his brother SE Spring-Rice and his sister-in-law Julia 1873-1902 (212 items).
John Rylands University Library of Manchester (Eng MS 1188). Presented by his niece Mrs Charles Booth 1957.

[321] **SPRING RICE, Hon Charles William Thomas** (1819-1870)
Entered the Foreign Office 1839; superintendent of the commercial and consular department 1866-9; assistant under secretary 1869-70.

Corresp 1834-69, mainly of him and his wife with his father, his brother Stephen and other members of the family, incl many references to Foreign Office business, politics and Irish affairs (304 items).
John Rylands University Library of Manchester (Eng MS 1187). Presented by his granddaughter Mrs Charles Booth 1957.

STAFFORD, Marquess of, see Leveson-Gower, George Granville.

STAIR, Earl of, see Dalrymple.

[322] **STANHOPE, Philip Henry** (1805-1875), styled Viscount Mahon 1816-55, 5th Earl Stanhope 1855
Parliamentary under secretary for foreign affairs 1834-5.

Political, literary, family and general corresp and papers 1812-75 incl letters from the 14th Earl of Derby 1840-69, WE Gladstone 1835-75 and Henry Hallam 1832-59 (11 vols, 14 boxes, *c*340 bundles, etc); corresp and papers rel to government office, membership of royal commissions and other public service 1834-73, incl material concerning the Spanish civil war and Turkish affairs 1835 (3 boxes, 22 bundles, etc);

misc personal papers 1810-75 (8 vols, 33 bundles, etc).
Kent AO (U1590/A122-3; C296-477, 714; O167-87). Deposited by the Administrative Trustees of the Chevening Estate 1971. NRA 25095.

Diary of appointments, addresses, etc 1875.
Lincolnshire AO (RA/4/A/3). Deposited 1971 by Mrs CWP Lee of Revesby Abbey, formerly the seat of his son Edward Stanhope. NRA 6329.

Letters to him or collected by him from politicians, authors and others.
Untraced. Sold at Sotheby's 23 Mar 1981, lot 16.

[323] **STANLEY, Edward Henry** (1826-1893), styled Lord Stanley 1851-69, 15th Earl of Derby 1869
Parliamentary under secretary for foreign affairs 1852; foreign secretary 1866-8, 1874-8.

Letters to him, drafts and copies of letters from him and notes and memoranda as under secretary 1852 (2 vols, several bundles); letters to him as foreign secretary 1866-8, 1874-8 from statesmen, diplomats, consuls and others, with a few drafts and copies of replies (86 vols, 5 bundles); drafts and copies of letters from him 1866-8, 1874-8 (46 vols); cabinet notes and memoranda 1866-8, 1874-8 (10 vols); cabinet and Foreign Office confidential print and parliamentary papers mainly rel to foreign affairs 1846-85 (171 vols, 1 box, 13 bundles); political journals, travel notes, etc 1849-93 (*c*44 vols).
Liverpool RO (920 Der (15)). Deposited by the 18th Earl of Derby 1968, 1980. NRA 20761 (partial list).

Letters from Queen Victoria 1870-6 (1 bundle); cabinet papers 1878 (1 bundle).
The Earl of Derby. Access restricted. Enquiries to the Librarian, The Estate Office, Knowsley, Prescot, Merseyside L34 4AG.

See also *Cabinet Ministers.*

[324] **STANLEY, Henry Edward John** (1827-1903), 3rd Baron Stanley of Alderley 1869
Précis writer in the Foreign Office 1847-51; attaché at Constantinople 1851-4; acting consul at Varna 1853; secretary of legation in Greece 1854-9; secretary to Sir WHLE Bulwer's mission to the Danubian principalities 1856-8.

Letters from his family 1849-52, 1873-97 (1 bundle); letters from various correspondents 1847-84, incl Lord and Lady Palmerston 1849-51, with press cuttings rel to his death 1903 (2 bundles); journal 1846, 1847 (1 bundle).
Cheshire RO (DSA 169-71, 203). Deposited by Lady Kathleen Stanley 1953, and by Mrs MFP Lubbock (née Stanley) 1972. NRA 17206.

Letters to him 1892-1902, mainly rel to Anglesey local affairs and the Penrhos estate (1 bundle, 65 items).

University College of North Wales, Bangor
(Penrhos VIII). Deposited by Mrs MFP
Lubbock 1972. NRA 21375.

[325] **STANTON, General Sir Edward**
(1827-1907)
Commissioner for the delimitation of the
Bessarabian boundary 1856-7; consul-general at
Warsaw 1860-5; agent and consul-general in
Egypt 1865-76; chargé d'affaires in Bavaria
1876-82.

Letters from CG Gordon 1874-9 (43 items).
Royal Engineers Museum, Chatham (4801-47).

[326] **STAUNTON, Sir George Leonard**
(1737-1801), 1st Bt 1785
Negotiated treaty with Tipu Sultan of Mysore
1783-4; secretary to Lord Macartney's embassy to
China 1792-4.

Family and other corresp 1743-1801, misc papers
rel to Mysore and China, and corresp, journals
and papers of Sir GT Staunton 1790-1858, incl
letters to his parents while in E India Co service
at Canton 1798-1817 (8 vols, 489 items).
*William R Perkins Library, Duke University,
Durham, N Carolina.* Mainly purchased at
Sotheby's 25 July 1960, lots 451-6, from Philip
Yorke, a descendant of his sister Lucy. NRA
25905.

Letters from Lord Macartney to Sir GL and Sir
GT Staunton 1780-1804 (20 items).
*Beinecke Library, Yale University, New Haven,
Connecticut* (Osborn Collection: Macartney
Papers). Purchased at Sotheby's 25 July 1960, lots
447-8. NRA 18661.

[327] **STAUNTON, Sir George Thomas**
(1781-1859), 2nd Bt 1801
King's commissioner of embassy to China
1816-17.

See Staunton GL.

[328] **STEPNEY, Sir John** (1743-1811), 7th Bt
1772
Envoy to Saxony 1776-82, to Prussia 1782-4.

Letters from Alleyne Fitzherbert, James Harris,
Sir RM Keith and other diplomats 1782-4 (2
bundles).
Sir HSP Monro (a descendant of his secretary
Joseph Ewart). Enquiries to NRA (Scotland).
NRA 11854 (bundles 129, 159).

[329] **STEWART, Robert** (1769-1822), styled
Viscount Castlereagh 1796-1821, 2nd Marquess of
Londonderry 1821
Foreign secretary 1812-22; plenipotentiary to the
congresses of Châtillon 1813-14, Paris 1814,
Vienna 1814-15, Paris 1815 and Aix-la-Chapelle
1818.

Drafts of memoranda and notes rel to the
congress of Amiens 1802-3 (23 items); corresp
and papers 1812-22, mainly as foreign secretary
and as plenipotentiary to the peace conferences
1814-15, incl corresp with British and foreign
diplomats and statesmen, memoranda, intelligence
reports, protocols and statistics, with some papers
rel to British and Irish affairs (*c*2,850 items);
printed official corresp rel to the United States
1810-12 (5 vols); Foreign Office secret service
accounts 1812-15, 1819-20 (3 vols).
Public Record Office of Northern Ireland (D3030).
Presented 1976 by the National Trust after
deposit 1974-5 by Lady Mairi Bury, daughter of
the 7th Marquess of Londonderry. NRA 12865.

Letters from Lord Stewart rel to the peninsular
war and as ambassador to Austria 1808-20 (2 vols,
123 bundles and items); misc corresp rel to
foreign affairs mainly 1812-22, incl intelligence
reports from France 1815-16 (110 bundles and
items); misc memoranda and other papers rel to
foreign affairs 1804-16 (27 bundles and items).
Durham County RO (D/Lo). Deposited by the
9th Marquess of Londonderry 1963. NRA 11528.

See also *Cabinet Ministers*.

STEWART, Baron, see Vane CW.

[330] **STRANGE, John** (1732-1799)
Resident at Venice 1773-90.

Literary, artistic, scientific and diplomatic corresp
1752-87, and misc papers rel to books and
pictures (8 vols); his collection of letters and
treatises by Italian authors on various subjects
(13 vols).
British Library (Add MSS 19309-15, 23729-30,
60537; Egerton MSS 1969-70, 1981, 2001-2, 2233;
King's MSS 290-4). Acquired by gift and
purchase 1823-1979.

STRANGFORD, Viscount, see Smythe.

STRATFORD DE REDCLIFFE, Viscount, see
Canning S.

STRATHNAIRN, Baron, see Rose HH.

[331] **STRATON, Alexander** (1763-1832)
Secretary of legation in Austria 1789-99
(intermittently in charge 1790-4); secretary of
embassy in Turkey 1801-6 (in charge 1802, 1803
and *minister ad interim* 1803-5); minister to
Sweden 1807-8.

Letter books, Austria and Turkey 1790-1807 (46
vols); corresp with diplomats, politicians, relatives,
friends and others, incl letters from Lord
Auckland, Lord Elgin, Sir RM Keith and Sir
Arthur Paget 1790-1827 (1,246 items); papers rel

to diplomatic conventions 1777-1823; personal and family papers 1778-1886; misc papers 1798-1819.
Suffolk RO, Ipswich (HA 239). Deposited 1971 by Commander PS Campbell whose wife was a descendant of Straton. NRA 25929.

[332] **STUART, Charles** (1779-1845), Baron Stuart de Rothesay 1828
Secretary of legation in Austria 1801-4 (in charge 1803-4); secretary of embassy in Russia 1804-8 (minister *ad interim* 1806-7); chargé d'affaires in Austria 1805-6; on a special mission to Spain 1808-9, to Austria 1809; minister to Portugal 1810-14, to France (*ad interim*) 1814; ambassador to the Netherlands 1815, to France 1815-24; ambassador on a special mission to Portugal 1825, to Brazil 1825-6; ambassador to France 1828-31, to Russia 1841-4.

After the deaths of his daughters the papers passed to EJ Montagu-Stuart-Wortley, whose son-in-law the 8th Earl of Abingdon sold them at Sotheby's 1 July 1935, except for 46 volumes of correspondence claimed by the Foreign Office. The papers were dispersed at this and later sales at Sotheby's, and many remain untraced.

Corresp with the Foreign Office, Austria 1801-4, 1809 (2 vols), Russia 1805-7 (6 vols), Spain 1808-10 (2 vols), Portugal 1810-14 (36 vols).
Public Record Office (FO 342). Acquired by the Foreign Office from the 8th Earl of Abingdon 1935. NRA 23466.

Corresp and papers 1800-46, mainly France 1816-30, incl letters from William IV, Lord Palmerston, the Duke of Wellington and other British and foreign statesmen and politicians (35 bundles); corresp with French ministers and British consuls 1815-30 (5 vols); copies of despatches to and from him, and some private corresp with foreign secretaries, 1814-24, 1828-31 (87 vols); misc corresp 1810-38, incl letters about Greek independence from Sir Frederick Adam 1828-30 (*c*55 items); account roll for supplies purchased as minister to Portugal 1811.
National Library of Scotland (MSS 3840, 6160-6246, 9818, 10997, 15386-90; Acc 7970; Dep 333). Partly purchased at Sotheby's 12 Feb 1951 (lot 327), 6 Nov 1951 (lot 371), 15 Dec 1980 (lots 14, 17), 20 July 1981 (lot 34); at Christie's 16 July 1969 (lot 1); at Phillips's 16 May 1978 (lot 101); from Bernard Quaritch Ltd 1952 and 1967 (catalogue 878, item 447). Partly deposited by Vizards, solicitors, 1982. *Catalogue of manuscripts*, ii, p305 and iv, pp117-20; *Annual report 1978-9*, p70, *1980-1*, p47, *1981-2*, p51; *Accessions of manuscripts 1965-1970*, p31.

Corresp with George Canning, Lord Castlereagh, the 5th Earl of Jersey, William Pitt and other politicians and diplomats, with misc printed papers 1785-1845 (450 items).

University of Minnesota Library, Minneapolis (MSS 24). Purchased 1962. *National union catalog*, MS 75-2025.

Misc corresp 1802-41, mainly with French ministers and with his family (84 items).
Edinburgh University Library (Dk 6.25). Purchased from a bookseller 1958. *Index to manuscripts*, pp570-3.

Letters to him, mainly of introduction, from the Foreign Office, politicians, friends and others 1814-30 (3 vols).
University of Chicago Library. Purchased from GH Last, bookseller, 1936. *National union catalog*, MS 64-169.

Travel journal, northern Europe 1801.
Bodleian Library, Oxford (MS Eng. misc. c.256). Purchased 1937.

[333] **STUART, John** (1744-1814), styled Viscount Mountstuart, 4th Earl of Bute 1792, 1st Marquess of Bute 1796
Envoy to Sardinia 1779-83; ambassador to Spain 1783 (did not proceed), 1795-6.

His papers passed to his daughter Frances, whose grandson the 5th Earl of Harrowby sold most of them at Sotheby's 9 May 1903, lots 19, 26-54. Some of the papers dispersed at this and subsequent sales remain untraced.

Letters to him as envoy to Sardinia 1779-83 (3 vols), letter books 1779-84 (3 vols), letter books of Sir William Lynch, envoy 1769-79 (2 vols), and of Louis Dutens and Robert Liston, chargés d'affaires 1780-3 (1 vol), register of corresp 1779-83 (1 vol), copies of despatches from him 1779-82 (1 vol), and misc papers rel to Sardinia 1760-83 (1 vol); letters to him, Spain 1783-4, 1795-6, with some related papers (3 vols), letter books 1795-7 (2 vols), despatches to him 1795-6 (3 vols), copies of despatches and a few private letters from him 1795-7 (1 vol) and of despatches between other diplomats and the Foreign Office 1792-5 (1 vol).
British Library (Add MSS 36799-36806, 36808-14, 37080-5, 38774). Purchased 1903-13 following sale at Sotheby's.

Letters from British consuls at Genoa, Leghorn, Nice and elsewhere to WD Poyntz as chargé d'affaires in Sardinia 1776-9 and to Mountstuart as envoy 1779-83 (3 vols); copies of enclosures in his despatches and of other diplomatic material incl papers rel to the capture of Fort St Philip, Minorca 1780-2 (1 vol).
John Rylands University Library of Manchester (Eng MSS 1145-8). Purchased at Sotheby's 27 Feb 1950, lot 268, after sale there on 9 May 1903, lots 28-30, 37. *Hand-list of additions to the collection of English manuscripts 1937-1951*, pp230-1.

Corresp rel to his appointment and mission to Sardinia 1779-83 (1 vol).
The Marquess of Bute. Purchased at Sotheby's 20 Feb 1978, lot 124.

Letters from relatives and others, with a few legal papers and other family corresp, 1787-1813 (2 vols); journal of his voyage to Spain 1795 (1 vol); observations on household management 1802 (1 vol); misc corresp and family papers.
Harrowby MSS Trust (vols 20-1, 306, 317 and *passim*). Enquiries to the Earl of Harrowby, Sandon Hall, Stafford ST18 0BZ. NRA 1561.

Estate papers rel to Luton Hoo incl letters to him from Samuel Whitbread and others concerning estate and local political affairs 1789-1859 (*c*750 items).
Bedfordshire RO (G/DDA). Deposited 1965, 1967 by Glamorgan RO to which they had been presented by Arthur Andrews following purchase at auction. NRA 10481.

[334] **STUART, Sir William** (1824-1896)
Secretary of legation in Brazil 1858-9, in the Two Sicilies 1859-61, in the United States 1861-4 (in charge 1863); secretary of embassy in Turkey 1864-6, in Russia 1866-8; minister to the Argentine Republic 1868-71, to Greece 1872-7, to the Netherlands 1877-88.

Copies of his despatches 1862-88 (11 vols); copies of private letters from him 1858-87, with a few letters to him (3 vols); confidential print, Greece 1870-1 (1 bundle).
Public Record Office (PRO 30/36). Presented by his wife's cousin SG Tremenheere 1931, 1933. NRA 23392.

SUTHERLAND, Duke of, see Leveson-Gower, George Granville.

[335] **SYKES, Lieutenant-Colonel Sir Percy Molesworth** (1867-1945)
Consul at Kerman 1894-1905; assistant commissioner for the delimitation of the Perso-Baluch boundary 1896; consul-general at Mashhad 1906-13, at Kashgar 1915.

Reports to the War Office, notes and maps rel to his travels in Persia 1892-4, papers rel to the Perso-Baluch boundary commission 1896 and the establishment of a consulate at Sistan 1898-9, copies of his despatches as consul and consul-general 1899-1900, 1910-12 and as commander of the South Persia Rifles 1917-18, and misc literary papers (2 boxes); corresp with Mohammed Halgh 1909, reports, despatches and other papers rel to the military situation in S Persia 1916-18, and miscellanea (1 box); corresp 1934-45 (1 box); press cuttings, articles and photographs 1897-1982 (2 boxes).
Middle East Centre, St Antony's College, Oxford. Deposited by his daughter Lady Reilly and his son Edward Sykes 1966, and by Edward Sykes 1982.

[336] **TAYLOR, Sir Brook** (1776-1846)
Minister to Cologne and Hesse-Cassel 1801-6, to Denmark 1807 (*ad interim*); on a special mission to the Netherlands 1814; minister to Württemberg 1814-20, to Bavaria 1820-8, to Prussia 1827-30; on a special mission to the Vatican 1831.

Corresp, despatches, memoranda and other papers (mainly copies), Württemberg 1816-19, mainly rel to the marriage of the Duke of Kent and Princess Victoria of Leiningen (*c*75 items); letters from British diplomats and others, Prussia 1828-30 (7 items); corresp, despatches to him, and misc papers, Rome 1830-1 (*c*40 items); letters from his brother Sir Herbert Taylor, diplomats and others 1830-9 (26 items); misc diplomatic and family papers 1805-59 (21 items).
British Library (Add MSS 62953-4). Presented by his great-great-great-nephew RT Holmes 1984. NRA 26578.

[337] **TEMPLE, Henry John** (1784-1865), 3rd Viscount Palmerston 1802
Foreign secretary 1830-4, 1835-41, 1846-51.

Royal corresp 1820-66, incl corresp as foreign secretary with William IV and Queen Victoria (29 files); general corresp 1807-65, incl private diplomatic corresp (278 files); patronage and misc corresp 1821-65, incl many letters from correspondents seeking diplomatic and consular posts mainly 1835-41 (15 files); drafts and copies of despatches 1822-51 (22 files); misc memoranda, etc on foreign affairs 1801-65 (14 files); corresp and papers rel to the slave trade 1806-65 (1 file); misc Foreign Office papers 1825-64 (4 files); cabinet papers 1828-65, incl some rel to foreign affairs (2 files).
Broadlands Archives Trust. Enquiries to the Historical Manuscripts Commission. NRA 12889.

Private letters from Lord Howard de Walden, Portugal 1835-40 (5 vols); précis and entry books 1830-50 (140 vols); drafts and copies of despatches, Foreign Office minutes, etc 1832-51 (1 vol).
British Library (Add MSS 48439-48577, 49963-9). Purchased 1954, 1958.

See also *Cabinet Ministers.*

[338] **TEMPLE, Sir William** (1788-1856)
Secretary of legation in Sweden 1815-17 (in charge 1815-16), in the Germanic Confederation 1817-23 (intermittently in charge), in Prussia 1823-8 (in charge 1826, 1827-8); secretary of embassy in Russia 1828-33 (minister *ad interim* 1828); minister to the Two Sicilies 1832-56.

Letters to him 1807-56, mainly from his brother Lord Palmerston (*c*260 items).
Broadlands Archives Trust (GC/TE/137-372 and *passim*). Enquiries to the Historical Manuscripts Commission. NRA 12889.

Letters to him *c*1796-1855, mainly from members of his family.
Hampshire RO (27M60). Deposited by the Broadlands Archives Trust 1960.

TENTERDEN, Baron, see Abbott.

[339] **THORNTON, Sir Edward** (1766-1852)
Secretary of legation in the United States 1796-1804 (intermittently in charge 1797-1803); resident in the Hanse Towns 1805-7; minister to Sweden 1807-8; plenipotentiary to Sweden 1811, 1812, to Russia 1812, to Denmark 1813, 1813-14; minister to Sweden 1812-17, to the Portuguese court in Brazil 1819-21, to Portugal 1823-4.

Corresp, despatches received and sent, intelligence reports, memoranda, treaty papers, etc 1793, 1803-4 (1 bundle), 1805-7 (24 bundles and vols), 1808-18 (51 bundles and vols), 1819-24 (14 bundles and vols); corresp 1825-6, 1834 (1 bundle); memoirs of his early life and diplomatic career in the United States (partly a photocopy of the volume in the Library of Congress).
Public Record Office (FO 933). Presented by EP Thornton 1970. NRA 23629.

Memoirs of his early life and diplomatic career in the United States (1 vol).
Library of Congress, Washington. Presented by Edward and Frances Thornton 1932.

[340] **THORNTON, Sir Edward** (1817-1906)
Attaché in Sardinia 1842-5, in Mexico 1845-51 (in charge 1847); secretary of legation in Mexico 1851-4; secretary to Sir Charles Hotham's mission to the River Plate 1852-3; consul-general and chargé d'affaires in Uruguay 1854-9; minister to the Argentine Republic 1859-63, to Paraguay 1863-5, to Brazil 1865-7, to the United States 1867-81; ambassador to Russia 1881-4, to Turkey 1884-6 (but was delayed in Russia until 1886).

Corresp, copies of his despatches, intelligence reports and other papers 1847, 1862-74 (1 bundle), 1875-81 (16 bundles), 1881-6 (7 bundles); corresp of his wife 1885 (1 bundle).
Public Record Office (FO 933). Presented by EP Thornton 1970. NRA 23629.

Copies of private letters 1870-2, mainly to Lords Clarendon and Granville and Edmund Hammond (1 vol).
Bodleian Library, Oxford (MS Eng. lett. c.193). Purchased 1960.

[341] **TIERNEY, George** (1800-1883)
Secretary of legation in Bavaria 1829-31.

Corresp with the Duke of Wellington and others, some rel to promotion in the diplomatic service, and misc papers, 1828-31, 1846 (23 items).
Hampshire RO (31M70). Deposited by Mrs LAH Wright 1970. NRA 14626.

TORRINGTON, Viscount, see Byng.

[342] **TOWER, Sir Reginald Thomas** (1860-1939)
Second secretary in Spain 1892-3 (in charge 1892), in Denmark 1893-4, in Germany 1894-6, in the United States 1896-1900 (in charge 1897, 1899); secretary of legation in China 1900-1; minister and consul-general in Siam 1901-3; minister resident in Bavaria and Württemberg 1903-6; minister to Mexico 1906-11, to the Argentine Republic and Paraguay 1911-19.

Notes by him on his career.
Foreign and Commonwealth Office Library.

A few personal papers, incl letters written from China 1901, notes on his career, letters of appointment, etc.
Miss Winifred Tower.

Notes by him on the Argentine Republic 1925 (3 vols).
London University Library (MS 813). Presented by his great-nephew the 28th Baron Dunboyne 1973.

ULLSWATER, Viscount, see Lowther.

[343] **URQUHART, David** (1805-1877)
British commissioner to accompany Prince Leopold to Greece 1830; attached to Sir Stratford Canning's mission to Turkey 1831-2; secretary of embassy in Turkey 1835-7.

Corresp and papers rel to the Greek war of independence and its aftermath 1822-37 (*c*32 bundles and items); corresp, memoranda and other papers rel to Turkey 1820-76, mainly 1832-8, incl corresp with James Hudson, Lord Ponsonby, Turkish diplomats and others, papers rel to his recall 1837, and to the commerce of the Ottoman Empire, particularly the Anglo-Turkish commercial treaty 1836-7 (*c*40 bundles and items); corresp and misc papers rel to foreign affairs 1834-75, the law of nations 1866-76, and the Vatican council 1867-76 (*c*25 bundles and items); corresp, reports, memoranda and literary MSS 1811-77, mainly rel to his concerns in Britain, incl chartism 1838-59, the Stafford election 1847 and working men's committees 1855-67.
Balliol College, Oxford. Bequeathed by FF Urquhart 1934. NRA 11691.

Corresp of Urquhart and his wife rel to the introduction of Turkish baths to Britain 1854-62 (52 items); notes, press cuttings and misc papers rel to Turkish baths, literary matters, etc (1 vol, 11 items).
Wellcome Historical Medical Library, London (Acc 67343). Purchased at Stevens's 5 Apr 1921, lot 6. NRA 26573.

[344] **VANE** (formerly **STEWART**), **General Charles William** (1778-1854), 1st Baron Stewart 1814, 3rd Marquess of Londonderry 1822
Minister to Prussia 1813-14; plenipotentiary to the congresses of Châtillon, Paris and Vienna 1814-15; ambassador to Austria 1814-22.

Political and personal corresp 1809-54, mainly after 1822 (*c*3,270 items); letters, despatches and memoranda from Lord Castlereagh 1815-16, with copies of Castlereagh's despatches to other diplomats 1816 (26 bundles); drafts and copies of his despatches to Castlereagh 1813-21 (917 bundles and items); corresp with diplomats elsewhere in Europe 1816-17, incl William A'Court, Lord Clancarty, FJ Lamb and GH Rose (93 bundles and items); misc despatches, letters, memoranda and papers rel to his diplomatic career 1813-23, incl papers rel to the financial and domestic arrangements of the Vienna embassy (93 bundles and items); memorandum and papers rel to Catholic emancipation 1815 (3 bundles); corresp rel to the co Down election 1852 (2 bundles, 170 items); business and estate corresp 1819-54 (4 vols, 3 bundles, *c*5,780 items); misc accounts and other papers 1809-49 (2 vols, 5 bundles, 40 items).
Durham County RO (D/Lo). Deposited by the 9th Marquess of Londonderry 1963, 1969. NRA 11528. (Most of the private letters that he received from his half-brother Castlereagh were lost at sea in 1829 while on loan to the bishop of Calcutta for a projected biography).

Corresp with Lord and Lady Castlereagh 1809-27 (242 items); copies of letters and despatches to Castlereagh 1808-12 (5 vols); letters from Edward Cooke 1808-16 (25 items); draft despatches and memoranda to George Canning rel to the Verona congress 1822 (25 items); letters, addresses and papers 1808-22, mainly rel to his military career (48 items); corresp, notes, press cuttings, etc 1822-54, mainly rel to British and Irish politics and foreign policy (329 items); corresp and papers of the Marquesses of Londonderry rel to co Down politics 1805-30 (196 items).
Public Record Office of Northern Ireland (D3030). Presented 1976 by the National Trust after deposit 1974-5 by Lady Mairi Bury, daughter of the 7th Marquess of Londonderry. NRA 12865.

[345] **VANE** (afterwards **POWLETT**), **Harry George** (1803-1891), 4th Duke of Cleveland 1864
Secretary of legation in Sweden 1839-41.

Corresp and papers 1858-91 and nd (1 vol); diary 1840 and journals 1856-87 and nd (10 vols).
National Library of Scotland (MSS 10206-16). Presented with the papers of his stepson the 5th Earl of Rosebery by Lord Primrose 1966. NRA 22490.

[346] **VANSITTART, Nicholas** (1766-1851), Baron Bexley 1823
On a special mission to Denmark 1801.

Copies of corresp and papers, Denmark 1801 (1 vol); corresp 1797-1835, incl some as chancellor of the exchequer rel to foreign affairs (6 vols); despatches from Sir Charles Stuart to Lord Castlereagh and WR Hamilton rel to Portuguese finances 1812 (1 vol); misc papers 1796-1844, incl some rel to S America (1 vol).
British Library (Add MSS 31229-37). Bequeathed by him and incorporated 1880.

[347] **VAUGHAN, Sir Charles Richard** (1774-1849)
Secretary of legation in Spain 1810-11, secretary of embassy 1811-20 (minister *ad interim* 1815-16); secretary of embassy in France 1820-2; minister to Switzerland 1823-5, to the United States 1825-36.

Private corresp, mainly diplomatic, 1807-48, with HU Addington, John Backhouse, George Canning, Lord Cowley, WR Hamilton, Richard Pakenham, Lord Fitzroy Somerset, Lord Stuart de Rothesay, Sir HWW Wynn and others (*c*1,130 items); general corresp 1805-48 (440 items); misc corresp, reports, memoranda, etc mainly rel to Spanish finances and commerce 1807-22, and copies of his despatches 1815-16 (*c*185 items); papers rel to Switzerland 1823-5, with a few rel to France 1820-3, and draft despatches 1823-5 (*c*135 items); memoranda, etc, United States 1824-46, mainly rel to Anglo-American commerce, suppression of the slave trade and boundary negotiations (1 vol, *c*240 items); drafts of his despatches 1825-35 (*c*700 items); lists and précis of despatches sent and received 1815-16, 1823-35, and of corresp with the United States government, George Canning and others 1825-34 (5 vols); corresp mainly with Lords Palmerston and Ponsonby and misc papers rel to his proposed mission to Turkey 1837 (*c*70 items); family corresp and genealogical papers 1794-1848 (*c*140 items); corresp and papers as a fellow of All Souls 1798-1848 (1 bundle, 45 items); papers rel to his Eastern travels *c*1804 (1 bundle); journals mainly of his travels in Britain, Europe, the Near East and the United States 1798-1843, and commonplace books (38 vols and bundles).
All Souls College, Oxford. NRA 10564.

[348] **VESEY-FITZGERALD** (formerly **FITZGERALD**), **William** (1783-1843), 2nd Baron Fitzgerald and Vesey 1832
Minister to Sweden 1820-3.

Copies of private corresp 1812-22 (47 vols).
National Library of Ireland (MSS 7813-59). Purchased at Sotheby's 28 Nov 1955, lot 83, from the library of Dr TPC Kirkpatrick. *Manuscript sources for the history of Irish civilisation*, ed RJ Hayes, ii, Boston 1965, p138.

See also *Cabinet Ministers.*

[349] **VILLIERS, Sir Francis Hyde** (1852-1925)
Assistant under secretary for foreign affairs
1896-1905; minister to Portugal 1905-11; minister
to Belgium 1911-19, ambassador 1919-20.

Letters from Sir Arthur Nicolson 1893-1908 (1
vol); corresp with Sir CA Spring-Rice and others
1895-1908, 1923 (1 vol); corresp with Sir Charles
Hardinge 1907-8 (1 vol).
Public Record Office (FO 800/22-4).

[350] **VILLIERS, George William Frederick**
(1800-1870), 4th Earl of Clarendon 1838
Minister to Spain 1833-9; foreign secretary
1853-8, 1865-6, 1868-70; plenipotentiary to the
congress of Paris 1856.

Corresp with Lord Palmerston, the Duke of
Wellington, British diplomats and consuls, army
and naval officers in Spain, Spanish and
Portuguese politicians and others, with related
papers 1833-9 (23 bundles, etc); copies of
despatches from him 1833-9 (10 bundles); corresp
as foreign secretary 1853-8 (104 vols), 1865-6 (18
vols), 1868-70 (4 vols, 35 bundles); registers of
corresp 1853-6 (49 vols); Foreign Office and
other printed papers 1848-58, 1867-70 (35 vols
and bundles); general corresp and papers 1820-70,
incl misc material rel to foreign affairs (2 vols,
2 boxes, 42 bundles).
Bodleian Library, Oxford (MSS Clar. dep.).
Deposited by the 7th Earl of Clarendon 1959-62.
NRA 6302.

Letters to him mainly from political colleagues
and British and foreign diplomats 1834-69 (c106
items).
RF Hobbs Esq (his great-great-grandson). NRA
12033.

Corresp with British diplomats 1867-70 (1 vol).
Public Record Office (FO 361). Transferred from
the Foreign Office 1921.

See also *Cabinet Ministers.*

[351] **WADE, Sir Thomas Francis** (1818-1895)
Vice-consul at Shanghai 1852-5; acting chargé
d'affaires in China 1864-5, 1869-71; minister to
China 1871-83.

Draft memorandum on the opium trade and notes
of current business 1881-2 (1 vol); misc notes on
Chinese and Tibetan history and geography (3
vols).
Cambridge University Library (Add 6318).

His MS copy of Robert Morrison's *Vocabulary of
the Canton dialect* (1828) with additions and
corrections 1843 (1 vol).
*School of Oriental and African Studies Library,
London* (MS 30368).

[352] **WALDEGRAVE, Admiral William**
(1753-1825), 1st Baron Radstock 1800
On a mission to Tunis 1796.

Corresp, incl letters from Lord Collingwood, DR
Morier, Lord Nelson and WE Parry, misc corresp
rel to the dey of Tunis and as governor of
Newfoundland, and corresp with his family
(11 boxes); account of proceedings at Tunis 1796
(1 vol).
National Maritime Museum (MS 82/077).
Deposited by Mrs OJ Diggle 1982. NRA 26356.

Account of his mission 1796 (1 vol).
Lewis Walpole Library, Farmington, Connecticut.

[353] **WALLACE, James** (fl 1803-26)
Vice-consul at Savannah 1804-24, consul 1824-6.

Letters from his brother Michael in Nova Scotia
rel to diplomatic, personal and business matters
1803-24, misc papers as vice-consul 1805-23, and
other family corresp and papers 1766-1885 (173
items).
In private possession. A microfilm is in the Wilson
Library, University of North Carolina, Chapel
Hill (M-747).

See also Molyneux.

[354] **WALLER, Sir Thomas Wathen**
(1805-1892), 2nd Bt 1853
Attaché in the Netherlands 1826-8, in France
1828-32, in Turkey 1832-4; secretary of legation
in Greece 1834-7, in Belgium 1837-58
(intermittently in charge).

Letters mainly from family and friends 1815,
1832-56 (c275 items); copies of his despatches
1838-48 (2 vols); commissions 1834, 1837 and
papers rel to his pension 1858 (6 items);
commonplace books c1834-7 (3 vols); notes of
income and investments 1844-90 (1 vol);
autograph collection and press cuttings (1 vol).
Warwick County RO (CR 341). Deposited by
Viola, Lady Waller 1955. NRA 0275.

[355] **WARD, Edward Michael** (1789-1832)
Secretary of legation and chargé d'affaires in
Portugal 1816-23; secretary of embassy in Russia
1824-5 (minister *ad interim* 1824-5); minister to
Saxony 1828-32.

Register of passports issued to British subjects
leaving Portugal 1814-16, and drafts of letters and
despatches 1817-18 (1 vol); copies of his
despatches 1820-3 (2 vols); journal 1828-31
(1 vol).
Public Record Office of Northern Ireland (D1205).
Presented by John Ross & Co 1961.

[356] **WARD, John** (1805-1890)
Commissioner for the revision of the Stade duties
1841-4, and for the settlement of the Portendic
claims on France 1844; consul-general at Leipzig
1845-60; secretary of legation in Saxony 1851;
consul-general and chargé d'affaires in the Hanse
Towns 1860-5, minister resident 1865-70.

Letters from statesmen, diplomats and others
1829-85 (89 items).
Cambridge University Library (Add 6157D).
Presented by Sir AW Ward 1918.

Memoranda, copies of despatches and misc papers
rel to the Stade duties, the Portendic claims, the
Schleswig-Holstein question, etc 1834-68 (*c*65
items); MS 'Recollections of Germany' and
'Memorials of Munster'.
Peterhouse, Cambridge. Bequeathed by Sir AW
Ward 1924.

[357] **WARREN, Admiral Sir John Borlase**
(1753-1822), Bt 1775
Ambassador to Russia 1802-4.

Corresp and papers rel to Russia 1802-4 (4 vols),
to naval operations 1781-1814 (30 vols), to naval
administration 1781-1821 (47 vols); misc papers
rel to dockyards, his appointments and his naval
service in N America and Jamaica and at
Portsmouth; family papers incl estate papers,
accounts, genealogical papers etc 1653-1839 (69
vols).
Lord Vernon (great-great-great-grandson of his
daughter Frances).

Household account books 1818-22 (3 vols).
Nottingham Central Library. Purchased 1957.
Annual report of the archives department 1957-58,
p5.

[358] **WELLESLEY** (formerly **WESLEY**),
Arthur (1769-1852), 1st Viscount Wellington
1809, 1st Earl of Wellington 1812, 1st Marquess
of Wellington 1812, 1st Duke of Wellington 1814
Ambassador to France 1814-15; plenipotentiary to
the congresses of Vienna 1815, Paris 1815, Aix-la-
Chapelle 1818 and Verona 1822; on a special
mission to Russia 1826; foreign secretary 1834-5.

Political and general corresp 1790-1852, incl
private corresp, drafts and copies of despatches
and memoranda rel to his diplomatic missions and
as foreign secretary (172 files, *c*995 bundles);
memoranda and papers mainly arranged by
subject 1791-1852, incl protocols, copies of
despatches, etc (22 files, *c*250 bundles); register of
corresp, Russia 1826 (1 vol); summaries of
despatches to France and from Spain 1834-5
(2 vols).
Southampton University Library. Among papers
allocated in 1983 after acceptance for the nation
in satisfaction of tax on the estate of the 7th
Duke of Wellington. NRA 20085.

See also *Cabinet Ministers.*

[359] **WELLESLEY, Colonel the Hon
Frederick Arthur** (1844-1931)
Military attaché in Russia 1871-8; secretary of
embassy in Austria-Hungary 1878-9.

Official and private letters mainly from the
Foreign Office 1877-9 (1 vol, 1 bundle); papers
mainly rel to his edition of the diaries and corresp
of the 1st Baron Cowley (1 box, 1 vol, 7
bundles).
Public Record Office (FO 519/281-3, 285-9,
302-4). Presented 1952 and bequeathed 1954 by
Sir VAAH Wellesley. NRA 23469.

[360] **WELLESLEY** (formerly **WESLEY**),
Henry (1773-1847), 1st Baron Cowley 1828
Secretary of legation in Sweden 1792-5 (in charge
1792-3); minister to Spain 1810-11, ambassador
1811-22; ambassador to Austria 1823-31, to
France 1835, 1841-6.

Copies of his letters to Lord Wellesley 1802 (1
vol); drafts and copies of private letters to Charles
Stuart and Lords Wellesley and Wellington
1810-11 (4 vols); papers rel to the commercial
treaty with Spain 1814-15 (1 bundle); drafts of
despatches and private letters to Lord Castlereagh
1817-20 (15 bundles); private corresp with Sir
William A'Court, George Canning, Sir Stratford
Canning, Friedrich von Gentz and other
diplomats 1823-31 (4 bundles); copies of his
despatches to foreign secretaries 1823-31 (9 vols);
private corresp with Lord Aberdeen and others
1842-5 (2 bundles); draft despatches to Aberdeen
1842-6 (15 bundles); diaries 1836, 1841-6 (3 vols,
15 bundles); misc notes and memoranda *c*1833-46
(2 vols, 1 bundle); memoirs 1773-1846 (2 vols).
Public Record Office (FO 519/17-88, 290-1).
Presented 1952 and bequeathed 1954 by Sir
VAAH Wellesley. NRA 23469.

Private letters from the Duke of Wellington
1810-15, with some letters from Lord Fitzroy
Somerset (9 vols); drafts and copies of private
letters to Wellington 1810-13 (3 vols); drafts of
official letters to Wellington 1813-14 (1 vol);
précis of despatches to Lord Wellesley 1810-12
and Lord Castlereagh 1813-15 (1 vol); copies of
private letters to George Canning 1823-6 (1 vol).
Southampton University Library (Wellington
Papers 12/1-3). Among papers allocated in 1983
after acceptance for the nation in satisfaction of
tax on the estate of the 7th Duke of Wellington,
to whom these papers were bequeathed by Sir
VAAH Wellesley in 1954. NRA 20085.

Copies of official corresp with Lord Wellesley and
others as lieutenant-governor of the ceded
provinces of Oudh 1801-3 (29 vols); misc private
letters from Indian administrators 1801-3, with a
few to Lord Wellesley from officials at the Cape
of Good Hope (1 vol).
British Library (Add MSS 13545, 13547-54,
13556-75, 13779). Presented among Lord
Wellesley's papers by his executors 1842.

Private and misc official corresp mainly with
Gerard Lake, John Malcolm, Archibald Seton,
Merrick Shawe and Lord Wellesley 1801-3 (10
vols).
India Office Library and Records (MSS Eur E
172-81). Purchased 1936. *Catalogue of European
manuscripts*, ii, pt 2, pp1541-66.

[361] **WELLESLEY, Henry Richard Charles**
(1804-1884), 2nd Baron Cowley 1847, 1st Earl
Cowley 1857
Secretary of legation in Württemberg 1832-43
(intermittently in charge 1833-43); secretary of
embassy in Turkey 1843-8 (minister *ad interim*
1846-8); on a special mission to the Germanic
Confederation 1848-51, minister 1851-2;
ambassador to France 1852-67; on a confidential
mission to Austria 1859.

Despatches to and from him 1833-43 (2 vols, 1
bundle); copies of his despatches 1846-8 (4 vols),
1848-52 (10 vols), 1852-67 (14 vols); corresp
with foreign secretaries, Foreign Office officials,
diplomats and others 1838-43 (2 bundles), 1846-8
(4 vols, 41 bundles), 1848-51 (2 vols, 9 bundles),
1852-72 (28 vols, 57 bundles); registers of corresp
and despatches 1852-67 (25 vols); telegrams
1859-60 (1 bundle); reports, memoranda and
other diplomatic papers 1844-71 (8 bundles);
misc personal papers 1829-66 (2 bundles).
Public Record Office (FO 519/1-16, 90-273,
292-301). Presented 1948 and 1952 and
bequeathed 1954 by Sir VAAH Wellesley. NRA
23469.

'Journal of a Paris Embassy' [1852] (1 vol).
Southampton University Library (Wellington
Papers 13/1). Among papers allocated in 1983
after acceptance for the nation in satisfaction of
tax on the estate of the 7th Duke of Wellington,
to whom this volume was bequeathed by Sir
VAAH Wellesley in 1954. NRA 20085.

[362] **WELLESLEY** (formerly **WESLEY**),
Richard Colley (1760-1842), styled Viscount
Wellesley 1760-81, 2nd Earl of Mornington 1781,
Marquess Wellesley 1799
Ambassador to Spain 1809; foreign secretary
1809-12.

Copies of his despatches, Spain 1809 (1 vol);
corresp and papers rel to foreign affairs
1793-1840, mainly 1809-12, incl the war in
Europe and at sea, and disputes with the United
States (5 vols); to Spain and Portugal, mainly
1809 (3 vols); to Persia, mainly 1809-14 (1 vol);
copies and abstracts of his corresp with British
diplomats in Spain 1809-12, Portugal and Brazil
1810-12, Persia 1810, the Two Sicilies 1811 and
the United States 1811-12 (14 vols); political
corresp 1799-1812, incl some as foreign secretary
with George Canning (2 vols).
British Library (Add MSS 37285-96, 49979-92).
Presented in 1906 by William Law, nephew of his
private secretary Alfred Montgomery, and in 1959
by the 7th Duke of Wellington.

Copies of corresp rel to Persia and Turkey
1809-11 (5 vols).
Huntington Library, San Marino, California.

See also *Cabinet Ministers.*

WELLINGTON, Duke of, see Wellesley A.

[363] **WERRY, Francis** (1745-1832)
Consul at Smyrna 1793-1829.

Family corresp and misc papers 1779-1885, mainly
of Werry and his son Francis during the
Napoleonic wars, incl letters from the 1st Earl
Cathcart, WR Hamilton and Sir WS Smith, and
reports on the congress of Vienna, the policy of
the allies and the Polish rising of 1830 (over 100
items).
Bodleian Library, Oxford (MSS Eng. hist. b.238,
c.1032). Purchased at Sotheby's 23 Mar 1981, lot
101.

[364] **WERRY, Francis Petre** (1788-1859)
Attached to the British missions to the congresses
of Châtillon, Paris and Vienna 1813-15; secretary
of legation in Saxony 1816-24.

See Werry F.

WESTMORLAND, Earl of, see Fane J.

[365] **WHITE, Sir Herbert Edward** (1855-1947)
Consul at Tangier 1885-1907 (intermittently
consul-general and chargé d'affaires in Morocco
1886-1905), consul-general 1908-14, agent
1914-21.

Corresp, papers, diaries and other papers mainly
rel to Morocco from the late 19th cent.
ARM White Esq.

[366] **WHITE, John** (d 1854)
Vice-consul at Valparaiso 1823-37.

Copies of official letters to him 1831-3 (1 vol).
Bodleian Library, Oxford (MS Eng. lett. c.197).
Purchased 1961.

[367] **WHITE, Sir William Arthur** (1824-1891)
On the consular staff at Warsaw 1857-64; consul
at Danzig 1864-75; agent and consul-general in
Serbia 1875-8; agent and consul-general in
Romania 1878-9, minister 1879-85; minister *ad
interim* to Turkey 1885-6, ambassador 1886-91.

Papers 1857-90, mainly Turkey, incl private
telegrams to and from Queen Victoria, other
members of the royal family and Lord Salisbury,
draft despatches, press cuttings and confidential
print (6 vols).

Public Record Office (FO 364/1-6). Sent to the Foreign Office from Constantinople after his death, and transferred 1921.

Letters from GW Buchanan, Lord Dufferin, Sir HG Elliot, Lords Granville and Iddesleigh, Sir AH Layard, Sir RBD Morier, Lord Odo Russell, Lords Salisbury and Tenterden and others 1851-91 (3 vols); letters from him to Layard 1877-91, and copies of his letters to Morier 1885-9 (1 bundle); letters of appointment as commissioner at the Suez Canal conference 1888. *Public Record Office* (FO 364/7-11). Presented to the Foreign Office in 1958 by the executor of his grandson Captain WA de Geijer. NRA 23625. See also CL Smith, *The embassy of Sir William White at Constantinople 1886-1891*, 1957.

[368] **WHITEFOORD, Caleb** (1734-1810)
Secretary to the commission to treat with United States envoys in Paris 1782-3.

Corresp with authors, politicians and others 1750-1810 (3 vols); treaty papers 1782-3, literary MSS and genealogical notes (1 vol).
British Library (Add MSS 36593-6). Purchased 1901.

[369] **WHITWORTH, Charles** (1752-1825), Baron Whitworth 1800, Viscount Whitworth 1813, Earl Whitworth 1815
Minister to Poland 1785-8, to Russia 1788-1800; plenipotentiary to Denmark 1800; ambassador to France 1802-3.

Corresp, instructions and other papers as minister to Russia mainly 1798-1800, incl papers rel to Malta, operations against the French and negotiations for French evacuation of Egypt (380 items); corresp and papers rel to Denmark 1800 and the capitulation of Copenhagen 1807 (1 vol, 1 bundle); corresp with Lord Hawkesbury and others, draft despatches, letter books, instructions and other papers, France 1802-3, with papers of Lord Cornwallis and Anthony Merry 1801-2 (4 vols, 17 bundles, 664 items); corresp with CW Flint, Robert Peel, Lord Sidmouth and others, letter books, audience books, memoranda, patronage papers and household accounts as lord-lieutenant of Ireland 1813-17, with papers of the 4th Duke of Richmond 1805-13 (52 vols, *c*240 bundles and items); personal and family corresp and papers 1778-1824, and misc papers rel to Kentish affairs 1802-15 (1 vol, 6 bundles, *c*140 items); household accounts 1800-1 and papers rel to his financial affairs 1797-1801 (1 vol, 2 bundles, *c*80 items).
Kent AO (U269/A263, C341-6, L67, O195-253). He married the widow of the 3rd Duke of Dorset, and his papers were deposited among those of the Sackville family by the 4th Baron Sackville 1950. NRA 8575.

Letters and instructions from Lords Hawkesbury and Liverpool, CM de Talleyrand and others 1802-3 (1 vol).

Public Record Office (FO 323/4). Purchased by the Foreign Office at Sotheby's 4 July 1932, lot 160.

[370] **WICKHAM, William** (1761-1840)
On a special mission to Switzerland 1794-5, chargé d'affaires 1795, minister 1795-7; on a confidential military mission to Switzerland 1799; joint plenipotentiary to Bavaria and Austria 1799-1801.

Political and diplomatic corresp and papers 1785-1839, incl letters from the 1st Baron Auckland, Francis Drake, Sir MF Eden, Lord Grenville, the 1st Baron Minto, the 3rd Duke of Portland, John Trevor, and other British and European politicians, diplomats and soldiers (170 bundles); despatches to and from him 1795-8 (8 bundles); corresp and papers rel to Ireland, mainly as chief secretary 1802-4, incl letters from Henry Addington, Lords Castlereagh and Colchester, Isaac Corry, John Foster, under secretaries and others (59 bundles); business papers mainly 1787-1834 (24 bundles); personal, family and estate papers 18th-19th cent.
Hampshire RO (38M49) Deposited at various dates by his great-great-granddaughter Lady Bonham Carter. NRA 0550.

[371] **WILLIAMS, Sir William Fenwick** (1800-1883), Bt 1856
Commissioner for the delimitation of the Turco-Persian boundary 1848; commissioner with the Turkish army in Anatolia 1854-6.

Private letters to him and draft despatches as lieutenant-governor of Nova Scotia 1865-7, personal corresp 1854-67, family corresp 1807-16, extracts from his journal, Ceylon 1839, commissions and addresses 1855-80.
New Brunswick Museum, Saint John. See *Union list of manuscripts in Canadian repositories*, 1975, p1323.

Misc letters, despatches and commissions 1825-70 (1 vol).
Royal Artillery Institution (MD/917). Access by written application.

[372] **WILLOCK, Sir Henry** (*c*1789-1858)
Chargé d'affaires in Persia 1815-26.

Letters from John Bidwell, Sir Robert Liston, JJ Morier, Sir RK Porter and others 1815-20 (47 items).
India Office Library and Records (MSS Eur D 527). Purchased 1957. NRA 27444.

[373] **WILSON, Francis** (fl 1789-93)
Chargé d'affaires in the Southern Netherlands
1789-92, 1792, 1793.

Corresp as chargé d'affaires 1791-2, incl letters
from Colonel William Gardiner, Lord Grenville,
Sir John Peter, Lord Torrington and others, notes
from the government of the Southern
Netherlands, and requests for passports and
assistance for British subjects (197 items).
Dr APW Malcomson. Photocopies are in the
Public Record Office of Northern Ireland
(T 2761). NRA 16314.

[374] **WILSON, General Sir Robert Thomas**
(1777-1849)
Attached to missions to Prussia 1806-7, to Turkey
1811-12; on a mission to Russia 1812-13.

Corresp with British and foreign statesmen,
politicians, military and naval officers, literary
figures and others 1799-1848 (15 vols); letters to
Lord Grey 1810-28 (7 vols); copies of his letters
to Lord Castlereagh 1814 (1 vol); journals and
memoranda 1800-1, 1805-9, 1812-14, 1816, 1823
(9 vols); papers rel to Russia and Turkey
1807-39, mainly 1812 (4 vols); to Portugal, Spain
and the Spanish colonies 1808-41 (4 vols, 1 item);
to France 1780-1819, incl intercepted French
corresp 1808-9, 1812, and material rel to his trial
at Paris 1816 (5 vols); military and political
papers 1798-1829 (3 vols); misc papers 18th-19th
cent (4 vols).
British Library (Add MSS 30095-30144, 30147-8).
Purchased from and presented by his son-in-law
the Revd Herbert Randolph 1876.

Letters from Lord Grey 1814-26 (120 items).
*Durham University Department of Palaeography
and Diplomatic* (Grey of Howick Collection).
Deposited by the 5th Earl Grey 1955. NRA 6228.

[375] **WODEHOUSE, John** (1826-1902), 3rd
Baron Wodehouse 1846, 1st Earl of Kimberley
1866
Parliamentary under secretary for foreign affairs
1852-6, 1859-61; minister to Russia 1856-8; on a
special mission to Denmark 1863-4; foreign
secretary 1894-5.

Corresp and memoranda rel to foreign affairs
1843-61 (5 bundles); copies of his despatches
1856-8, 1863-4 (3 vols); Foreign Office
memoranda rel to Schleswig-Holstein 1861-3 (1
bundle); cabinet and Foreign Office memoranda
1893-5 (1 vol, 1 bundle); corresp 1894-5 with
Queen Victoria, cabinet colleagues, diplomats and
officials of the Foreign Office and other
departments (37 vols); 'conversations' 1894-5 (1
vol); Foreign Office confidential print 1893-5, and
other printed papers rel to foreign affairs 1863-95
(49 vols, 21 bundles).
In family possession. Not open for research. NRA
1274.

Letters from Liberal statesmen and others 1881,
1891-1901 (6 vols); copies of his letters to Lord
Rosebery 1894-5 (2 vols).
National Library of Scotland (MSS 10242-9).
Purchased 1973 from Mr and Mrs C Kohler, who
had bought them at Christie's 12 July 1972, lot
219. NRA 22490.

Corresp, Russia 1856-8, mainly with Lord
Clarendon (3 vols).
British Library (Add MSS 46692-4). Purchased
1948.

Letters from foreign diplomats in London 1854-6
(20 items).
Leicestershire RO (DE 1749/34). Deposited 1977
by his great-grandson SJ Packe-Drury-Lowe.
NRA 21104.

See also *Cabinet Ministers*.

[376] **WOLFF, Sir Henry Drummond Charles**
(1830-1908)
Commissioner for the organisation of the province
of Eastern Roumelia 1878-9; on a special mission
to Turkey 1885-7; minister to Persia 1887-91, to
Romania 1891-2; ambassador to Spain 1892-1900.

Corresp and papers, Eastern Roumelia 1878-9,
comprising despatches and telegrams to and from
Lord Salisbury (15 vols), corresp mainly with his
assistant commissioner Lord Donoughmore
(2 vols), misc corresp (3 vols) and printed papers
(2 vols).
Public Record Office (FO 901). Received from
Lovell White & King, solicitors, on behalf of his
heirs 1966.

[377] **WOOD, Sir Richard** (1806-1900)
Attaché in Turkey from 1824, dragoman 1834-41;
consul at Damascus 1841-55; agent and consul-
general at Tunis 1855-79.

Official reports and corresp 1831-41, incl letters
from Major-General JB Estcourt, William Lyon,
Lord Ponsonby and Colonel RL Taylor (2
boxes); official reports, papers in Arabic and
Turkish, and corresp mainly with Sir Stratford
Canning, Lord Dufferin, Colonel RL Taylor and
Turkish officials 1840-98 (2 boxes); personal and
family corresp, accounts and papers rel to his
career (1 box); journals, notebooks, memoranda
and misc papers mainly rel to his travels in the
Middle East c1830-46 (2 boxes).
Middle East Centre, St Antony's College, Oxford.
Deposited by his descendant P Plunkett 1972,
1981.

[378] **WORSLEY, Sir Richard** (1751-1805), 7th
Bt 1768
Resident at Venice 1793-7.

Letters from British diplomats, consuls, agents,
naval officers, etc 1793-6 (3 vols); copies of
corresp 1795-6 (1 vol); papers mainly of previous
residents, incl instructions and copies of corresp
1756-94 (2 vols); appointments, etc 1780-93 (1
vol); travel journals, Europe and the Near East
1765-87 (5 vols); catalogue of drawings by Willey
Reveley 1785-7 (1 vol); letters to him rel to his
art collection and *Museum Worsleyanum* 1778-1805
(1 vol, 20 items); inventory of his paintings at
Venice 1797; poll book, Hampshire 1779.
Lincolnshire AO. Deposited 1957 by the 6th Earl
of Yarborough, a descendant of his niece
Henrietta Bridgeman Simpson. NRA 5950.
Lincolnshire *Archivists' Report 15, 1963-4,*
pp15-22.

Papers rel to his marriage settlement and the
administration of his estate, incl valuations of his
paintings, marbles, etc 1755-1858.
Lincolnshire AO. Deposited 1961 by the 6th Earl
of Bradford, a trustee of Henrietta Bridgeman
Simpson's marriage settlement. NRA 9551.
Lincolnshire *Archivists' Report 15, 1963-4,*
pp15-22.

Materials for his *History of the Isle of Wight*
(1781), with other family corresp and papers
1322-1830 (1 vol).
British Library (Add MS 46501). Presented by
CF Worsley 1948.

Passports, commissions, quietus roll as sheriff of
Hampshire 1773, corresp rel to his *History of the
Isle of Wight,* and other misc papers 1773-1803
(70 items).
Isle of Wight RO (JER/WA/36/17-20, 37/22-31,
39/5). Deposited with other family papers in
various institutions by CF Worsley 1948 and later
reunited in Isle of Wight RO. NRA 26748.

[379] **WYNDHAM, Sir George Hugh**
(1836-1916)
Attaché in China 1858-63, in Prussia 1863-5;
acting consul-general at Warsaw 1865-8; second
secretary in Belgium 1868-71 (in charge 1868), in
France 1871-5; secretary of legation in Greece
1875-8 (intermittently in charge 1876-8), in Spain
1878-81 (in charge 1879, 1880); chargé d'affaires
in Russia 1881; secretary of embassy in Turkey
1881-5 (intermittently in charge 1882-5); minister
resident in Serbia 1885-6, minister 1886-8;
minister to Brazil 1888-91, to Romania 1894-7.

Journal, China 1861-3 and letters from CG
Gordon 1862 (1 vol, 2 items).
Untraced. Sold at Sotheby's 20 Dec 1965, lots 719-
21.

[380] **WYNN, Sir Henry Watkin Williams**
(1783-1856)
Envoy to Saxony 1803-6; minister to Switzerland
1822-3, to Württemberg 1823-5, to Denmark
1824-53.

Letters to him and his wife 1795-1856, mainly
from his family, incl his uncles Lords
Buckingham and Grenville and Thomas
Grenville, and from diplomats and politicians incl
Lord Bloomfield, Sir Brook Taylor, and Lords
Wellesley and Whitworth (14 vols); letters from
him to his brother Charles 1803-50 (4 vols).
National Library of Wales, Aberystwyth (MSS
2789-2806). Presented 1918 by his granddaughter
Mrs Stanley Leighton and his great-
granddaughter Miss Rachel Leighton. *Handlist of
manuscripts,* i, pp242-5.

Draft despatches from him 1849-51 (3 vols);
copies of private letters to Lords Cowley and
Palmerston and others 1831-7, 1849-50 (3 vols).
National Library of Wales, Aberystwyth (Sweeney
Hall MSS A14-19). Deposited by his great-
grandson Major BEP Leighton 1949-50, 1969.
Annual report 1949-50, p41.

Letters to him mainly from his brother Charles
1820-53 (3 vols).
National Library of Wales, Aberystwyth (MSS
4816-18). Presented 1922-3 by AW Williams
Wynn. *Handlist of manuscripts,* ii, p44.

Copies and drafts of despatches, Saxony 1804-6
(2 vols).
British Library (Add MSS 43353-4). Presented
1932 with papers of Sir Robert Gordon by the 1st
Marquess of Aberdeen.

Copies of his despatches 1823-31 (1 vol).
Public Record Office (FO 323/9). Acquired 1976.

Travel journal, mainly Greece, Cyprus, the Near
East and Egypt 1811-12 (1 vol).
Bodleian Library, Oxford (MS Eng. misc. c.488).
Purchased 1969.

[381] **WYSE, Sir Thomas** (1791-1862)
Minister to Greece 1849-62.

Corresp with his brother George, British and Irish
politicians and others mainly rel to Irish politics
and local affairs c1808-61, but incl some corresp
as minister to Greece (52 bundles, etc); papers rel
to elections, public works, etc in Ireland
c1826-1844 (11 bundles, etc); financial papers
c1830-50 (c100 items); literary papers (13
bundles); journals 1830-57 (13 bundles); misc
corresp and papers c1825-55.
National Library of Ireland. Deposited
1951-2 by WL Bonaparte Wyse. *Manuscript
sources for the history of Irish civilisation,* ed RJ
Hayes, iv, Boston 1965, p925 and *Supplement,* i,
1979, pp793-4.

Diaries (26 vols), notebooks and other papers rel
to his travels in Europe, the Middle East and
elsewhere 1817-60; political diaries 1829-30,

1839-40, 1845; notebook containing an essay on Irish politics.
In private possession. A microfilm is in the National Library of Ireland (n 4984-5, p 5077-8).

Political memoranda 1826-8 (3 vols).
In private possession. Purchased among books and papers of his son WC Bonaparte Wyse at Sotheby's (Hodgson's Rooms) c1979.

Letters to him and his wife from members of the Bonaparte family 1821-49 and related family corresp (c370 items).
Untraced. Sold at Sotheby's 17 Nov 1983, lots 223, 225, 305, and 10 May 1984, lot 236.

YARMOUTH, Earls of, see Seymour-Conway.

[382] **YOUNG, Horace** (1823-1900)
Consul at Bilbao 1859-93.

Letters from AH Layard 1873-7 (81 items) and other diplomats 1859-90 (c80 items); corresp with his family c1840-1893 (c260 items).
British Library (Add MSS 63476-85). Purchased at Sotheby's 6 Nov 1984, lot 978.

ZOUCHE, Baron, see Curzon R.

Index of institutions

The references are to entry numbers

SAN MARINO, California
Huntington Library 36, 146, 152, 186, 205, 220, 287, 315, 362

SAVANNAH
Georgia Historical Society 244

SHREWSBURY
Shropshire Record Office 256, 314

SOUTHAMPTON
University Library 317, 358, 360, 361

STAFFORD
Staffordshire Record Office 53, 188, 207
William Salt Library 310

SWANSEA
University College 239

SYDNEY
Mitchell Library 214

SYRACUSE, New York
University Library 52

TAUNTON
Somerset Record Office 98

TOKYO
Tôyô Bunko (Oriental Library) 220

TROWBRIDGE
Wiltshire Record Office 3, 168, 169

VANCOUVER
University of British Columbia Library 263

WARWICK
Warwick County Record Office 307, 354

WASHINGTON, DC
Library of Congress 128, 183, 220, 339

WIGAN
Wigan Record Office 130

WINCHESTER
Hampshire Record Office 74, 158, 159, 160, 198, 260, 274, 338, 341, 370

Printed for Her Majesty's Stationery Office by Burgess & Son (Abingdon) Ltd.
Dd 737355   C20   4/85   Job No. 842749P